Research and
Technical Writing
for Science and
Engineering

Research and Technical Writing for Science and Engineering

Meikang Qiu
Han Qiu
Yi Zeng

CRC Press
Taylor & Francis Group
Boca Raton London New York

CRC Press is an imprint of the
Taylor & Francis Group, an **informa** business

First edition published 2022
by CRC Press
6000 Broken Sound Parkway NW, Suite 300, Boca Raton, FL 33487-2742

and by CRC Press
2 Park Square, Milton Park, Abingdon, Oxon, OX14 4RN

CRC Press is an imprint of Taylor & Francis Group, LLC

Library of Congress Cataloging-in-Publication Data

Names: Qiu, Meikang, author. | Qiu, Han, author. | Zeng, Yi (Computer engineer), author.
Title: Research and technical writing for science and engineering / Meikang Qiu, Han Qiu, Yi Zeng.
Description: First edition. | Boca Raton : CRC Press, 2022. | Includes bibliographical references and index.
Identifiers: LCCN 2021042783 | ISBN 9780367687847 (hardback) | ISBN 9780367686406 (paperback) | ISBN 9781003139058 (ebook)
Subjects: LCSH: Research--Methodology. |
Engineering--Research--Methodology. | Technical writing.
Classification: LCC Q180.55.M4 Q58 2022 | DDC 001.4/2--dc23/eng/20211108
LC record available at https://lccn.loc.gov/2021042783

ISBN: 978-0-367-68784-7 (hbk)
ISBN: 978-0-367-68640-6 (pbk)
ISBN: 978-1-003-13905-8 (ebk)

DOI: 10.1201/9781003139058

Typeset in CMR10
by KnowledgeWorks Global Ltd.

Publisher's note: This book has been prepared from camera-ready copy provided by the authors.

Dedications

We are enormously grateful to numerous individuals for their assistance in creating this book. We would like acknowledge those who have provided insights or feedback to this creation and the immeasurable helps and supports from the editors and anonymous reviewers.

Contents

SECTION III Bring Your Idea to the Reality

CHAPTER 6 ▪ How to Design Algorithms 117

CHAPTER 7 ▪ How to Do Experiments 137

SECTION IV Put Your Work Out and Make Impacts

CHAPTER 9 ▪ Paper Submission and Publication 179

CHAPTER 10 ▪ Reference and Research Impact 197

List of Figures

Preface

The rapid advancement of science and engineering in recent years has increased by the publication of research papers. As the number of students studying science and engineering grows, so does the number of novel research findings. However, in order to better understand these research findings, academia still requires the ability to organize and write research papers. Because there is no efficient textbook designed to illustrate all details of science and engineering paper writing comprehensively, students will typically learn how to write a research paper piece by piece from their advisors.

The main motivation is to write a textbook focusing on illustrating how science and engineering papers are written to assist graduate-level students majoring in Science and Engineering to efficiently and systematically learn how to conduct research and then how to write research papers. A basic understanding of selecting research topics, conducting a literature review, formulating research problems, generating novel ideas, designing algorithms, and conducting experiments are required for science and engineering research. These objectives are critical for higher education institutions that want to prepare students to conduct successful scientific research.

This book, in particular, has four main parts (eleven chapters) that follow the general pipeline of research in the science and engineering field. We begin with an overview of the research itself and the importance of research integrity; then we emphasize how you can find new ideas and form your own problem; then we explain possible ways for you to bring your idea to reality by conducting solid experiments and paper writing; and finally, we explain how you can put your work out there and make an impact on the world of science.

The book is meant for graduate students or junior/senior undergraduate students in the fields of science and engineering, including computer science/engineering, electrical engineering, mechanical engineering, applied mathematics, economics, etc. The target readers also include researchers and engineers in the fields related to RL, CPS and cybersecurity.

Meikang Qiu, Texas A&M University-Commerce,
Commerce, TX, USA
Han Qiu
Tsinghua University, Beijing, China
Yi Zeng
Virginia Tech University, Blacksburg, VA, USA

Author Bios

Meikang Qiu earned BE and ME degrees from Shanghai Jiao Tong University and obtained Ph.D. degree of Computer Science from University of Texas at Dallas. Currently, he is the Department Head and tenured full professor of Texas A&M University Commerce. He is an ACM Distinguished Member and IEEE Senior member. He is also the Highly Cited Researcher in 2021 from Web of Science and IEEE Distinguished Visitor in 2021–2022. He is the Chair of IEEE Smart Computing Technical Committee.

His research interests include Cyber Security, Big Data Analysis, Cloud Computing, Smarting Computing, Intelligent Data, Embedded systems, etc. Many novel results have been produced and most of them have already been reported to research community through high-quality journal and conference papers. He has published 20+ books, 600+ peer-reviewed journal and conference papers (including 300+ journal articles, 300+ conference papers, 100+ IEEE/ACM Transactions papers). His paper on Telehealth system has won IEEE Systems Journal 2018 Best Paper Award. His paper about data allocation for hybrid memory has been published in IEEE Transactions on Computers has been selected as IEEE TCSC 2016 Best Journal Paper and hot paper (1 in 1000 papers by Web of Science) in 2017. His paper published in IEEE Transactions on Computers about privacy protection for smart phones has been selected as a Highly Cited Paper in 2017–2020. He also won ACM Transactions on Design Automation of Electrical Systems (TODAES) 2011 Best Paper Award. He has won another 10+ Conference Best Paper Awards in recent years.

Currently he is/was an associate editor of 10+ international journals, including IEEE Transactions on Computers, IEEE Transactions on Cloud Computing, IEEE Transactions on Big Data, and IEEE Transactions on System, Man, and Cybernetics (A). He has served as leading guest editor for IEEE Transactions on Dependable and Secure Computing (TDSC), special issue on Social Network Security. He is the General Chair/Program Chair of a dozen of IEEE/ACM international conferences, such as IEEE TrustCom, IEEE BigDataSecurity, IEEE CSCloud, and IEEE HPCC.

As of this printing, his Google scholar citation is 14000+ and H-index 70. He is ranked within the top 1000 scientists in US. He has won Navy Summer Faculty Award in 2012 and Air Force Summer Faculty Award in 2009. His research is supported by US government such as NSF, NSA, Air Force, Navy and companies such as GE, Nokia, TCL, and Cavium.

Han Qiu earned the BE degree from Beijing University of Posts and Telecommunications and obtained the ME degree and Ph.D. degree in Computer Networks from Telecom-ParisTech. He is currently an assistant professor in the Institute for Network Sciences and Cyberspace at Tsinghua University. His research interests include AI Security, Big Data Security, Internet of Things, Cloud Computing, etc. He won the best paper awards of the ICA3PP 2020 and SmartCom 2019. He has published 40+ peer-reviewed journal and conference papers. He served as the program chair for the KSEM 2021 and the IEEE ISPA 2021.

Yi Zeng is a first-year Ph.D. student in Computer Engineering at Virginia Tech. He earned his BE in Electronic and Information Engineering from Xidian University and his MS in Machine Learning and Data Science from the University of California, San Diego. His research interests include trustworthy machine learning, AI security, and the reliable data market for ML. He received the best paper award at the ICA3PP 2020.

He currently has over ten peer-reviewed journal and conference papers to his credit, including top-tier platforms such as ICCV, IJCAI, IEEE Access, IEEE Transactions on Computers, AsiaCCS, etc.

I

Introduction

Overview of Research

CONTENTS

"Research is a systematic inquiry to describe, explain, predict, and control the observed phenomenon. It involves inductive and deductive methods."

Earl Robert Babbie
American Sociologist

RESEARCH is the process of developing new ideas that have an effect on others by using methodical techniques in particular areas within academic disciplines to accomplish. This chapter provides an overview of the writing process for scientific and technical papers. A detailed explanation of all topics covered in this book is provided to

DOI: 10.1201/9781003139058-1

help students in obtaining a comprehensive understanding of how to write a research paper for science and engineering from the very beginning of the idea generation process. In this chapter, the instructional goal is to aid students in comprehending the basic knowledge of what a research paper should look like and how this book is structured to guide them through the process of writing a research paper from start to finish. Reading this chapter may also be an effective way for teachers or students to choose where the most engaging chapters should be placed.

1.1 WHAT IS RESEARCH?

You may wonder, "what exactly is research, anyway?" For the purpose of providing the most comprehensive response to this topic, we have included this specific section to split the term "research" into smaller functional components, and we will examine each distinct element from an overview perspective.

1.1.1 Definition

Whenever we begin to work on anything new, it is always beneficial to begin by reading the definition of the word in its entirety as a first step. Type the word "research" into your browser and you'll be brought to Wikipedia, which describes it as "**creative** and **systematic** work undertaken to **increase** the **stock of knowledge** [54]." Four key terms in this definition have been italicized for emphasis; **creative**, **systematic**, **increase** and **stock of knowledge**. These concepts are critical to the definition of research and will be explored in detail in the following sections.

1.1.2 Creative–Build Something New

The term "creative" refers to the fact that successful research must provide results that were not previously achieved via previous study. The phrase refers to an effort to be unique in a previously unexplored area. There are three kinds of originalities that may be found in the fields of science and engineering.

1. **New tools, approaches, or procedures should be implemented that have not been used before.** To put it another way, this kind of investigation is required to design a certain

application situation. To demonstrate why and how the suggested method is appropriate, evidence must be provided.

2. Another approach to be "creative" is to "**investigate new fields**." A new method to addressing issues that have not been successfully handled or addressed by previous study may be proposed by the researchers themselves.

3. **Studying unexpected issues** is another kind of creativity, since it allows academics to explore a subject that has already been covered by previous research. When compared to exploratory expeditions into new territory, this kind of originality allows researchers to investigate an established research subject by using a novel method of investigation.

In terms of the project's outcomes, the creativity and originality will be judged based on the findings themselves as well as any unique by-products of the study. A new product, theory, concept, or technique, to name a few examples of novel results, may be created. Although not all experiments result in the desired results, by-products may still be considered innovative – for example, learning why a certain experiment failed or why a specific method did not work in a new setting.

1.1.3 Systematic–General Pattern

Research must be a deliberate activity that adheres to a well-established set of steps and procedures. Only original work that follows a systematic process for doing research may then directly transfer the creativity and knowledge into works that have the potential to impact others and are simple to follow for others to replicate. This critical nature is not restricted to scientific and technical study, but may be seen in a wide range of areas, including business.

After you have a good understanding of the subject you want to investigate, you may begin doing your research in accordance with the general research pattern. From an overview, the following is the typical pattern for studying the background of science and engineering:

1. A review of the literature and a survey on a particular area or issue;

2. Using your knowledge and actual data, develop your own hypothesis;

3. Empirically or theoretically test the theory with a comprehensive experimentation/implementation;

4. Reflect on and integrate the information you have gathered as a result of your observations, and consider how your findings may affect others in the domain.

As long as one adheres to this basic pattern, one may build innovations while standing on the shoulders of giants. Meanwhile, their effort is having an effect on more individuals in the same domain, and they are utilizing the same technique to construct taller structures.

1.1.4 Increase–Acquire and Contribute

It is possible to interpret the phrase "increase" in the definition of research as a "contributing to knowledge." The act of doing a unique piece of study and learning something new for oneself is standard practice. In contrast, unless you are able to communicate this information to others, the findings of your study are essentially pointless. With this in mind, the next debate will center on the word "contribute", which conveys a much clearer message that research should contribute to global knowledge so that it is available to everyone, rather than just the researchers themselves.

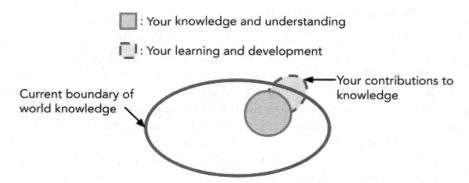

Figure 1.1: The relationship between acquiring and contributing

Figure 1.1 represents the world's body of knowledge and the many ways in which contributions may be made to it. It can also be viewed as the connection between gaining information and contributing. It is this corpus of knowledge that reflects global understanding, theories, ideas, and models, as well as the sciences, the arts, and other disciplines. Books, journal articles, conference proceedings, papers, reports, the Internet, art, and people's thoughts, among other things, serve as repositories for knowledge. You can see that your own knowledge, which is represented by the dark area, is absorbed inside this domain. You may learn things that others already know, which allows you to broaden your own knowledge, as shown by the bright yellow area inside the bounding box. In the same way, your study may result in contributions to global knowledge in the form of inventions, new theories, and other innovations. As a result of the bright yellow area extending beyond the border, they are shown as additions to the global body of knowledge. For this reason, a contribution refers to the dissemination of new ideas, theories, and research findings with the rest of the world while also extending the scope of what is already known.

1.1.5 The Stock of Knowledge

To explain what is meant by the stock of knowledge, it will be discussed in terms of a hierarchy consisting of **data**, **information**, **knowledge**, and **wisdom**. Here we elaborate the meaning of these terms with the perspective of research in science and engineering as:

- **Data.** When it comes to data, they are the factual components that describe things or events that take place under particular conditions. Their raw statistics and raw observations reflect the raw data you have gathered through your studies. For example, as part of your research assignment, you may be required to gather pictures of cats from various sources online. The information you gathered may have originated from a variety of sources, including various breeds and images of varied sizes. They are collected in the form of raw pictures that, in their current state, signify practically nothing.

- **Information.** The information represents data that has been processed in order to give you with some insight into the significance of the information. To put it another way, the data has been preprocessed, examined, summarized, and otherwise processed into a more intelligible and usable manner. Information may be passed on to other individuals in this format, which can include books, articles, recordings, speeches, and other forms of communication.

Processing your raw cat pictures into something useful may lead to the development of feature extraction algorithms, the identification of various cat kinds and patterns, the identification of the most significant differences between each species of cat, and other applications. In these forms, the data would have some significance, and you now have some understanding of what these data represent or might lead to in the future.

- **Knowledge.** Knowledge is your more in-depth knowledge of a subject or situation. While information provides you with a grasp of the "what" (i.e., what is occurring in the actual world), knowledge reflects your comprehension of the "why." Information is a method of communication that is used to convey information. In other words, knowledge is your own interpretation of what you learn through information in the form of rules or patterns or choices or models or ideas or other forms of expression.

  When looking at cat pictures on the internet, your knowledge about them will provide you a general idea of what you're getting at with your comprehension. Knowing why and how something works represents your understanding of why and how something works, for example, how your classification model can work over those cats, why similar cats can still be classified correctly, why the samples of each breed of cat collected are of different sizes, and how the difference in size may impact your learning model Those pieces of knowledge you gained throughout your journey are essential and lead to wisdom.

- **Wisdom.** Your capacity to put your knowledge into action is represented by your wisdom level. That capacity to use your abilities and experiences in new ways to generate new knowledge and adapt to new circumstances is represented by this symbol.

  Regarding the information you gained from the cat pictures, wisdom would reflect your capacity to design and improve a more accurate and efficient cat classification model, or to extend your investigations to other objects such as dog classification models, among other things.

Another area that ought to be included is theoretical considerations. While data, information, knowledge, and wisdom represent a relatively "firm understanding of what is going on and how things can be applied, theory means ideas, opinions, and suppositions based on your observations of the world. A theory is not always correct, but it does offer the most reasonable explanation for what you are seeing at the time.

Despite the fact that knowledge has been defined from a human perspective, global knowledge may be described in a similar manner. This definition of global knowledge includes all understanding, wisdom, and interpretation of the world by everyone and everything that has been recorded or documented someplace and in some manner.

The act of collecting data and information on one's own is referred to as "intelligence gathering." In order to answer issues such as what is going on in the world, what we don't know, and what we can find out, these data are utilized. Research, on the other hand, must go beyond just collecting data and must also explain what you observe. It is required to make an addition to the existing body of knowledge. It is on the lookout for explanations, connections, analogies, generalizations, and hypotheses, among other things. As a result, research seeks to answer issues such as "why do things happen the way they do?" What is the root of the current situation? And so on. While facts and information may only answer the question "what?" on their own, knowledge and insight can answer the question "why?"

1.1.6 Summary

As previously stated, the four major elements of "research" have been thoroughly examined. During our study, we discovered that scientific and engineering research need creative and methodical approach, and the findings should be able to add to the body of information already available. Afterwards, we'll go into more depth about the research method itself.

1.2 THE PROCESS OF RESEARCH

We have mentioned the general pattern in Section 1.1.3. Now, we will dive deep into the process of researching science and engineering environments. Blaxter et al. [12] identify four standard views of the research process: **sequential**, **generalized**, **circulatory**, and **evolutionary**. We will now break each phase down into details.

- **Sequential.** The sequential process is the simplest view of all. In this process, a series of activities are performed one after another as a "fixed, linear series of stages." An example of such a process consists of seven unique, sequential steps:

1. Identify the broad area of study.
2. Select a research topic.
3. Decide on an approach.
4. Plan how you will perform the research.
5. Gather data and information.
6. Analyse and interpret these data.
7. Present the results and findings.

- **Generalized.** The generalized research process is similar to the sequential research process in that a specified series of actions is carried out one after the other in a sequential fashion. However, the generalized model acknowledges that not all phases are relevant in all situations, and that certain processes may need alternative approaches depending on the nature of the study. This is accomplished by creating alternate paths that may be followed at various phases of the research process based on the nature and results of the study.

- **Circulatory.** This method acknowledges that each study is actually just a part of a continual cycle of discovery and inquiry, which is what the circulatory approach emphasizes. Quite frequently, research will reveal more questions than it will provide answers, and the research process may be restarted by trying to answer the new questions that have been discovered. It is possible that your study experiences may prompt you to review or reinterpret previous phases of your work. The circulatory interpretation also allows participants to join the research process at any stage in the process and acknowledges that the process is never-ending.

- **Evolutionary.** As a step further than the circulatory interpretation concept, the evolutionary concept emphasizes the importance of research evolving and changing over time. Research should not be limited to following a defined circulatory pattern or repeating the same forms of analysis and interpretation that have previously been performed. The results of each evolution have an effect on the outcomes of subsequent evolutions to a greater or lesser degree.

1.2.1 Intellectual Discovery

Although the research process may be represented by a model of some kind or another, your individual thinking processes and intellectual breakthroughs are frequently far more complicated and personal in nature. When you are searching for questions to answer and solutions to those questions, you will often go through a complicated process of inductive and deductive reasoning to get the information you need.

– **Inductive reasoning.** Observations of the world lead you to general judgments about it, which you then communicate to others. For want of a better expression, you construct models and hypotheses based on your interpretation of the world. The data and information you may gather from the world, the subject/problem you are investigating, and most significantly, your prior knowledge and beliefs will all influence your interpretation.

Epistemology is the study of the knowledge that can be gained from the subject matter that you are studying. Depending on your perspective (positivism or realism), you can either draw general conclusions from what you observe and what you are studying and apply them to other situations, or you can only infer information that is exclusive to yourself and the particular scenario under investigation (anti-positivism).

– **Deductive reasoning.** You begin with your current knowledge and comprehension of the world and make predictions about likely observations that will occur inside it, even if you have never encountered them before.

Deductive reasoning is influenced by your theory of reality, your own personal understanding of the universe, and your underlying beliefs about the subject matter you are examining, among other factors. An ontology is a formalized description of what exists. Because their comprehension differs from yours and they view things in various ways, different people may draw different conclusions from the same information.

The application of inductive and deductive reasoning to complex situations may necessitate a lengthy and complicated chain of reasoning. Knowing something is what you get from inductive reasoning, as we've discussed previously. For better or worse, you construct your ideas, models, theories, and understandings on the foundation of your inductive reasoning about the world. Wisdom, on the other hand, can be seen in your deductive reasoning talents, which allow you to apply what you know to situations and issues you haven't yet faced.

Additionally, before devoting several months to your research, it is important to evaluate where you want to go with your findings. For example, research students frequently come up with a topic for their investigation and are passionate about pursuing it. However, when they eventually get their hands on the "solution," they realize that it was of little use in the first place and discard it. Take a deep breath and try to visualize where you're going. Assume you've already arrived at your destination and ask yourself, "What's the point?."

1.3 CLASSIFYING RESEARCH

Research can be divided into three categories based on three separate perspectives: the field, the approach, and the character of the research.

- **Field.** The area of research is little more than a nomenclature that allows groups of academics with similar interests to be identified and grouped together in one place (Sharp et al., loc. cit.). As an example, if you were researching the topic of computers, you may find research topics in areas such as information systems, artificial intelligence, software engineering, and so forth. These subjects may be further subdivided into more particular topics in order to assist the more specialized researcher or expert in distinguishing features of a field of study.

- **Approach.** Approaches indicate the different types of research methodologies that were used as part of the research process – for example, case studies, experiments, and surveys. The following section goes into greater depth about each of these methods and their advantages and disadvantages.

- **Nature.** The type of contribution that research contributes to knowledge is determined by the nature of the investigation. Three categories can be used to categorize the nature of research in the context of science and engineering: basic, applied, and interdisciplinary.

1. Pure theoretical development.
2. Research that examines and evaluates pure theory, as well as the potential for its application in real-world situations.
3. Applied research has some practical application or outcome.

1.3.1 So, What is Good Research?

While it is important to understand what research is about and how to define it, you need also understand what constitutes effective research. As from a general perspective, we highlight three criteria of excellent research:

- **Open minds.** You should employ a "open system of thought" when conducting your work. Be receptive to the questions that are being offered. "Conventional wisdom and established belief... may prove to be insufficient", says the author.

- **Critical analysis.** Examine the information with a critical eye. If so, are these numbers correct? Have they been negatively impacted in any way? What are the implications of these findings? Is it possible to obtain alternate data? Is it possible to interpret these data in a different way?

- **Generalisations.** Researchers make broad generalizations and then specify restrictions on the scope of the generalizations they identify. Generalization enables for the interpretation and application of research findings to a wide range of scenarios. However, researchers must know the limitations of these generalizations. Generalizations are derived from your personal experience and develop as a result of your deductive reasoning. This process helps you to generate concepts about things you have never encountered before, with some caveats.

Failure to apply these traits results in the perpetuation of the status quo – everything continues to be uncontested and unchanged. You will not contribute to knowledge if you do not keep an open mind to new ideas, do not examine them critically, and do not have the ability to generalize your learning to diverse situations. After all, this is the primary goal of your investigation.

1.4   RESEARCH METHODS

According to general classification, there are two major types of research methods: quantitative and qualitative. Numeric scales are related with quantitative research methodologies because they allow for
the measurement of items on them. The natural sciences, according to
Berndtsson et al., are the origin of these methodologies, which are focused with knowing "how something is produced, built, or functions."
In the natural sciences, it is common to be concerned with testing
hypotheses, and the repeatability of experiments as well as the testing
of hypotheses are critical to the reliability of the outcomes.

However, qualitative approaches have their roots in the social
sciences, as opposed to quantitative methods. In the discipline of information science, they are increasingly widespread, and they include
approaches such as case studies and surveys. These techniques, as well
as a number of others, are explained in greater detail in the next section.

Below, we list out four of the most common research methods that
you might use (either individually or combined) are action research,
experiment, case study, and survey:

- **Action research.** Includes the meticulously documented (and
closely supervised) examination of an attempt by you... to actively address a problem or improve an existing situation known
as participant observation in some circles, it entails working on
a specific topic or project with a subject or, more commonly, an
organization, and then analyzing the results. It is important to
remember that when conducting action research, you must avoid
becoming overly fixated with the action itself and losing sight of
the underlying reason for performing it – that is, analyzing it as
part of your academic project.

- **Experiment.** It entails the exploration of causal linkages
through the use of tests that you design and control. It is quite
common for quasi-experimental research to be required due to
a lack of access to samples, ethical concerns, and other factors,
among others. Typical experiments include the following steps:

  1. defining a theoretical hypothesis;

  2. selecting samples from known populations;

  3. allocating samples to different experimental conditions;

4. introducing planned changes to one or more variables;

5. measuring a small number of variables;

6. controlling all other variables.

Experiments are usually performed in development, evaluation, and problem-solving projects.

– **Case study.** A case study is a comprehensive examination of a specific scenario. A specific issue, problem, firm, or set of companies is being investigated as part of the investigation. This inquiry can be carried out directly, for example, through interviews, observation, and so on, or indirectly, for example, through the analysis of corporate reports or company paperwork. Instead of simply reporting on the findings of a case study research, one should strive to draw broad conclusions from the specific features of the investigated environment. A common occurrence is the attempt to characterize the situation for a given examined organization.

Case studies create a considerable amount of subjective data, which needs to be sifted and analyzed before being interpreted in order to come up with conclusive, accurate, and fair conclusions. If you are personally involved in the case study, you should be conscious of the fact that you have an impact on it. Consider the following scenario: when you questioned employees at a local company, did they tell you what they thought you wanted to hear rather than the truth about the situation? Is there a way to "triangulate" your data – that is, to receive the data from two or three separate sources to validate that what you are told is true (and therefore, eliminate any possible influence you may be exerting on the data collection process)?

– **Survey.** Studies in the fields of science and engineering typically place a greater emphasis on the most recent developments in a certain domain of community. In order to gain an understanding of the situation you are working with and to gain some preliminary perspective based on other people's contributions, this research method is essential as a first step.

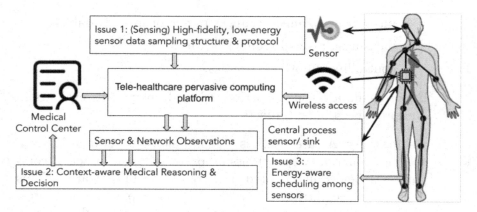

Figure 1.2: Main problems and issues in telehealth systems

1.5 OVERVIEW OF THE TELEHEALTH SYSTEMS

Now, we put ourselves in the position of a newbie who was so interested in the future health systems and trying to conduct their first research under the topic of telehealth systems as illustrated in Figure 1.2. Though the telehealth system is already a sub-topic among future healthy systems [76], this topic still covers a wide range of problems that you can work on. We break the major issues and directions of research in telehealth in Figure 1.2 based on the implementation place. The first thing that comes to a system is building a well-recognized structure or protocol upon which the future applications and users and exchange their information. If you find yourself really interested in this direction, then you can apply a wide range of techniques for better efficiency and security of the systems' platforms and protocols [167, 180, 294]. In the next step, we can intuitively think of the context-aware end of decision making, which is also the application end of making solid output base on the acquired information from the system. As a critical function of the whole system, decision-making is required to be robust and accurate [66, 105]. When you get your hands over topics that fall in this range; you can easily think of adopting most state-of-art classifiers, say deep neural networks, graphical neural networks for reasoning each connected relationships of the given data, or using transformers as a tool to effectively predicting a potential decision, etc. This is the most interesting end to myself, as you can find various ways and tools to apply to these topics. Finally, we see the issues over the sensors, which is the hardware end of bio-human interaction [81]. You will also find a list of interesting topics ranging from material, system processing, system transmitting, etc. This is merely a small fraction of what you can do within the context of telehealth.

For deeper diving, we may first find ourselves encountering a list of specific sub-topics within the context from a more generalized overview, and we can summarize those range of topics as follows: 1) data formation and integration, namely Electronic Health Record (EHR) syntax and semantic validation and integration and EHR automatic translation among proprietary EHR formats and HL7 EHR standard [140]; 2) system integration, which covers the topic of Interoperability: HL7 (Health Level 7), Web services (WSDL), and Fault-tolerance, response time, system scalability, etc. [191]; 3) then is topics around the telehealth systems' sensor platforms, namely, Mica 2, Crossbow Inc. Central processor: Atmel mega 128L microprocessor, PSoC (Programmable System on Chip), Cypress, San Jose, and UART (Universal Asynchronous Receive/Transmit) serial comm [244].

Screening through those topics can be burdensome but also full of fun. The next step is to screen out a specific topic that most interests you. Now, we adopt another topic in the telehealth systems as examples, the monitoring systems of telehealth systems.

Within the context of telehealth monitoring, there is a list of data that are valuable to the telehealth systems: e.g., blood pressure, electrocardiogram, pulse, and body temperature [263, 170]. All those data enable better medical care and helps. However, simply recording those data is only one small step towards the whole process; the next specific context is the framework of implementing such a health data gathering procedure. We need to ensure that the remote sensor (mote) must be programmed such that it is able to: 1) Receive the data serially from the PSoC; 2) Transmit the data wirelessly to the base mote [214]. Finally, we must include the base mote and the requirement that it should be considered: 1) it can receive data from the remote mote; 2) it can transmit the data to the computer. And even now, we can just say that we are halfway to the whole process [24]. We then need a TinyOS to control the whole system: 1) Bridge the serial and wireless channel. Whenever a mote receives a packet, it transmits wirelessly to the other mote or base station [213]; 2) For the base station, TinyOS will receive data from the remote mote and transmit it to the central computer; 3) Stored with XML format at the central computer [25, 167]. And all the information and details are the scope we tuned over the telehealth monitoring system, which is a small fraction of the whole picture.

Figure 1.3: Three basic steps of a standard remote health diagnostic system

Now, we are going to dive into the context of telehealth systems from the perspective of a person with particular cyber security interests. So, in general, a remote health diagnostic system consists of three basic steps [242], as shown in Figure 1.3: 1) Measure (M): different medical devices available, with different cost and time features, need to translate and select; 2) Data Transmit (T): heterogeneous network paths available, with different cost and time requirements (diversify); 3) Experts diagnose (E): local or around-world experts, with different costs and time.

A remote health diagnostic system's ultimate goal/object is to minimize the total cost while finishing the whole diagnosis within specific time constraints, e.g., before delivering to the next shift in a 24-hour knowledge factory [201]. We take a type of attack that exists under this context as an example, namely, the buffer overflow attack towards telehealth systems. Buffer overflow attack is a serious attack over telehealth systems, targeted at the software, computer, routers, network base stations, wireless devices, sensors, etc. [29, 243]. Attackers exploit buffer overflow issues by overwriting the memory of an application. This changes the execution path of the program, triggering a response that damages files or exposes private information [62, 166]. Figure 1.4 demonstrates a direct way to conduct such a buffer overflow attack. As illustrated, a buffer overflow attack is an attack in which a malicious user exploits an unchecked buffer in a program and overwrites the program code with their own data [288]. If the program code is overwritten with new executable code, the effect changes the program's operation as dictated by the attacker. If overwritten with other data, the likely effect is to cause the program to crash [287].

Thus, we can find a list of interesting this that we can focus on to prevent the buffer overflow attack:

1. Use Different Language Tools. Language tools that provide automatic bounds checking such as Perl, Python, and Java. True, these are available. However, this is usually not possible or practical when you consider almost all modern operating systems in use today are

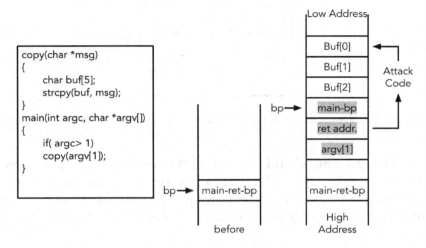

Figure 1.4: Illustration of a buffer overflow attack.

written in the C language. The language tool becomes particularly critical when low-level hardware access is necessary. The good news is with languages evolving, language and code security has become a serious issue. For example, Microsoft, in their .NET initiative, has completely rewritten Visual Basic and Visual C++ with "string safe" security in mind. Additionally, they have added the Visual C# tool, which was designed from the ground up with security in mind.

2. Eliminate the Use of Flawed Library Functions. Programming languages are only as flawed as the programmer allows them to be. Our demonstration utilized three flawed functions from the Standard C Library (gets(), strcpy, and strcmp). These are just three of many such functions that fail to check the length or bounds of their arguments. For instance, we could have completely eliminated the buffer overflow vulnerability in our demonstration by changing one line of code. This simple change informs strcpy() that it only has an eight-byte destination buffer and that it must discontinue raw copy at eight bytes.

The persistence of programming errors of this nature may indeed be related to how we train and educate young programmers. One can pick up an introductory college textbook on C or C++ and find this set of flawed functions introduced in the Chapter 3. Sure, they make great training aids. However, humans are creatures of habit and tend to use what they know best and are most comfortable with.

```
#replace line 49 from
strcpy (buffer2, string2);

#to
strncpy(buffer2, string2, 8)
```

Figure 1.5: Demonstration of eliminating the use of flawed library

3. Design and Build Security Within Code. It takes more work, and it takes more effort, but software can be designed with security foremost in mind. If the previous example, we could have yet added one extra step to assure complete buffer safety: Again, this may

```
strncpy(buffer2, string2, sizeof(buffer2))
```

Figure 1.6: Demonstration of using specific design to mitigate the attack.

go back to how we train programmers. Is code security taught and encouraged? Are they given the extra time to design security within their code? Typically, and unfortunately, the answer to these questions is no.

4. Use Safe Library Modules. String safe library modules are available for use, even in problematic languages such as C++. For instance, the C++ Standard Template Library offers the Class String in its standard namespace. The String Class provides bounds checking within its functions and be preferred for use over the standard string handling functions.

5. Use Available Middleware Libraries. Several freeware offerings of "safe libraries" are available for use. For instance, Bell Labs developed the "libsafe24" library to guard against unsafe function use. libsafe works on the structure of stack frame linkage through frame pointers by following frame pointer to the stack frame that allocated a buffer. When a function executes, it can then prevent the return address from being overwritten. However, libsafe is not without security problems of its own, as it has been reported that libsafe's protections can be bypassed in a format-string-based attack by using flag characters that are used by Glibc but not libsafe. Users of libsafe should upgrade to version 2.0-12.

6. Use Source Code Scanning Tools. Several attempts have been made to design a tool that performs analysis on raw source code with the hope of identifying undesirable constructs to include buffer vulnerabilities. The boys at L0pht Heavy Industries (now a white hat group called @atstake) produced one such tool called "Slint" a few years back, but it was never released. Probably the most successful tool to date is Rational's (http://www.rational.com) PurifyPlus Software Suite that capably performs a dynamic analysis of Java, C, or C++ source code. Although the specialty of PurifyPlus is memory leak detection, it is capable of hunting down unchecked buffers and other coding errors that could possibly lead to buffer overrun conditions

7. Use Compiler Enhancement Tools. Although a relatively new concept, several compiler add-on tools have recently been made available that work closely with function return address space to prevent overwriting. One such tool, Stack Shield (http://www.angelfire.com/sk/stackshield), provides protection by taking a copy of RET and temporarily placing it in a location not subject to overflow attacks. Upon return, the two address values are compared. If they are different, the return address has been modified, and Stack Shield terminates the program. A somewhat similar tool, Stack Guard (http://www.immunix.org/stackguard.html), is able to detect a return address being overwritten in real-time. When it does, it proceeds to terminate the program.

8. Disable Stack Execution. Although it requires the operating system kernel to be recompiled, patches are available for some versions of UNIX that render the stack non-executable. Since most buffer overrun exploits depend on an executable stack, this modification will essentially stop them dead in their tracks. A patch for the Linux kernel has been made available by the Openwall Project (http://www.openwall.com).

9. Know What is on Your System. Awareness of what is on your system and who has the privileges to execute it is essential. SUID root executable and root-owned world-writable files and directories are the favorite targets of many attacks. Find them, list them, and know them. Once your list is complete and in hand, programs are available to test each for buffer overrun vulnerabilities. Should a "segmentation fault" occur during testing, chances are you have just discovered a vulnerable program.

10. Patch the Operating System and Application. Perhaps the very best defense is to stay informed and remain "offensive." As new vulnerabilities are discovered and reported, apply the necessary patches and fixes promptly. If you are in a Microsoft shop, this may get very tiresome very quickly. It may even seem like an endless task. But cheer up. Knowledge in increasing and understanding is improving. The diseased will be cured.

Treat those ideas as the starting points of countering the buffer overflow attack, which can lead you to state-of-art research covering the topics you are most interested in. You can easily generalize this kind of procedure to other use cases, jump on a specific idea, brainstorm over potential solutions, and then dig deeper for more specific and state-of-art solutions that could inspire you in the best ways.

1.6 KEYWORD EXPLANATION

Telehealth: Telehealth refers to the delivery of health-related services and information via the use of electronic information and telecommunications technologies. Communication between patients and doctors across long distances, care, advice, reminders, education, intervention, monitoring, and remote admission are all advantages that may be given via the use of telemedicine. When discussing remote clinical services such as diagnosis and monitoring, the term "telemedicine" may refer to either a broad category of remote clinical services or a more specific category of distant clinical services such as monitoring. When individuals are unable to receive care because of their location, lack of transportation, a limited budget, or staffing constraints, telehealth may assist to bridge the gap. Auphonic provides services such as meeting, supervision, and presentations among practitioners, as well as provider distance-learning, online information, and healthcare system integration, among other things. Telecommunications health (telehealth) can include anything from a live video conference with two clinicians discussing a case to a robotic surgery performed remotely, physical therapy administered through digital monitoring instruments, tests sent between facilities for interpretation by a higher specialist, home monitoring, and online consultation.

Telehealth vs. telemedicine: The terms telehealth and telemedicine are often used interchangeably, despite the fact that telemedicine is much more common. While telemedicine involves the provision of remote clinical services such as diagnosis and monitoring, telehealth involves the provision of preventive, promotive, and curative care to patients over long distances. Non-clinical applications include administration and teaching for healthcare professionals. The United States Department of Health and Human Services uses the term telehealth to designate services such as training and administrative meetings, while the term telemedicine refers to treatment such as remote clinical services provided by physicians. When it comes to the World Health Organization's perspective of health care, the word "telemedicine" is used to refer to all aspects of it, including preventive care. Telecommunications medicine and telehealth are terms that are used interchangeably by the American Telemedicine Association, but the organization recognizes that the term "telehealth" may refer to more broadly remote health that does not involve any medical treatment activities. eHealth, which is particularly popular in the United Kingdom and Europe, as well as telehealth, electronic medical records, and other components of health information technology are some of the additional terms used to describe electronic health records and other components of health information technology.

Buffer overflow: The term "buffer overflow" refers to the situation when a program writes data to a buffer but the buffer border is exceeded, resulting in data being transferred to adjacent memory areas.

In computer programming, a buffer is a section of memory dedicated to storing data while it is being moved or transferred from one part of a program to another. Buffer overflows may occur when abnormal transactions produce extra data, and the buffer was designed with the assumption that all inputs would be smaller than a certain size, resulting in the overflow. If this overwrites adjacent data or executable code, it may result in erroneous program behavior, such as memory access issues, erroneous results, and crashes.

Buffer overflows are a popular and well-known attack vector for exploiting security weaknesses. On many systems, the memory layout of a program, or the memory layout of the system as a whole, is typically well-defined. The data we bring in may be used to cause a buffer overflow, which can then be used to write malicious code or selectively change program state data, resulting in behaviors that were not intended by the original creator. When it comes to operating system (OS) code, buffers are frequently utilized, which makes it simple to perform privilege escalation attacks and, as a consequence, get access to the computer's resources regardless of the user's rights on the system. This was one of the worm's methods of attack in the notorious Morris worm event that occurred in 1988.

The fact that there are no built-in checks to ensure that data delivered to an array (the built-in buffer type) is within the boundaries of that array means that programming languages such as C and C++ that enable buffer overflows are often used in conjunction with these languages. A buffer overflow may occur as a result of the additional code and processing time needed by bounds checking. Modern operating systems use a variety of techniques to prevent malicious buffer overflows, including random memory layout and intentionally leaving buffer and pointer space to detect activities that write into such areas ("canaries").

1.7 SUMMARY

1. Research is defined as "**creative** and **systematic** work undertaken to **increase** the **stock of knowledge**."

2. The research process can be **sequential, generalized, circulatory**, or **evolutionary**.

3. Research can be classified according to its **field, approach**, and **nature**.

4. Research approaches include **case studies, experiments, surveys**, and **action research**.

We have covered the scientific and technical writing process in the first chapter. At the start of the concept development process, students will be provided with a comprehensive description of everything covered in this book, helping them to fully understand how to compose a scientific and engineering research paper. Our study has shown that scientific and engineering research necessitates the use of innovative and systematic approaches, as well as the use of discoveries that add to the current body of knowledge. Research methods may be classified according to whether they use quantitative or qualitative approaches, with quantitative techniques being more prevalent. Any of these may be used to do action research, experimental research, case studies, and surveys. Three different perspectives enable researchers to place research into three categories: work that is done in a certain region, work that is done via a particular technique, and work that is performed by certain characters. Keep in mind that your activities have a direct impact on the case study. The security issues surrounding Telehealth Systems were briefly mentioned in the technical section. An overflow attack is outlined in this post on Telehealth Systems. Despite the fact that this is a novel concept, compiler add-on tools are already widely available that deal with the function return address space to prevent security issues in Telehealth Systems.

Research Integrity

CONTENTS

Scientific research is built on integrity. Without it, the intricate interweaving of the fragile fabric that is scientific inquiry begins to unravel in unexpected and unfavorable ways. Every day, what we do as individual scientists in terms of the experimental protocols and materials we use, the "facts" on which we base our work, the quality of the materials we produce (software, drugs and reagents, materials, and technical data), and the communications we have with others about our work and theirs has an impact on untold others. Individually and collectively, we rely heavily on the fragile link of trust and honesty between us as members of the larger scientific community to grow and innovate.

In this chapter, we will look at some of the most important concerns that you should be aware of as an apprentice in the larger scientific research community. Our objective here isn't to tell you what to believe or do or to provide you any magical algorithms or formulae for deciding what's good and wrong in each scenario. You will rapidly discover that the terrain in scientific research is riddled with complicated, multi-faceted difficulties due to its undiscovered and frequently unforeseen character. Such problems necessitate consideration and may need to be addressed when new data becomes available. You will discover that past experience, family, culture, and religious views may drive you to agree with your peers at times yet to a different opinion and/or behavior at other times. As a result, the goal is to prepare you to think first, inquire second, and act third when confronted with new, unfamiliar, and frequently difficult concepts and circumstances. This will allow you to avoid problems when possible/practical, make sound decisions when challenges arise (and they will), and, in the long run, equip you to act with moral leadership when called upon to adjudicate the complex challenges of modern research with wisdom, compassion, and personal integrity.

2.1 WHY IS RESEARCH INTEGRITY SO IMPORTANT?

The broader scientific community's dedication to the reliability of the research process, sometimes in the face of hardship, is referred to as research integrity. It is critical because the greater scientific community can only innovate and flourish when its members work together as a body to ensure a climate that promotes confidence and trust in our research findings, encourages a free and open exchange of research materials and new ideas, upholds personal and corporate accountability, and recognizes and respects intellectual congruence.

2.2 BE THE WHISTLEBLOWER WHEN YOU SEE IT

As members of the scientific community, we are all responsible for maintaining the integrity of the research process and the scholarship that comes from it. It is critical that we do not overlook or tolerate misbehavior when it occurs and take corrective action when necessary. When research misconduct happens, research integrity requires every one of us as members of the larger scientific community to take responsible action rather than apathy. Speaking up about ethical problems, while emotionally and ethically rewarding, frequently has harmful repercussions. As a result, it is critical to consider the consequences before speaking up. Please don't take it for granted that your privacy will or can be safeguarded. That is not to suggest that you should not speak up for fear of personal repercussions, but instead that you should ensure that you are prepared to cope with the consequences of your actions. Those who expose wrongdoing are frequently labeled as "whistleblowers." There may also be substantial personal and professional consequences, such as the introduction of unpleasant and hostile working circumstances, job loss or demotion, and so on. The basic line is that speaking up requires guts and conviction.

When should you speak out? When:

Criminal action is involved;

Research misconduct has occurred;

Physical injury or loss of life could result; and/or

Facilities, equipment or materials and resources are at risk.

If you want to report an allegation, you should do so in writing and include as much detail as possible, such as the nature of the alleged misconduct, the name of the individual(s) involved and their role(s) in the incident, the date and location of the incident, and a detailed description of the incident. Any written material that supports your concerns should also be mentioned and given. Depending on the gravity of the incident, your institution or university may create a committee to investigate the alleged misbehavior right away. Because severe charges are not common in academia, it is difficult to detail the intricacies of the inquiry process here, but you should expect it to be lengthy and possibly controversial due to the gravity of the allegations involved. When charges of research misconduct are made in federally funded facilities, the Office of Research Integrity has developed standard processes that should be followed.

Genuine cases of scientific misconduct are uncommon. The National Institutes of Health's Office of Research Integrity (NIH ORI) provides summaries of recently closed cases that resulted in administrative action but did not find that misconduct had occurred on the ORI's website.

2.3 FUNDAMENTAL TYPES OF RESEARCH DILEMMAS

Research poses a distinct set of ethical issues. Being aware of these difficulties and prepared to cope with them is critical to your success as a researcher. Do you believe you're ready? Can you answer all of the questions below?

Who owns the laboratory notebook?

With whom can you discuss your research? What can you tell these individuals about your research?

Who owns the creative findings that will result from your work in the laboratory?

What is required for authorship in your laboratory? Will your name go on the by-line of any papers or presentations that result from your work?

What is required for inventorship in your laboratory? Will you be listed as an inventor or any new intellectual property that results from your work this summer?

Is it ever "OK" to copy something you read in print? What information should you cite (credit) when you write up your work? Do you know how to properly cite the work of others in any presentations and/or publications you will create?

Is it ever "OK" to "modify" data, omit data, or make up data?

What relationships if any do you have that might bias you or appear to bias you in the conduct or reporting of your research?

What, if any, are the hazards that are presented by your research project (reagents, products) to you, your colleagues, your institution, and the world? How will you minimize these dangers to yourself and others?

2.4 FALSIFICATION/FABRICATION OF DATA

The integrity of research is dependent on the accuracy of the data and the accuracy of the data record. Falsification and fabrication are important concerns in scientific ethics because they call into question the integrity of data and the data record. Falsification is the practice of deleting or changing research materials, equipment, data, or methods so that the study results are no longer correctly reflected in the research record. Fabrication is the process of making up data or outcomes and then recording and/or reporting them in the research record. Both of these techniques are likely to be among the most serious crimes in scientific research since they call into question the legitimacy of everyone and everything participating in a study effort. These crimes make it difficult for scientists to move forward since no one knows what, if anything, is true and can be trusted – which may lead students and colleagues to squander valuable time, effort, and money exploring dead ends. Because we are all interrelated, when one of us behaves recklessly, we are all susceptible.

The instance of Bell Laboratories' wunderkind physicist Dr. Jan Hendrick Schon is an excellent illustration of this. Allegations of data fabrication and falsification initially surfaced in 2002, when academics contacted Bells Laboratories with evidence that data given in five publications published over two years were suspect. Noise, which is normally random in pattern, seemed similar on data in two of the pictures. Only a short time afterward, the physics community called into doubt the veracity of data in nine more figures published in eight further articles. Bell Laboratories eventually found that Dr. Schon manipulated or misrepresented data appearing in papers between 1998 and 2001 and fired him. Co-authors withdrew seven Nature publications and eight Science articles. Independent efforts by IBM and Delft University (Netherlands) experts failed to replicate results from multiple investigations. The executive summary and report of the inquiry by Lucent Technologies may be read here. Schon and colleagues had published a huge body of work in recent years, and the work was regarded groundbreaking; thus, the impact of his misbehavior on research in the field of Field-Effect Transistors (FETs) was believed to be immense. Govert Schilling estimated in a 2002 article in Science magazine (G. Schilling (2002) Science 296, 1584–1585) that over 100 groups worldwide were engaged in comparative research when the misbehavior was discovered. Postdoctoral and graduate students had been working unsuccessfully in many of these facilities to reproduce and expand on Schon's findings.

2.5 OWNERSHIP OF RESEARCH MATERIALS AND DATA

Normally, your research adviser and workplace will supply you with research materials such as chemical reagents, solvents, and other miscellaneous supplies such as notebooks, pens, zip disks, CDs, paper, and so on for use in carrying out your research project. These supplies are acquired with internal or external money that have been earmarked especially to assist the project on which you are working. This implies that the materials you are using are the property of the research facility and/or institution where you are doing your study. The laboratory notebook is perhaps the most essential of these resources. It has enormous value in terms of intellectual property (research ideas, evidence of reduction to practice, etc.) for your advisor and your employer since it is a record of all of the work that has been completed on a given project. As a result, it is not acceptable to remove laboratory notebooks or any other materials and supplies from the research lab without the express consent of your advisor, nor is it permissible to remove pages from the notebook or photocopy pages without the express approval of your advisor. It is important to note that many laboratory notebooks, particularly those necessary for scientific and engineering laboratory courses, are intended to allow the user to create a duplicate of the notebook's contents. Don't think that just because the notebook design allows you to create a copy means you have permission from your adviser and/or your company to make and keep photocopies of the notebook contents.

Borrowing and using research materials for demonstrations, scientific fairs, or any other projects and/or activities outside of the workplace is also not permitted without the specific consent of your advisor and workplace. There are two possible difficulties here: intellectual property rights and laboratory safety (which also raises liability concerns). In certain circumstances, the resources you utilize in your study may have been obtained from other research organizations and/or corporations via legally signed "transfer of materials" agreements that limit their usage. Even if no formal agreements exist, unforeseen difficulties caused by the abuse of research materials may pose health concerns that might result in significant legal responsibility issues for you and your company.

Advice:

> As a student working in someone else's research laboratory, it is critical that you understand and adhere to your advisor's regulations governing the ownership of research items and data.
>
> Always seek and get written permission from your advisor before using or removing any materials from the laboratory.

2.6 PLAGIARISM

If there is one topic with which you are almost certainly familiar, it is plagiarism. Having said that, while many students have heard the term "plagiarism," many are unsure exactly what it is and why it is treated so severely in academia and the scientific community as a whole. In this part, we'll talk about plagiarism and detail some practical methods you may apply right now to avoid difficulties in the future.

Plagiarism-related events abound on most college campuses. The emergence of the internet and computers and computer technology's capacity to copy and paste from printed materials has undoubtedly exacerbated the problem of plagiarism. Simultaneously, computer technology has proved beneficial in facilitating the identification of plagiarism. Julianne Basinger's essay in the Chronicle of Higher Education in 2000 provided a nice illustration of this. Then freshman Seth Weitberg was researching schooling on the internet. Seth noticed that the text of a paper allegedly written by Mr. Scott D. Miller, President of Wesley College (Delaware), was strikingly similar in content and form to a speech written eight years earlier by Claire Gaudiani, President of Connecticut College, and e-mailed both Mr. Miller and Ms. Gaudiani about his discovery. Following that, inconsistencies were discovered in Mr. Miller's biography published on the Wesley College website. The Chronicle of Higher Education article includes links to the original articles as well as a side-by-side comparison of many extracts from the two publications.

Assistant Professor of Political Science Kim Lanegran discusses her emotional brush with plagiarism from the victim's perspective in a more recent essay published in the Chronicle of Higher Education. Dr. Lanegran received a phone call shortly after defending her dissertation from a doctorate student at another university who had read one of her articles and was curious whether she had published any additional papers on the same topic. Dr. Lanegran transcribed her dissertation onto a diskette and forwarded it to a fellow student who expressed interest in her work. Three years later, she received a copy of the student's dissertation through interlibrary loan and was astounded to find that much of it was copied word for word from her dissertation. Her work was not credited anywhere in the volume. Dr. Lanegran then contacted the student's graduate school and provided proof that the dissertation had been plagiarized, and the student's Ph.D. was discreetly removed. The experience jolted her to the core. In her Chronicle of Higher Education piece, she recounts how it "almost defeated me, questioning my trust in academe's basic ideals as well as my capacity to convert my students into honest academics."

Plagiarism is defined as "the appropriation of another person's ideas, processes, results, or words without giving appropriate credit, including those obtained through confidential review of others" research proposals and manuscripts' by the National Science Foundation's Office of Science and Technology. Plagiarism is primarily an intellectual property issue founded on the concept that words represent ideas, which are a type of intellectual property. The unique representation of those ideas in written form belongs to and is held by the person who expressed them. As a result, copying phrases (small groupings of words), sentences, paragraphs, or entire articles authored by another individual or group of people is not allowed.

If someone truly feels that using that person's words is required in order to correctly and sufficiently express the thoughts involved, then two things must be done:

1. Put quote marks around all of the words borrowed from the original work.

2. In your bibliography, include a reference to the originally published work(s).

2.6.1   Ignorance Is Not a Valid Excuse for Plagiarism

Students may unintentionally plagiarize. Many individuals make the error of copying down the writer's words with the intention of subsequently modifying the wording when they read something and don't comprehend what they've read. Regrettably, later never comes. The majority of individuals just forget that the words scribbled in their notebooks aren't their own. In this situation, ignorance is neither bliss nor a valid explanation for plagiarism. A better option is to just resolve to always write in your own words. If you don't understand anything and feel driven to copy the author's words down, put them in quote marks to know they aren't your own and include the citation for the original work, so you don't have to fight later to find the original citation source.

If you are having difficulty articulating your views clear using your own words, this is most certainly an indication that you do not grasp the subject as well as you believe you do. If you don't understand what you're reading, talk to your adviser, other professors, or classmates about it. When you believe you have grasped the concept, write it down in your own words and contact your adviser, professors, or others if you are unsure whether you have represented the new ideas correctly.

2.6.2 Paraphrasing

People will sometimes substitute one or more words in a phrase or longer portion of another person's work that preserves the original author's sentence structure, arrangement of thoughts and ideas, and lacks proper credit of the borrowed work. This is known as paraphrasing, and it is usually considered a kind of plagiarism. It is not an acceptable practice in the sciences and engineering.

2.6.3 Summary of Useful Guidelines for Writing

1. When writing, always use your own words;

2. If you must utilize someone else's words, put them in quotation marks and include a reference to the original work in your bibliography;

3. Cite, cite, and cite when you write about facts that are the thoughts or efforts of another!

2.7 AUTHORSHIP/ASSIGNMENT OF CREDIT

Authorship is an essential technique of identifying persons responsible for the ideas, experimental work, interpretation, and written representation of work submitted for presentation at professional conferences and/or publishing in a technical journal. As a result, authorship carries a considerable deal of responsibility for the authors listed on the paper, the institutions with which they are connected, and the publisher or professional organization involved with the conference or technical journal. Authorship is critical to the professional reputations of all parties concerned. The criteria for authorship differ slightly between fields, organizations, and individual laboratories. Criteria, on the other hand, typically necessitate that an individual:

1. Contributed a substantial, distinguishable, and unique intellectual contribution to the project. This indicates that the individual must have done more than just act as a pair of hands (following SOPs, capturing data, conducting data entry, performing data analysis, typing, and so on) while carrying out a series of tests.

2. Understands the study as a whole, as stated in the publication, and that he/she

3. Participated in the writing of the technical paper

As such, the author is capable of defending the study's quality, technical interpretation of the data, and written articulation of the work as expressed in the article.

In science and engineering, the order of authorship is also an essential consideration. In general, the order of the names represents the relative importance of each person's contributions to the article. The first person mentioned on a paper's byline is the individual recognized for making the most important contributions to that study. The last name on the report is frequently that of the primary investigator or academic circles, the professor whose work the research study was conducted.

The standards apply to everyone participating in the research endeavor, including supervisors and researchers. In other words, giving mentoring does not qualify someone for authorship on a publication any more than being a laboratory technician does. Being a part of a team working on a research topic does not inevitably transfer into authorship on a paper for the same reasons. All contributors are given authorship based on their professional contributions to the work detailed in the paper in question. Another critical aspect to remember is that age is not a criterion for authorship. High school and undergraduate students have become writers – even first authors – on technical articles published in peer-reviewed journals. Neither the length of time spent nor the amount of effort put into work is a valid justification for authorship. Authorship is determined by the quality of the contributions. Employment status, whether you work on a project as a volunteer, for academic credit, or for money, is also not taken into account when assessing authorship. Finally, keep in mind that even if your advisor first offers you authorship on a publication, the offer may be revoked if your intellectual contributions to the work do not turn out to be as anticipated for any reason.

Advice:

1. Make sure you understand what it takes to be an author on a publication in your lab.

2. To avoid misunderstandings, discuss the requirements for authorship with your adviser before the start of your research project or as soon as feasible.

3. Keep careful notes in your laboratory notebook and write down your contributions to the research.

2.8   CONFIDENTIALITY

Another concept you may be unfamiliar with is confidentiality. If your research project is sponsored by a private enterprise, your institution, and your adviser may have signed a confidentiality agreement, which limits or prohibits some or all spoken and/or written contact with people outside the financial/research connection about the study. These agreements frequently restrict the presentation and/or publishing of research findings to individuals who are not bound by the confidentiality agreement. As a result, you may be unable to discuss your findings at professional conferences or publish them in peer-reviewed journals. As a result, it is critical to inquire about any restricted criteria that may influence your study and/or your capacity to communicate your results at the start of any research project.

Advice:

1. Make sure that you understand your advisor's confidentiality policies.

2. Without initially getting permission from your research adviser, do not discuss details about your study with anybody outside your research group.

3. If someone shares a research funding application, an unpublished paper, or unpublished research results, keep this material secret until the individual permits you to do otherwise.

2.9 INTRODUCTION TO CPU SCHEDULING IN OPERATING SYSTEM

As usual, we will use the last section of this chapter to draw some preliminary ideas on interesting topics of the computer science world. For this chapter, we will use task scheduling in CPUs as a case study.

Task scheduling is a basic technique in computer science that permits better use of the restricted resources of a particular CPU, i.e., one method to use the CPU while another process is on hold. Task scheduling in CPUs tries to improve the system's efficiency, speed, and fairness. When the CPU becomes idle, the operating system must choose one of the processes in the ready queue to run.

There are three basic concepts of CPU scheduling in Operating Systems:

1. Aiming to Maximum CPU utilization obtained with multiprogramming;

2. CPU-I/0 Brust Cycle-Process execution consists of a cycle of CPU execution and I/O wait;

3. Scheduling is central to OS design: CPU and almost all computer resources are scheduled before use.

2.9.1 CPU Scheduling: Schedulers

CPU schedulers carry out the selecting procedure. The scheduler chooses one of the tasks in memory that is ready to execute and assigns the CPU to it [157]. As a CPU scheduler, it chooses one of the processes in memory that is ready to execute and assigns the CPU to it [158].

CPU scheduling decisions may take place when a process:

1. Switches from running to waiting state

2. Switches from running to ready state

3. Switches from waiting to ready

4. Terminates

It is worth mentioning that scheduling tasks 1 and 4 are non-preemptive, which means that a new process must be chosen for execution. Once a process has been assigned a CPU, the process retains the CPU until it releases it by terminating or transitioning to a waiting state. Windows OS 3.1 and Apple Macintosh OS are two well-known instances of employing such a scheduling mechanism.

Non-preemptive scheduling does not interrupt a running CPU process in the middle of its execution [252]. Instead, it waits until the process's CPU burst period is complete before allocating the CPU to another process. Some non-preemptive scheduling algorithms include: Shortest Job First (SJF) Scheduling and Priority (non-preemptive version) Scheduling, among others [247, 248].

Process	Arrival time	CPU Burst Time (in millisecond
P0	2	8
P1	3	6
P2	0	9
P3	1	4

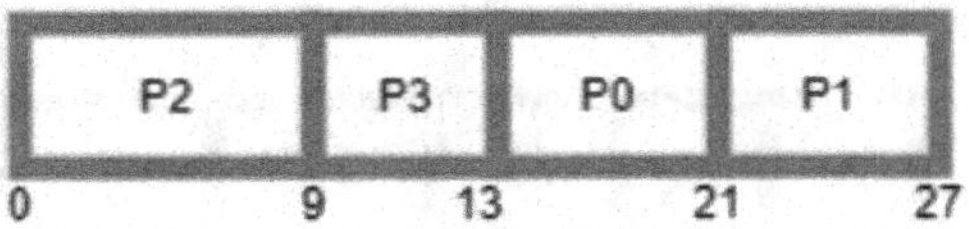

P2	P3	P0	P1
0	9 13	21	27

Figure 2.1: An example of non-preemptive scheduling

Meanwhile, all other scheduling is preemptive, which considers:

1. access to shared data

2. preemption while in kernel mode

3. interrupts occurring during crucial OS activities

Tasks are generally allocated with priorities in this form of Scheduling. Although another job is running, it is sometimes essential to run a task with a higher priority before another task. As a result, the current job is paused for a short time before restarting after the priority task has completed its execution [248].

As a result, this form of scheduling is mostly utilized when a process transitions from a running state to a ready state or from a waiting state to a ready state. The resources (that is, CPU cycles) are primarily provided to the process for a short length of time before being removed, and the process is then placed back in the ready queue if it still has CPU burst time remaining [124]. That process remains in the ready queue until it is given the opportunity to execute again.

Round Robin Scheduling (RR), Shortest Remaining Time First (SRTF), Priority (preemptive version) Scheduling, and others are preemptive scheduling algorithms [109].

Process	Arrival time	CPU Burst Time (in millisecond)
P0	2	3
P1	3	5
P2	0	6
P3	1	5

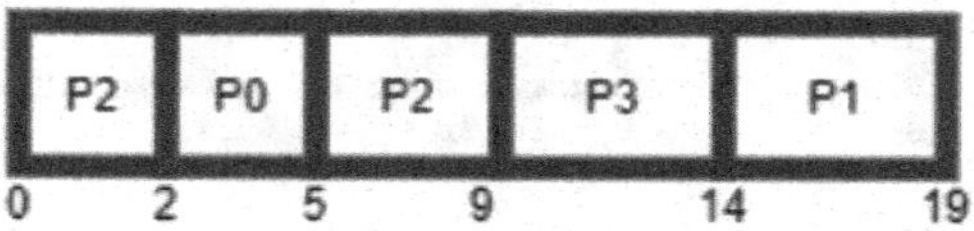

P2	P0	P2	P3	P1
0	2	5	9	14	19

Figure 2.2: An example of preemptive scheduling

2.9.2 CPU Scheduling: Dispatcher

Another component involved in the CPU scheduling process is the dispatcher. The dispatcher is the module that allocates CPU control to the process selected by the short-term scheduler. This function involves the following responsibilities:

1. Switching context

2. Switching to user mode

3. Jumping to the proper location in the user program to restart that program from where it left last time.

As a result, given that it is called at each process change, the dispatcher should be as responsive as possible. Dispatch Latency is the amount of time it takes the dispatcher to stop one operation and begin another. Figure 2.3 describes dispatch latency in further detail:

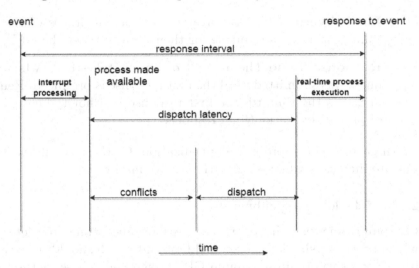

Figure 2.3: An explanation of the dispatch latency

2.9.3 CPU Scheduling: Scheduling Criteria

When looking for the "best" scheduling method, consider the following criteria:

CPU Utilization To make the most use of the CPU and avoid wasting any CPU cycles, the CPU would remain active the majority of the time (Ideally 100% of the time). In a real-world system, CPU use should range from 40% (lightly loaded) to 90%. (heavily loaded.)

Throughput It is the total number of processes accomplished per unit of time, or the total quantity of work completed in a unit of time. Depending on the procedure, this can range from 10/second to 1 hour.

Turnaround Time It is the amount of time required to carry out a specific process, i.e. the time elapsed between the time of process submission and the time of process completion (wall clock time).

Waiting Time The total of the periods spent waiting in the ready queue is the length of time a process has been waiting in the ready queue to get CPU control.

Load Average It is the average number of processes that are waiting in the ready queue for their turn to enter the CPU.

Response Time The amount of time it takes from when a request was submitted until the first response is produced. Remember, it is the time till the first response and not the completion of process execution(final response).

In general, for appropriate optimization, CPU usage and throughput are increased while other variables are minimized.

2.9.4 Scheduling Algorithms

Computer scientists have created various algorithms to determine which processes should be executed first and which should be executed last in order to obtain maximum CPU usage [39]. These methods are:

1. First Come First Serve (FCFS) Scheduling;

2. Shortest-Job-First (SJF) Scheduling;

3. Priority Scheduling;

4. Round Robin (RR) Scheduling;

5. Multilevel Queue Scheduling;

6. Multilevel Feedback Queue Scheduling;

7. Shortest Remaining Time First (SRTF);

8. Longest Remaining Time First (LRTF);

9. Highest Response Ratio Next (HRRN).

In this part, we will go through the two most representative scheduling algorithems as a totorial.

2.9.4.1 First Come First Serve Scheduling

The "First come, first served" scheduling method, as the name implies, executes the process that comes first, or we may say that the process that wants the CPU first, gets the CPU allotted first.

First Come, First Serve is similar to the FIFO (First in, First Out) Queue data structure, in which the data piece added to the queue first is the one that departs the queue first.

It's simple to comprehend and implement programmatically, utilizing a Queue data structure in which a new process enters through the tail of the queue and the scheduler picks a process from the head of the queue. Purchasing tickets at a ticket counter is an excellent illustration of FCFS scheduling in action [251].

Average waiting time (AWT) is a critical statistic for evaluating the performance of any scheduling method [113].

The average waiting time, abbreviated as AWT, is the sum of the waiting periods of the processes in the queue, waiting for the scheduler to choose them for execution.

The scheduling method performs better when the average waiting time is reduced.

Consider the processes P1, P2, P3, and P4 in the table below, which come for execution in the same sequence, with Arrival Time 0, and given Burst Time, calculate the average waiting time using the FCFS scheduling method we can acquire the average waiting time as 18.75 ms.

P1 will be granted CPU resources first; hence, P1's waiting time will be zero. P1 takes 21 ms to complete; hence, the waiting time for P2 is 21 ms. Similarly, the waiting time for process P3 will equal the sum of the execution times of P1 and P2, which is $(21 + 3)$ ms $= 24$ ms. It will be the total execution times for processes P1, P2, and P3. The waiting time for each procedure is accurately represented by the GANTT chart above.

Here are a few flaws or issues with the FCFS scheduling algorithm:

1. It is a non-preemptive algorithm, which implies that the process priority is irrelevant [33]. If a process with the lowest priority is being executed, such as a daily routine backup process that takes more time, and then another high priority process arrives, such as an interrupt to avoid a system crash, the high priority

PROCESS	BURST TIME
P1	21
P2	3
P3	6
P4	2

The average waiting time will be = (0 + 21 + 24 + 30)/4 = 18.75 ms

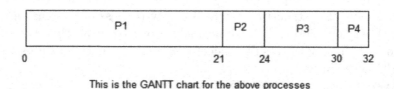

This is the GANTT chart for the above processes

Figure 2.4: An exampling of using FCFS for task schduling

process will have to wait, and the system will crash as a result of improper process scheduling [106].

2. Average Waiting Time is not optimum.

3. Parallel resource usage is not feasible, resulting in the Convoy Effect[1] and, as a result, inefficient resource (CPU, I/O, etc.) utilization.

2.9.4.2 Shortest Job First Scheduling

Shortest Job First (SJF) scheduling prioritizes processes with the lowest burst time or length [189].

SJF is well-known for being the most effective method of reducing waiting time. It is of two types: Non-preemptive and preemptive. To properly implement SJF scheduling, the burst time/duration time of the processes must be known in advance to the processor, which is not always possible [217]. This scheduling technique works best when all jobs/processes are available at the same time (either all arrival times are 0 or all arrival times are the same) [254].

---

[1]The Convoy Effect occurs when numerous processes that require a resource for a short period of time are stymied by a single process that holds that resource for an extended period of time.

Non-preemptive SJF Consider the following processes, which are available for execution in the ready queue, with arrival times of 0 for all and given burst times.

PROCESS	BURST TIME
P1	21
P2	3
P3	6
P4	2

In Shortest Job First Scheduling, the shortest Process is executed first.

Hence the GANTT chart will be following :

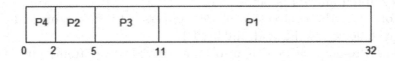

Now, the average waiting time will be = (0 + 2 + 5 + 11)/4 = 4.5 ms

Figure 2.5: An exampling of using SJF for task schduling

As seen in the GANTT chart above, process P4 will be selected first since it has the lowest burst period, followed by P2, P3, and finally P1.

In the last subsection, we scheduled the same set of processes using the first come first serve method and received an average waiting time of 18.75 ms, but with SJF, the average waiting time is 4.5 ms.

Non-preemptive SJF also has its own draw backs. If the arrival times for processes differ, which means that not all processes are available in the ready queue at time 0, and some jobs arrive after some time, a process with a short burst time may have to wait for the current process's execution to finish, because in non-preemptive SJF, when a process with a short duration arrives, the existing job/execution process's is interrupted [101, 193].

This causes the problem of starvation, in which a shorter process must wait for a long period for the present larger process to complete [270]. This occurs if shorter occupations continue to be created, however it is a problem that may be remedied by employing the notion of aging [207].

Pre-emptive SJF Jobs are placed in the ready queue as they come in Preemptive Shortest Task First Scheduling, but when a process with a short burst time arrives, the existing process is preempted or withdrawn from execution, and the shorter job is completed first [226]. In result, the above task's AWT would be $((5-3)+(6-2)+(12-1))/4 = 8.75$. Preemptive shortest job first scheduling has a shorter average waiting time than both non-preemptive SJF scheduling and FCFS scheduling [216].

Because P1 comes first, its execution begins immediately, but shortly after 1 ms, process P2 arrives with a burst time of 3 ms, which is less than P1's burst time, thus P1 is preempted (1 ms done, 20 ms left) and process P2 is run.

P3 comes after 1 ms of P2 execution, but it has a burst time bigger than P2, thus P2 execution continues. However, P4 comes after another millisecond with a burst time of 2 ms, thus P2(2 ms done, 1 ms left) is preempted and P4 is performed.

Following the completion of P4, process P2 is taken up and completed, followed by P2 and, finally, P1.

The Pre-emptive SJF is also known as Shortest Remaining Time First because the job with the shortest remaining time is done first at any given moment in time [262].

2.10 KEYWORD EXPLANATION

Central Processing Unit (CPU): When a computer program is executed, the CPU, also known as a central processor, is responsible for executing the instructions that make up the computer program. Because the program code incorporates all of these activities, the CPU will execute the appropriate arithmetic, logic, controlling and I/O instructions as specified by the program's instruction set. Comparing internal components to external components (such as the main memory and I/O circuits) and specialized processors (such as the graphics processing unit) may help you understand what you're looking at (GPUs).

Operating System: An operating system (OS) is a kind of software that is responsible for managing computer hardware as well as other software resources. It is also often used to provide services to computer programs, such as the Windows operating system. Systems that enable a large number of users to use the computer's resources in an efficient way, such as mass storage, printing, and computing power, may also include software for keeping track of how much time and money each user has spent on the computer. Depending on how the operating system is utilized, an OS function may be called by the application code or halted by the code. Operating systems are used by a wide range of computer-based devices, including mobile phones, video game consoles, web servers, and supercomputers, among others.

2.11 SUMMARY

This chapter discussed academic integrity, which is one of the most important issues that you should be aware of as a newcomer to the scientific research community as well as a scientist in training. When presented with new, unfamiliar, and sometimes difficult topics, the objective is to prepare you to think first, question second, and act third in order to maximize your chances of success. As a case study for the technical portion of this chapter, we explored task scheduling in Central Processing Units (CPUs).

II

Find Your Idea of Research

How to Select Research Topics

CONTENTS

This chapter explains how to choose research directions and specific subjects. Choosing study directions and subjects for scientific and engineering research is influenced not only by personal interests, but also by the authors' previous knowledge and current research trends. Following the key research trends will be highly essential in many science and engineering disciplines because research trends change very fast. This chapter will provide some instances relating to various research trends.

DOI: 10.1201/9781003139058-3

3.1 OVERVIEW

Once you have decided to gain experience by being involved in research, you have to face the huge question: What will I study? If you have decided to join a research lab or jump on board with research that a particular professor is conducting, this question will be answered for you. However, if you will conduct research through an independent study of your own under the advisement of a faculty member, or if you have joined a lab designed to facilitate students' independent research endeavors, this question will probably consume much of your time. However, consider this approach if this is your first research project: look at research that others around you are doing. If any of it interests you, approach that researcher about working together and maybe even adding a variable that you can make your own. There are some significant advantages to identifying a topic this way. If you are interested in an area, work with another researcher on their project. This means you know more about it from the beginning, and whomever you are working with can point you toward key journals, authors, and measures. Also, someone with increased exposure to the area you want to study will be able to help you identify possible problems with your design. After all, they have already had to develop an idea, decide how to approach it, and iron out all the kinks.

If, however, you want to conduct your first project independently, you are likely to have quite a task ahead of you. And if you plan to jump onto someone else's research team, it is always nice to bring fresh ideas to the table when you come. Generally, the identification of a research topic for a new researcher can be broken down into a five-step process:

3.2 IDENTIFY AN AREA OF INTEREST

Selecting a topic is possibly the most challenging part of doing research. Is it too big? Is it too narrow? Will I be able to find enough on it? Start by choosing a topic that you like or are curious about. You're going to be working on it for quite a while, so try and find one that's interesting and that you can reasonably cover in the time and space available.

Indeed, your progress will be faster (and more fulfilling) if you are genuinely interested in your topic, and you may also learn something valuable in the process. Is there an event or problem in your life that's related to the course you are taking? By choosing a topic that has meaning in the broader context of your own life, you may find the answer to a question or solve a problem, in addition to advancing your studies. Don't overlook the importance of motivation because research often requires persistence, and you are more likely to keep looking if you care about finding the answer.

Here are some tips for you to choose your first research topic:

1. Choose a topic that you are interested in! The research process is more relevant if you care about your topic.

2. Narrow your topic to something manageable:

   If your topic is too broad, you will find too much information and not be able to focus.

   Background reading can help you choose and limit the scope of your topic

3. Review the guidelines on topic selection outlined in your assignment.Ask your professor or TA for suggestions.

4. Refer to lecture notes and required texts to refresh your knowledge of the course and assignment.

5. Talk about research ideas with a friend. S/he may help focus your topic by discussing issues that didn't occur to you at first.

6. Think of the who, what, when, where, and why questions:

   WHY did you choose the topic? What interests you about it? Do you have an opinion about the issues involved?

   WHO are the information providers on this topic? Who might publish information about it? Who is affected by the topic? Do you know of organizations or institutions affiliated with the topic?

   WHAT are the major questions for this topic? Is there a debate about the topic? Are there a range of issues and viewpoints to consider?

   WHERE is your topic important: at the local, national or international level? Are there specific places affected by the topic?

WHEN is/was your topic important? Is it a current event or an historical issue? Do you want to compare your topic by time periods?

Also, keep in mind that each area under the science and engineering umbrella has the potential to offer exciting insights into your own research, such as an applicable theory, different statistical methods, or a unique perspective from which to think critically about your own research. This is an essential aspect when you are writing a paper that should accompany major research projects you undertake.

3.3 BROWSE THE LITERATURE

Often, the simple act of reviewing literature that is already out there will spark a flame for a new research idea. Simply by browsing through abstracts from a few key journals in the area you are interested in, you will learn not only about what has been studied but also what has been studied a lot and what has been somewhat ignored. Just browse through journal articles until you come across something that interests you. When you read an abstract and are so interested in the topic that you find yourself wanting to read the whole article, you are there.

Over and above, read a general encyclopedia article on the top two or three topics you are considering. Reading a broad summary enables you to get an overview of the topic and see how your idea relates to more general, narrower and related issues. It also provides an excellent source for finding words commonly used to describe the topic. These keywords may be beneficial to your later research. If you can't find an article on your topic, try using broader terms and ask for help from a librarian.

Here are some tips for getting your hands on browsing the literature to find topics that interest you:

Use the article database that most famous in your domain to scan top-tier conferences, journals. E.g., suppose your research topic or interested domain is within the scope of computer science or electronic engineering. In that case, you might find IEEE explore as a great tool to get yourself to dive into the most recent articles. Meanwhile, google scholar and arXiv are also helpful tools to explore new ideas and topics before official publications.

Use Web search engines to find Web sites on the topic. It is also helpful for you to scan through the industrial needs by exploring articles and news from the internet.

3.4 PICK A TOPIC AND DIVE

After you have a clear awareness of the current status of the wide range of topics, you should start to question yourself on one crucial question: What do you want to study in one word or less?

As you browse through past issues of key journals, write down everything you find interesting. No paragraphs or dissertations for this, just a list of topics or concepts – but be sure to include enough information that you will remember what the items in your list mean. Suppose you write down SQL but don't remember later that SQL stands for Structured Query Language. In that case, you will end up having to go back through journals to find that exciting tidbit again. Now that you have this list, read over it several times put it down, and walk away. The topic(s) you can't stop thinking about is probably the one you want to pursue.

After you have a clear mind on what most interests you, the procedure is to dive and explore more. One thing that we highly recommend is that you should keep your topic manageable. A topic will be challenging to research if it is too broad or too narrow. One way to narrow a broad topic such as "the environment" is to limit your topic. Common ways to limit a topic are:

by geographic region: E.g., what environmental issues are most important in the Southwestern United States?

by culture: E.g., how does the environment fit into the Navajo world view?

by time frame: E.g., what are the most prominent environmental issues of the last 10 years?

by discipline: E.g., how does environmental awareness effect business practices today?

by population group: E.g., what are the effects of air pollution on seniors citizens?

Remember that a topic will be more difficult to research if it is too:

locally confined: Topics this specific may only be covered in local newspapers, if at all! E.g., what sources of pollution affect the Ogden valley water supply?

recent: Be aware if a topic is very recent, books and journal articles will not be available, but newspaper and magazine articles will. Web sites may or may not be available. E.g., events that happened yesterday or last week

broadly interdisciplinary: You could be overwhelmed with superficial information. E.g., how can the environment contribute to the culture, politics and society of the Western states?

popular: E.g., how does environmental awareness effect business practices today?

by population group: E.g., what are the effects of air pollution on seniors citizens?

Also, if you have any uncertainties about the focus of your topic, you should always discuss your topic with your instructors to have their opinons.

3.5 IDENTIFY A RESEARCH QUESTION

Once you have read through your lit search findings, you will have a pretty clear picture of what you want to study, and possibly even how you are going to measure or study it. Your research question is exactly what it sounds like – a statement about the relationship between two variables. For instance, suppose I decided that I am interested in social psychology, browsed the literature, made my list, conducted a lit search, and now know that I want to study prejudice and privilege awareness. A research question might look something like this: How are prejudice and privilege awareness related? The downfall to this question is that it is too broad and lacks a lot of information. Your goal for the research question is not to predict cause and effect, or even the direction of a relationship. Save that stuff for the hypothesis. Instead, the research question should be a semi-broad question that includes all the variables (or factors) you want your research design to consider. A better research question is something like this: How does increased privilege awareness in undergraduate men and women relate to levels of prejudice toward classmates who are members of minority ethnic groups?

This is just a general model to help you get through the process of deciding what to study. In practice, you will probably find that you combine a couple of steps, or do things in a different order. For instance, I often find that research I have done leads me to identify a new research question, and then I have to go back to see what literature is available that relates to that question. This process does not consist of five clear-cut steps for every project, or even for every researcher. However, if you are starting at the beginning, this model will guide you flawlessly through the process.

Before leaving this topic, there are tow other points that I want to make about choosing a research topic. First, It is important to have a solid interest in a topic so that you don't lose interest in the project halfway through. Being passionate about a topic is okay, but don't pick one that is extremely emotional for you. While a huge personal investment in the topic might give be a driving force when you first start out, there is a danger that the continued emotional arousal will produce overwhelming stress over time. Remember that research is an involved process, and can take a long time to complete. Initiating and conducting research is a huge responsibility, which can also be stressful. Wait until you are a little more comfortable with research the way it is before making it more stressful than it has to be. If you enjoy your first project, you are more likely to do a second.

The final thing you should consider when selecting a research topic is this: Do not try to solve all the problems of the world in your first study! There are a lot of problems in this world and it will take at least a dozen studies to solve them all. Of course, this is a joke. You cannot solve all the problems of the world through what research you can accomplish during your lifetime. Accept (and appreciate) the fact that small questions have scientific impact. This is a hard fact for many students to accept. Hanging out with other student researchers, there is this running joke that someday my name will be included in the list of researchers that all dedicated psychology students are familiar with: Freud, Zimbardo, Milgram, Bandura, Chumney.... Yes, this delusion is nice and it always gets a few giggles, but it is not realistic. The goal of your research should be to enhance psychology as a science, not revolutionize it.

3.6 LIST OF RESEARCH TOPICS AND KEYWORDS IN COMPUTER SCIENCE

This section aims not to provide strict guidelines for you to stick with the following topics. But, we would like to provide you with some of the trending topics and domains that fall into the range of computer science and technology, which might shed some light and help you when you are trying to decide what you might want to do for your first project.

3.6.1 Artificial Intelligence

When most people hear the term "artificial intelligence," they usually envision robots from the film "Terminator." However, this is far from the case. AI is intended to be as near to logical thinking as feasible. It employs binary logic (much like computers) to assist in the resolution of a wide range of issues. Applied AI is limited to a single job. A branch of generalized AI involves researching a human-like machine that can learn to do anything. Artificial intelligence is already assisting researchers in quantum physics and medicine. Every day, you interact with AI when online stores recommend goods based on your prior purchases. Siri and self-driving cars are more instances of AI in action.

The goal of generalized AI is to mimic multitasking human intellect. It is, however, still in the early stages of development. Computer technology has yet to reach the level required for its development. Improving healthcare management is one of the most recent advances in this field. It is accomplished by digitizing all of the information in hospitals and even assisting in the diagnosis of patients. Privacy concerns and facial recognition technology are also being investigated [80, 82]. Some governments, for example, gather biometric data in order to minimize and even anticipate crime [5].

Because AI development is so important right now, it's a good idea to put some time and effort into investigating it. Here are some suggestions for artificial intelligence research areas to consider:

1. What are the most influential areas of life where machine learning is used?

2. How do you pick the best machine learning algorithm?

3. Compare and contrast supervised vs. unsupervised machine learning Algorithms for reinforcement learning in machine learning [97]

4. As a subset of machine learning, deep learning [177]

5. Artificial neural networks and deep learning

6. What is the operation of artificial neural networks?

7. Model-free and model-based reinforcement learning methods are compared.

8. Single-agent vs. multi-agent reinforcement learning

9. What kind of interactions do social robots have with humans?

10. Natural language processing [301]

11. Computer Vision [205]

12. Applications of computer vision: self-driving automobiles

13. Recommender systems [85, 132, 260, 295]

14. The link between the Internet of Things and artificial intelligence [19, 134, 176, 258]

15. How much data is generated by Internet of Things devices [73, 152]

3.6.2 Communications and Media

As a result of technology, communications and media were one of the first areas to be affected. Previous-generation people had no idea how easy it would be to make connections now [290]. Even in the most distant locations, internet access is becoming more prevalent. Aside from social contact, media is being employed for corporate growth and education. Starting a fully online business or promoting an existing one is now possible. Many prestigious institutions also offer online degrees as well [259].

Recently, AI has being used to boost communications and media [53]. For customers who are always demanding, the technology allows for the creation of tailored content. Multiple career opportunities are created by the growth of the media. Influencers, for example, have been a popular professional path in recent years. Always, influencers make use of the most appropriate communication instruments at their disposal [268]. Live video and podcasting are currently the most popular forms of media [264]. Now, all you have to do is grab your smartphone to take advantage of all of the aforementioned options. Online, you may apply for a college, look for a career, or reach out to all of your followers, among other things. How far communication and media can advance is difficult to conceive...

Research subjects in media and communications technology may be easy and interesting. Hopefully, you'll find THE ONE among these ICT research tpoics:

1. Communication ethics in new media [221]

2. During the last decade, computer-mediated communication has become increasingly commonplace.

3. The social media revolution has altered the way we communicate.

4. What role does the media play during disasters? Does it increase or decrease panic?

5. A comparative study of authorities' media portrayals throughout the world

6. Does the public begin to choose newspapers over new media once more?

7. What is the impact of the Internet on media [90]?

8. Networks for communication [63].

9. Super Bowl advertisements and social media.

10. Technology and personal touch are two methods of communication.

11. Content marketing concepts that are new.

12. Adolescents' media exposure and its influence.

13. Personal socialization and the effect of mass media

14. A tool for advertising using the Internet and interactive media.

15. A digital universe of music promotion When it comes to the media, how do individuals make use of hype?

16. Videoblog communication psychology.

17. Speaking out: The media and the right to free speech Trust may be built through virtual communication, but can it be earned?

18. When it comes to social media, how can you retain privacy?

19. Technology and cyberbullying.

20. How has the development of computers affected interpersonal communication?

21. Communication technology in the future [169, 187].

22. The use of ICT by businesses to gain a competitive edge.

23. Healthcare and Information and Communications Technology [117, 170, 178].

24. Without mainstream media, can we survive?

25. 21st century mass media and morals

3.6.3 Computer Science and Engineering

"I think computer viruses should count as life, it says something about human nature that the only form of life we have created so far is purely destructive"

Stephen Hawking
Theoretical Physicist & Cosmologist

If you've ever questioned how computers operate, you'd be wise to consult a computer science engineering expert. This major brings together two distinct, but linked, worlds of machines.

Computer science is concerned with the brain of the computer. It often encompasses disciplines like as programming languages and algorithms. Additionally, scientists identify three paradigms within the area of computer science. Computer science, according to the rationalist paradigm, is a subset of mathematics. While the technocratic paradigm is concerned with software engineering, the scientific paradigm is concerned with natural sciences. Surprisingly, the latter also exists in the field of artificial intelligence!

On the other side, computer engineering is responsible for the physical structure of a computer – its hardware and software. It is highly reliant on electrical engineering. And only by combining computer science and engineering can the machine be fully understood. When it comes to trends and breakthroughs, the growth of artificial intelligence is perhaps the most significant in the field of computer scientific technology. Big data is a subject that has exploded in popularity over the last several years. Cybersecurity is and will continue to be a major area of study in our Information Age [165, 192]. Virtual reality is also the newest trend in computer science and engineering.

If you're looking for a decent thesis subject or are just preparing for a speech, have a look at this list of computer science and engineering research topics:

1. What is the relationship between virtual reality and human perception?

2. Computer-assisted education's future.

3. Computer science and data modeling on a large scale.

4. Implicit vs. declarative languages in computer science.

5. The use of blockchain and artificial intelligence to algorithmic regulation [79, 171, 199, 233].

6. Banking sector & distributed ledger technology [212].

7. How does the architecture of the machine impact the efficiency of code?

8. Parallel computing languages [164, 213].

9. What is the purpose of mesh creation in computational domains?

10. Methods for optimizing persistent data structures [42, 179].

11. Cyber-physical systems vs. sensor networks [31, 70, 77, 118].

12. The evolution of computer graphics: a case study in non-photorealistic rendering [116].

13. The evolution of programming languages for systems [14].

14. Network economics & game theory [282, 291].

15. What impact does computational thinking have on science?

16. Computer science theory applied to functional analysis [145, 186, 302].

17. Cryptographic methods that are the most efficient [114, 168, 170, 296].

18. An overview of the many kinds of software security [197].

19. Is it feasible to eradicate phishing completely?

20. Floating point and programming

3.7 DYNAMIC PROGRAMMING IN RESEARCH AND PROBLEM SOLVING

Dynamic Programming is one of the fundamental optimization methods over plain recursion [210, 249]. We may use Dynamic Programming to optimize recursive solutions with repeated calls for the same inputs. The goal is to save the outcomes of subproblems so that we don't have to recompute them later. This straightforward improvement decreases the time complexity from exponential to polynomial. Let's build a basic recursive solution for Fibonacci Numbers, for example. We obtain exponential time complexity, and if we optimize it by storing subproblem answers, we get linear time complexity.

This fundamental optimization method has a great impact on almost all computer programmers. You can see tons of real-life cases and industrial problems that fall into the scale that can adopt dynamic programming [185].

3.7.1 An Example for Cost Minimization

Figure 3.1 shows an example of a cost minimization problem, where each node represents a specific task. And tasks of the same column can be conducted simultaneously, i.e., task A, B, and D can be parallel conducted. Each task can be settled using different approaches with a different time overhead and costs shown in the tables in Figure 3.1. The total time constraint for accomplishing these three-level six jobs is six time units. The goal of such a problem is to minimize the total cost subject to the time constraint.

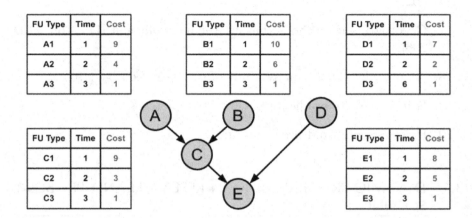

Figure 3.1: An example of a cost minimization problem.

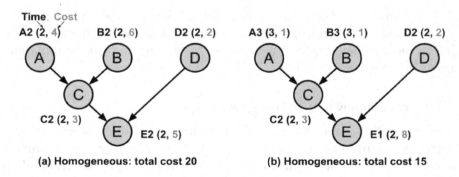

Figure 3.2: Two assignment examples.

Figure 3.2 illustrates two possible assignment of the tasks that satisfies the time units constraints. Where we find assignment (a) within the time constraint, the cost is 20; meanwhile, assignment (b) only costs 15.

Now, we will elaborate on the specific procedure of conducting dynamic computing using a simpler example, as shown in Figure 3.3. Here, we only have three different levels of tasks that need to be done. The time constraint is seven-time units. Each task can be addressed using two different approaches as shown in the tables in Figure 3.3. In Figure 3.3 (b), we show the best assignment of this whole task, which has a total cost (TC) of seven.

To compute such optimum results, instead of computing the total cost of the three tasks for each iteration, we use dynamic programming to store the sub-problem's results and simply deploy them when we need them [125]. For example, we first calculate all the possible approaches' costs that satisfy the total time constraints regarding just task A, which would be 4 (A1, 1) (cost (task, time)), and 1 (A2, 3). Then we based on those recorded results of task A to compute the possible approachs' costs from A to B, which would then be 9 (B1, 3), 5 (B2, 5), 6 (B1, 5), 2 (B2, 7). Finally, we include task C and compute the minimum cost that satisfies the time constraint based on merely the records above (A to B), which would be 12 (C1, 5), 10 (C2, 6), 9 (C1, 7), and finally 8 (C1, 7).

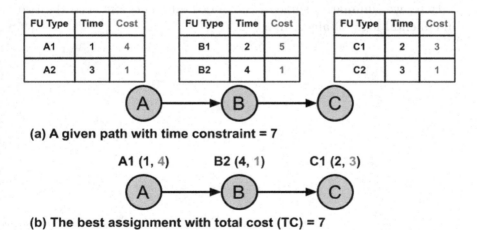

FU Type	Time	Cost
A1	1	4
A2	3	1

FU Type	Time	Cost
B1	2	5
B2	4	1

FU Type	Time	Cost
C1	2	3
C2	3	1

(a) A given path with time constraint = 7

A1 (1, 4) B2 (4, 1) C1 (2, 3)

(b) The best assignment with total cost (TC) = 7

Figure 3.3: A simple path example.

The core idea of dynamic programming is to avoid repeated work by remembering partial results [78, 126]. This is a very common technique whenever performance problems arise. In fact figuring out how to effectively cache stuff is the single most leveraged thing you can do to often dramatically improve performance with a small amount of work.

3.7.2   Greedy vs. Dynamic

Document Distance Algorithms- to identify the extent of similarity between two text documents used by Search engines like Google, Wikipedia, Quora and other websites.

For example, consider the Fractional Knapsack Problem. The local optimal strategy is to choose the item that has maximum value vs weight ratio. This strategy also leads to global optimal solution because we allowed taking fractions of an item.

Dynamic programming is mainly an optimization over plain recursion. Wherever we see a recursive solution that has repeated calls for the same inputs, we can optimize it using Dynamic Programming. The idea is to simply store the results of subproblems so that we do not have to re-compute them when needed later. This simple optimization reduces time complexities from exponential to polynomial. For example, if we write a simple recursive solution for Fibonacci Numbers, we get exponential time complexity and if we optimize it by storing solutions of subproblems, time complexity reduces to linear.

Here, we summarize some of the major difference between the two fundamental logic of algorithm:

Feature	Greedy method	Dynamic programming
Feasibility	In a greedy Algorithm, we make whatever choice seems best at the moment in the hope that it will lead to global optimal solution [22].	In Dynamic Programming we make decision at each step considering current problem and solution to previously solved sub problem to calculate optimal solution [69].
Optimality	In Greedy. Method, sometimes there is no such guarantee of getting Optimal Solution.	It is guaranteed that Dynamic Programming will generate an optimal solution as it generally considers all possible cases and then choose the best.
Recursion	A greedy method follows the problem solving heuristic of making the locally optimal choice at each stage.	A Dynamic programming is an algorithmic technique which is usually based on a recurrent formula that uses some previously calculated states.
Memoization	It is more efficient in terms of memory as it never look back or revise previous choices	It requires dp table for memoization and it increases it's memory complexity.
Time complexity	Greedy methods are generally faster. For example, Dijkstra's shortest path algorithm takes O(ELogV + VLogV) time.	Dynamic Programming is generally slower. For example, Bellman Ford algorithm takes O(VE) time.
Fashion	The greedy method computes its solution by making its choices in a serial forward fashion, never looking back or revising previous choices.	Dynamic programming computes its solution bottom up or top down by synthesizing them from smaller optimal sub solutions.

3.7.3 Industrial and Research Applications of Dynamic Programming

Industrial people love using DP, and most of the requests people make will execute many instances of it. Starting with databases caching common queries in memory, through dedicated cache tiers storing data to avoid DB access, web servers store common data like configuration that can be used across requests [299]. Then multiple levels of caching in code abstractions within every request prevent fetching the same data multiple times and save CPU cycles by avoiding recomputation. Finally, caches within users browser or mobile phones that keep the data that doesn't need to be fetched from the server every time [73].

As for the field of artificial intelligence research, automatic speech recognition is an extremely important area of research. To transition from systems using hybrid models that exploit HMMs for data segmentation into a pure end-to-end deep learning system, we needed to introduce a method for automatically segmenting input data and post-processing output data [181].

In 2006, Alex Graves introduced a method that allowed modern deep recurrent architectures to represent a probability distribution over all possible label sequences [32]. His idea, at its core, automated the requirement of pre-segmenting training data and post-processing outputs into labeled sequences (and it did so exceptionally efficiently). This method is called connectionist temporal classification.

Using the magic of dynamic programming, CTC computes a forward pass that denotes the total probability of a particular label prefix at time-step t and a backward pass that denotes the total probability of a particular label suffix at time t. Both forward and backward computations are built, time-step by time-step, by applying the concept of dynamic programming [240, 297].

DP simplifies CTC from a combinatorial problem (compute the distributions for all viable paths of a certain length) into a polynomial problem, making training deep CTC models computationally tractable [297].

Here, we list a bunch or more state-of-art applications of dynamic programming for reders' interests:

1. In Google Maps to find the shortest path between source and the series of destination (one by one) out of the various available paths.

2. In networking to transfer data from a sender to various receivers in a sequential manner.

3. Multi stage graph

4. Travelling salesman problem

5. Largest common subsequence – to identify similar videos used by youtube

6. Optimal search binary tree

7. Single source shortest path-Bellman Ford Algorithm.

8. Document Distance Algorithms- to identify the extent of similarity between two text documents used by Search engines like Google, Wikipedia, Quora and other websites.

3.8 SUMMARY

Lists of recommendations for computer science research topics were offered to you in this chapter, along with detailed explanations of each suggestion. We have provided you with a selection of computer science subjects that appear to be promising. In the technique part, we briefly covered dynamic programming and how it may be used in research and problem-solving situations.

CHAPTER 4

Literature Review and Formulating a Problem

CONTENTS

DOI: 10.1201/9781003139058-4

This chapter describes the suggestion on how to do a comprehensive literature review and to summarize the research challenge from the previous publications. In the science and engineering area, understanding the previous publications' research background, research motivation, contribution, and future work will be vital for building basic knowledge on the current research. By reviewing the previous works and the novel problem can be summarized. Then, the next step is to formulate this problem with a clear description. A few examples will be given in this chapter for showing how to do a thorough literature review and problem formulation.

4.1 WHAT IS A LITERATURE REVIEW?

A literature review is much more than a list of separate reviews of articles and books. They are common and very important in the sciences. A literature review is a critical, analytical summary and synthesis of the current knowledge of a topic. It should compare and relate different theories, findings, and so on, rather than just summarize them individually. It should also have a particular focus or theme to organize the review. It does not have to be an exhaustive account of everything published on the topic. But it should discuss all the more significant academic literature important for that focus.

The organization of a review depends on the type and purpose of the review, as well as on the specific field or topic being reviewed. But in general, it is a relatively brief but thorough exploration of past and current work on a topic. Literature reviews are usually organized thematically, such as different theoretical approaches, methodologies, or specific issues or concepts involved in the topic – rather than a chronological listing of previous work.

A thematic organization makes it easier to examine contrasting perspectives, approaches, methodologies, findings, etc., and to analyze the strengths and weaknesses of, and point out any gaps in previous research. This is the heart of what a literature review is all about. A literature review may offer new interpretations, theoretical approaches, or other ideas. If it's intended to be part of a research proposal or report, it should demonstrate the relationship of the research to others' work. But whatever else it does, it must provide a critical overview of the current state of research efforts.

4.2 TYPES OF LITERATURE REVIEWS

There are different types of literature reviews and different purposes. The most common are:

4.2.1 Stand-Alone Literature Review Articles

These provide an overview and analysis of the current state of research on a topic. The goal is to evaluate and compare previous research on a topic to provide an analysis of what is currently known and to reveal controversies, weaknesses, and gaps in current work – pointing to directions for future research.

Writing a stand-alone review can be an effective way to get a good handle on a topic and to develop ideas for your own research. E.g., the basis of your research project can be contrasting theoretical approaches or conflicting interpretations of findings.

Can you find evidence supporting one interpretation vs. another, or can you propose an alternative interpretation that overcomes their limitations?

You can find examples published in countless academic journals. There is a well known journal series called Annual Reviews: http://www.annualreviews.org/ specifically devoted to literature review articles. The best known literature review journal for computer science is called Computing Reviews: http://reviews.com/

4.2.2 Research Proposal

This could be a proposal for a Ph.D. dissertation, a senior thesis, or a class project. It could also be a submission for a grant.

The literature review, by pointing out the current issues and questions about a topic, is a crucial part of demonstrating how your proposed research will contribute to the field, and hopefully convince your thesis committee to allow you to pursue the topic of your interest or a grant funding agency to pay for your research efforts.

4.2.3 Research Report in the Workplace

When you finish your research and write your thesis or paper to present your findings, it should include a literature review to provide the context in which your work is a contribution. Your report should show how your work relates to others' work, in addition to detailing the methods, results, etc. of your research.

This kind of literature review is often a revision of the review for a research proposal, which may be a revision of a stand-alone review. Each revision should be a fairly extensive revision. With the increased knowledge and experience in the topic as you proceed, your understanding of the topic will increase. So you will be in a better position to analyze and critique the literature. Also, your focus will change as you proceed in your research. Some areas of the literature you initially reviewed will be marginal or irrelevant for your eventual research and you will need to explore other areas more thoroughly.

4.3 COMMON STRUCTURE OF LITERATURE REVIEWS

Dr. Mankoff provided you with some examples of how your literature reviews should look. They may vary in how they are organized. But a common general structure is to have sections such as:

Abstract – Brief summary of the contents of the article

Introduction – An explanation of the purpose of the study; a statement of the research question(s) you intend to address

Literature review – A critical assessment of the work done so far on this topic – to show how the current study relates to what has already been done

Methods – How the study was carried out (e.g. instruments or equipment, procedures, methods to gather and analyze data)

Results – What was found in the course of the study

Discussion – What do the results mean

Conclusion – State the conclusions and implications of the results; discuss how it relates to the work reviewed in the literature review; also point to directions for further work in the area

4.4 WHAT IS THE LITERATURE?

The "literature" that is reviewed should be written by scientists and researchers for scientists and researchers. They may include any of the following:

1. Academic, scholarly journal articles (i.e., peer-reviewed)

2. Books

3. Conference Proceedings

4. Dissertations

5. Patents

6. Standards

7. Technical Reports

8. Websites and other Internet Resources

4.5 THE "INFORMATION CYCLE"

The diagram below is a brief picture of how scholarly literature is produced and used. Research does not have a beginning or an end. Researchers build upon work that has already been done in order to add to it, providing more resources for other researchers to build on.

They read the literature of their field to see what issues, questions, and problems are current, then formulate a plan to address one or more of those issues. Then they make a more focused review of the literature, which they use to refine their research plan. After performing their research, they present their results (such as presentations at conferences and/or published articles) to other scientists in the field. So they add to the general subject reading ("the literature").

Research may not have a beginning or an end. But researchers have to begin somewhere. There are three categories of types of literature: primary, secondary, and tertiary. Let me explain these in more detail.

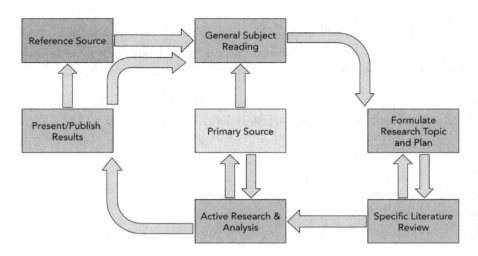

Figure 4.1: Illustration of information cycle

4.5.1 Primary Sources

Direct, uninterpreted records of the subject of a research project. Primary sources are what you perform your research work on. So a primary source can be almost anything, depending on the subject and purpose of your research.

A few examples of what can count as primary sources would be:

1. **Lab Reports** – Records of the results of experiments

2. **Field Notes**, Measurements, etc. – Records of observations of the natural world (electrons, elephants, earthquakes, etc).

3. **Conference Proceedings** – Scientists and researchers getting together and presenting their latest ideas and findings

4. **Articles of Original Research** – Published in peer-reviewed journals

5. **Dissertations**

6. **Patents**

7. **Internet** – Websites that publish the author's findings or research; e.g., your professor's home page listing research results. But remember, use extreme caution when using the Internet as a primary source . . . anyone with a computer can put up a website.

4.5.2 Secondary Sources

Books, articles, and other writings by scientists and researchers reporting their work to others. They may be reporting the results of their own primary research or critiquing the work of others.

So these sources are usually the focus of a literature review: this is where you go to find out in detail what has been and is being done in a field, and therefore to see how your work can contribute to the field.

4.5.3 Tertiary

These include encyclopedias, indexes, textbooks, and other reference sources. In general, there are two types of tertiary (reference) sources:

Summaries/Introductions – Encyclopedias, dictionaries, textbooks, yearbooks, and other sources that provide an introduction or summary "state of the art" of the research in the subject areas covered. They are an efficient means to quickly build a general framework for understanding a field.

Databases/Indexes – Provide lists of primary and secondary sources of more extensive information. They are an excellent way of finding books, articles, conference proceedings and other publications in which scientists report the results of their research.

4.6 WORKING BACKWARDS

Usually, here's how your research process for a literature review will work:

Tertiary – Start by finding background information on your topic by consulting reference sources for introductions and summaries. Find bibliographies or citations of secondary and primary sources.

Secondary – Find books, articles, and other sources providing more extensive and thorough analyses of your topic. Check to see what other scientists have to say about your topic. Find out what has been done and where there is a need for further research. Discover appropriate methodologies for carrying out that research.

Primary – Now that you have a solid background knowledge of your topic and a plan for your own research, you're in a better position to understand, interpret, and analyze the primary source information. Find primary source evidence to support or refute what other scientists have said about your topic. Or posit an interpretation of your own and look for more primary sources. Or create more original data to confirm or refute your thesis. When you present your conclusions, you will have produced another secondary source to aid others in their research.

4.7 THE PUBLISHED LITERATURE

Let's get a better understanding of how scientists publish and report the results of their research.

4.7.1 Peer Review

An important part of academic publishing is the peer review, or refereeing, process. When a scientist submits an article to an academic journal or a book manuscript to a publisher, the editors or publishers send copies to other scientists and experts in that field who review it.

The reviewers check to make sure the author has used methodologies appropriate to the topic, that they've used those methodologies properly, taken other relevant work into account, and adequately supported the conclusions, as well as considered the relevance and importance to the field. A submission may be rejected or sent back for revisions before being accepted for publication.

Peer review does not guarantee that an article or book is 100% correct. Instead, it provides a "stamp of approval" saying that experts in the field have judged this to be a worthy contribution to the discussion of an academic field.

Peer reviewed journals typically note that they are peer-reviewed, usually somewhere in the first few pages of each issue. Books published by university and most association presses typically go through a similar review process (e.g., IEEE Press). Other book publishers may also have a peer review process. But the quality of the reviewing can vary among different book or journal publishers. Use academic book reviews or check how often and in what sources articles in a journal are cited. Ask a professor or two in the field, to get an idea of the reliability and importance of different authors, journals, and publishers.

Informal Sharing – Scientists discuss their ongoing projects to let others know what they are up to or to give or receive assistance with their work. Conferences and online discussion forums (blogs, wikis, etc.) are common ways for these discussions. Increasingly, scientists are using personal websites to present their work.

Conference Presentations – Many organizations sponsor conferences at which scientists read papers, or display at poster sessions to present the results of their work. To give a presentation, scientists submit a proposal which is reviewed by those sponsoring the conference. Some databases list conference proceedings along with the author and contact information.

Journals – Articles in journals contain specific analyses of particular aspects of a topic. Since these can be written and published more quickly than books, academic libraries subscribe to many journals and the contents are indexed in databases and elsewhere so you can easily find them.

Books – Books take a longer time to get from research to publication. But they can cover a broader range of topics, or cover a topic more thoroughly than articles or conference presentations. Always remember to search your library catalog for titles. Librarians can show you how to search for books elsewhere beyond simply Google Books and you can request to borrow them through the Interlibrary Loan process usually at no cost.

Dissertations/Theses – Graduate students earning advanced degrees typically write a substantial piece of original work and then present the results in the form of a thesis or dissertation. Usually, only the library and/or department at the school where the work was done has copies of the dissertation. But once again, the library can usually get you a copy of most dissertations at no cost.

Websites – In the process of tracking down journal articles and conference proceedings, you'll learn who the better known scientists are in your particular field of research. Look for their personal websites to see if you can find additional sources that you haven't found elsewhere.

Reference Sources – Encyclopedias, dictionaries, and other reference sources provide introductions or summaries of the current work in a field or on a topic. These are usually written by a scientist and/or publisher serving as an editor who invites submissions for articles from experts on the topics covered.

4.8 HOW TO FIND THE LITERATURE

OK, so how to find the literature?

4.8.1 Computer Science Research Databases

1. **ACM Digital Library:** Full text of journal articles, conference proceedings, and reviews published by the Association for Computing Machinery (ACM).

2. **CiteSeerX:** Free computer science citation database with some full text available. Lists the most frequently cited authors and documents in computer science, as well as impact ratings. Also provides algorithms, metadata, services, techniques, and software.

3. **IEEE Xplore:** Full text of all IEEE journals and conference proceedings published since 1988. Also includes all current IEEE standards. Some titles available pre-1988.

4. **Lecture Notes in Computer Science:** Full text of conference proceedings in computer science from Springer. About 100 conferences published per year.

5. **ScienceDirect:** A full text scientific database offering science, medical, and technical (STM) journal articles and book chapters from more than 2,500 peer-reviewed journals and over 11,000 books.

6. **Scopus:** Supports research needs in the scientific, technical, medical, and social sciences fields and, more recently, also in the arts and humanities. Contains both peer-reviewed research literature and quality web sources. Includes citation linking and citation tracking for patents.

4.8.2 Footnote Chasing

The key articles in encyclopedias, books, or journals are always helping. The bibliography at the end of each paper or article is another way to help you chase the most interesting topics. In such a way, you can access more articles that interest you by tracking down existing ones.

4.9 WRITING THE LITERATURE REVIEW

Keep these points in mind as you are writing your literature review:

1. What is the purpose for the literature review and make sure your review specifically addresses your purpose(s).

2. Write as you read, and revise as you read more. Rather than wait until you have read everything you are planning to review, start writing as soon as you start reading.

3. You will need to reorganize and revise it all later. But writing a summary of an article when you read it helps you to think more carefully about the article.

4. Having drafts and annotations to work with will also make writing the full review easier since you won't have to rely completely on your memory or have to keep thumbing back through all the articles.

5. The first draft is for you, so you can tell yourself what you are thinking. Later you can rewrite it for others to tell them what you think.

Here are some general steps that one can follow when you writing a literature review:

Stage One: Annotated Biblography. As you read articles, books, etc., on your topic, write a brief critical synopsis of each. After going through your reading list, you will have an abstract or annotation of each source you read. Later annotations are likely to include more references to other works since you will have your previous readings to compare. But at this point the goal is to get accurate critical summaries of each individual work.

Stage Two: Thematic Organization. Find common themes in the works you read and organize them into categories. Usually, each work in your review can fit into one category or sub-theme of your main theme. But sometimes a work can fit in more than one. Write some brief paragraphs outlining your categories, how in general the works in each category relate to each other, and how the categories relate to each other and to your overall theme.

Stage Three: More Reading. Based on the knowledge you have gained in your reading, you should have a better understanding of the topic and of the literature. You have discovered specific researchers who are important to the field or methodologies you were not aware of. Look for more literature by those authors, on those methodologies, etc. You may be able to set aside some less relevant areas or articles which you pursued initially. Integrate the new readings into your literature review draft. Reorganize themes and read more as appropriate.

Stage Four: Write Individual Sections. For each section, use your annotations to write a section which discusses the articles relevant to that theme. Focus your writing on the theme of that section, showing how the articles relate to each other and to the theme, rather than focusing your writing on each individual article. Use the articles as evidence to support your critique of the theme rather than using the theme as an angle to discuss each article individually.

Stage Five: Integrate Sections. Now that you have the thematic sections, tie them together with an introduction, conclusion, and some additions/revisions in the sections to show how they relate to each other and to your overall theme.

4.10   KEY POINTS WHEN WRITING A LITERATURE REVIEW

More specifically, here are some points to address when writing about works you are reviewing. In dealing with a paper or an argument or theory, you need to assess it (clearly understand and state the claim) and analyze it (evaluate its reliability, usefulness, and validity). Look for the following points as you assess and analyze papers, arguments, etc. You do not need to state them all explicitly, but keep them in mind as you write your review:

> **Be specific and be succinct.** Briefly state specific findings listed in an article, specific methodologies used in a study, or other important points. Literature reviews are not the place for long quotes or in-depth analysis of each point.

> **Be selective.** You are trying to boil down a lot of information into a small space. Mention just the most important points in each work you review.

> **Is it a current article?** How old is it? Have its claims, evidence, or arguments been superseded by more recent work? If it is not current, is it important for historical background?

> **What specific claims are made?** Are they stated clearly?

> **What support is given for those claims?** E.g., what evidence, and what type (experimental, statistical, anecdotal, etc.)

is offered? Is the evidence relevant? Sufficient? What arguments are given? What assumptions are made and are they warranted?

What is the source of the evidence or other information? The author's own experiments, surveys, etc.? Government documents? How reliable are the sources?

Does the author take into account contrary or conflicting evidence and arguments? I.e., how does the author address disagreements with other researchers?

What specific conclusions are drawn? Are they warranted by the evidence?

How does this article, argument, theory, etc., relate to other work?

However, these are just the points that should be addressed when writing about a specific work. It is not an outline of how to organize your writing. Your overall theme and categories within that theme should organize your writing and the above points should be integrated into that organization.

4.11 ADAPTIVE RESOURCE ALLOCATION IN CLOUD SYSTEMS

From an overview, cloud computing is an exciting trend in the IT community. In cloud computing, people move computing and data from local to large data centers [227]; then, the service is conducted through the Internet and provided by the data centers [298].

Cloud computing in 2021 has become the go-to model for information technology as companies prioritize as-a-service providers over traditional vendors, accelerate digital transformation projects, and enable the new normal of work following the COVID-19 pandemic [74].

And while enterprises are deploying more multicloud arrangements the IT budgets are increasingly going to cloud giants. According to a recent survey from Flexera on IT budgets for 2021, money is flowing toward Microsoft Azure and its software-as-service offerings as well as Amazon Web Services [304]. Google Cloud Platform is also garnering interest for big data and analytics workloads. But hybrid cloud and traditional data center vendors such as IBM, Dell Technologies, Hewlett-Packard Enterprise, and VMware have a role too.

Below we list out some of the most popular cloud computing examples:

4.11.1 Types of Cloud Computing

There are three types of cloud deployment models: private, public, or hybrid; and with three types of cloud computing: Infrastructure as a Service (IaaS), Platform as a Service (PaaS), and Software as a Service (SaaS). With IaaS, companies control their own computing, networking, and storing components without having to manage them on-premises physically. PaaS, provides developers with a framework to build custom applications, while SaaS avails internet-enabled software to organizations via a third party [110, 271].

The three main types of cloud deployment models are private, public, or hybrid. One can select your desired model depends on your specific requirements.

Private cloud consists of an infrastructure that is owned by a single business. This model can be hosted in-house or can be externally hosted. Although expensive, the private cloud model is well suited for large organizations with a focus on security, customizability, and computing power.

Pros of a private cloud:

· Highest level of security;

· Better autonomy over the servers;

· Highly customizable;

· No risk of sudden changes that can disrupt company operations;

Cons of a private cloud:

· Requires extensive expertise of IT personnel;

· Comparatively expensive;

Public cloud consists of services and infrastructure that are shared by all organizations. With huge available space, scalability becomes easier in public cloud solutions. Organizations pay public cloud models on a pay-per-use basis, making it a suitable solution for smaller businesses looking out to save money.

Pros of a public cloud:

> · Highly scalable;
>
> · Cost-effective;
>
> · Management is delegated to the cloud service provider;
>
> · Not bound by geographical restrictions;

Cons of a public cloud:

> · Offers less customization;
>
> · Sudden changes by cloud provider can have dire impacts;
>
> · Lesser autonomy over servers;
>
> · Since the server is shared, it is less secure;

Hybrid Cloud is a combination of both public and private clouds, which combines the two models to create a tailored solution that allows both platforms to interact seamlessly.

Pros of a hybrid cloud:

> · Highly secure, flexible, and economic;
>
> · Better security than pure public cloud solutions;

Cons of a hybrid cloud:

> · Since communication occurs between public and private clouds, it can become conflicted at times.

Most of the universities that students can access are considered private clouds or hybrid clouds.

4.11.1.1 IaaS (Infrastructure as a Service)

IaaS provides an on-demand infrastructure to organizations on a pay-as-you-go basis over the Internet instead of via a traditional datacenter. IaaS has the following physical and virtual resources that allow organizations to run workloads in the cloud:

Physical datacenters. IaaS providers have tens of powerful servers spread across the world to provide on-demand and scalable computing. IaaS provisions these components as a service rather than users interacting with them directly.

Compute resources. IaaS compute resources are Virtual Machines (VMs) that are managed by hypervisors. IaaS providers provision VMs based on CPU, GPU, and memory consumption for various workloads. Organizations can auto-scale and load-balance different workloads based on the performance characteristic they want to achieve [108].

Networks. Software-defined networking programmatically manages network hardware such as switches and routers [26, 27, 76].

Storage. IaaS providers offer highly distributed storage technologies such as file storage, block storage and object storage that are resilient and easily accessible over Hypertext Transfer Protocol (HTTP).

Startups can opt for the IaaS model to avoid the costly and tedious process of setting up on-premises IT infrastructure. Similarly, large corporations that want to retain control over their IT infrastructure, but with the flexibility of paying only for resources consumed, can also use this model.

Common examples of IaaS include Amazon Web Services (AWS), Microsoft Azure, Google Cloud Platform (GCP), Rackspace and Alibaba Cloud.

Disadvantages of IaaS:

1. Because IaaS has a multi-tenant architecture, there are data security issues associated with it.

2. If there are vendor outages in IaaS solutions, users might be unable to access their data for some time.

3. Managing a new infrastructure can be challenging, thus giving rise to the need for team training.

4.11.1.2 PaaS (*Platform as a Service*)

In a PaaS model, developers lease the infrastructure they need for a complete application lifecycle: development, testing, deployment and maintenance [84]. Like IaaS, developers rent the servers, networking and storage components. In addition, they also lease items like middleware, development tools, and database management systems (DBMSs) from the PaaS provider [190].

PaaS allows an organization to avoid the often costly and complex process of purchasing and managing software licenses. Essentially,

PaaS providers manage everything else related to the application life-cycle while allowing developers to focus on applications they are de-veloping [230]. PaaS is particularly useful for organizations that want to streamline workflows in a production environment that has multiple developers [253].

PaaS can also minimize costs greatly and simplify the application development lifecycle in a Rapid Application Development (RAD) envi-ronment [229]. Common examples of PaaS include Google App Engine, Apache Stratos, OpenShift, AWS Elastic Beanstalk, and Heroku.

Disadvantages of PaaS:

1. PaaS can have data security issues.

2. Since not every element of existing infrastructure can be cloud-enabled, there might be compatibility issues with adopting PaaS solutions.

3. The speed, support, and reliability of PaaS depend on the vendor.

4.11.1.3 SaaS (Software as a Service)

In this model, SaaS providers host software on their servers and lease it to organizations on a subscription basis [67]. Rather than IT admin-istrators installing the software on individual workstations, the SaaS model allows users to access the application via a web browser where they log in with their usernames and passwords [133].

Under the SaaS model, organizations can lease productivity soft-ware such as email, collaboration and calendaring. Also, they can lease other business applications, including enterprise resource plan-ning (ERP), document management, and customer relationship man-agement (CRM) [136].

Startups can use the SaaS model to launch enterprise applications quickly if they do not have the time to set up the server or software. Common examples of SaaS include Dropbox, Google GSuite (applica-tions), Cisco Webex, and GoToMeeting.

Disadvantages of SaaS:

1. There is a limited range of solutions with SaaS.

2. Network connectivity is a must when it comes to using SaaS solutions.

3. There is a loss of control when using SaaS solutions.

4.11.1.4 Cloud Computing vs. Traditional Web Hosting

A cloud service has three distinct characteristics that differentiate it from traditional web hosting:

1. Users can access large amounts of computing power on demand. It is typically sold by the minute or the hour.

2. It is elastic – a user can have as much or as little of a service as they want at any given time.

3. The service is fully managed by the provider (the consumer needs nothing but a personal computer and internet access). Significant innovations in virtualization and distributed computing, as well as improved access to high-speed internet, have accelerated interest in cloud computing [36].

4.11.2 Task Scheduling in Cloud Computing Systems

Task scheduling is the main problem in cloud computing which reduces system performance [121]. When we discuss task scheduling in cloud computing, we are referring the task scheduling in IaaS cloud computing systems.

In IaaS, applications can be partitioned into several tasks. From an overview, we can specialize the problem of parallel processing of those tasks:

1. How to allocate resources to the tasks?

2. In what order the clouds should execute the tasks?

3. How to schedule overheads when VMs prepare, terminate or switch tasks?

Most of those tasks can be regarded as optimization tasks but with no straightforward solutions. Two major focuses on this study are: 1. Developing efficient task scheduling mechanism in IaaS cloud system; 2. Developing feedback dynamic scheduling algorithms for scheduling tasks.

4.11.2.1 Model of Task Scheduling

Figure 4.2 presents an example of an IaaS cloud computing model. The clouds are connected via the Internet.

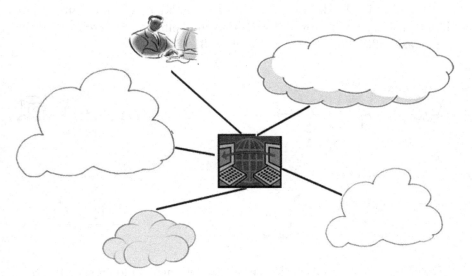

Figure 4.2: An example of a cloud model

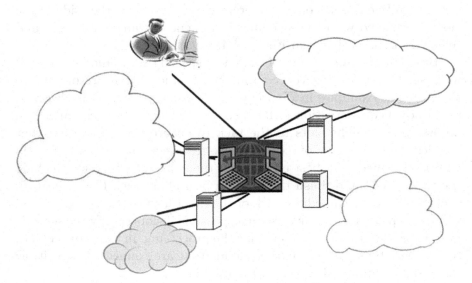

Figure 4.3: An example of a cloud model with build-in schedulers

The purpose of the cloud scheduling mechanism is to build schedulers running in the data center of every provider, which communicate with each other, thus provide reliable and efficient schedules for the users' tasks [265], as shown in Figure 4.3.

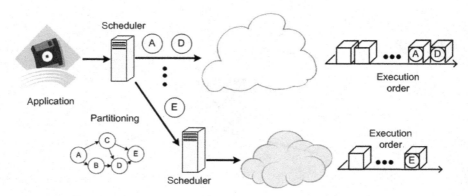

Figure 4.4: An example of a cloud model with build-in schedulers

To be more specific, the scheduler partitions the job requested from the users into several smaller tasks [120]. And the schedulers decide where a given task is executed in the cloud, i.e., they assign the tasks towards different parts of the different clouds. On the other side of the cloud-connected with the scheduler is a queue of waiting for tasks and rejected tasks, as shown in Figure 4.4.

Based on the importance of those tasks, each task would be assigned with slots representing the computational and storage resources, as shown in the examples in Figure 4.5. Suppose a given task is classified as an advance reservation (AR) task. In that case, the scheduler will be assigning specific slots to the tack to ensure the reservation that enables the tasks to be processed in the reserved time being. If a given task is classified as a best-effort task, then the scheduler will include the task at last and finish the job in a best-effort way. If a given task is classified as an immediate task of the highest importance, the model will try to process the task as soon as possible if slots satisfy the server's job. If the resource is not enough for the processing, in that given cloud, reject the job as pass it to other clouds that are connected with it, as the assignment case 3 shown in Figure 4.5.

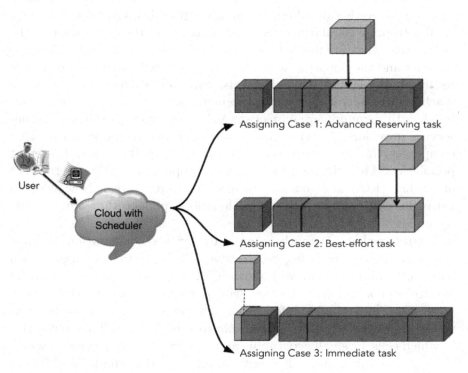

Figure 4.5: An example of assigning tasks based on importance

4.12   KEYWORD EXPLANATION

5G (network): Known as 5G, this technology is the fifth-generation broadband cellular network technology that mobile phone operators across the world began deploying in 2019. It will ultimately replace the fourth-generation (4G) networks that now service the vast majority of mobile phones. It is predicted that there will be more than 1.7 billion users of 5G networks by 2025, according to the GSM Association. 5G networks, like previous cellular networks, are cellular networks in which service delivery is carried out in small geographic areas known as cells, similar to prior cellular networks. An antenna in the cell transmits the radio waves that are needed to connect wireless devices in a cell to the Internet and the phone network. New networks will have more capacity, resulting in faster download speeds, with some networks capable of reaching 10 Gbit/s. Because of the increased availability of networks, bandwidth demands are expected to rise, prompting existing internet service providers (ISPs) such as cable internet to merge with other companies that can meet the needs of the rapidly growing internet population. This will open the door to new opportunities in the Internet of Things (IoT) and machine-to-machine applications. New wireless networks can only be utilized with mobile phones that support 5G technology.

6G (network): Currently, standards for sixth-generation wireless communications are being created for cellular data networks, which will use technology that will allow 6G. It will be the next generation of wireless communications that will be much faster than the current generation. [unverifiable information] Previous versions of the 6G networks are expected to be comparable to broadband cellular networks, in which cells, or small geographic areas, serve the service area in which they are deployed. Many different companies and a number of different countries have shown an interest in the development of sixth-generation networks (also known as 6G networks).

In the near future, 6G networks will likely support virtual and augmented reality (VR/AR), omnipresent instant communications, pervasive intelligence, and the Internet of Things, among other applications (IoT).

Due to the widespread use of mobile edge computing, artificial intelligence, short-packet communication, and blockchain technologies, network operators can expect to adopt flexible, decentralized business models for 6G, including local spectrum licensing, spectrum sharing, infrastructure sharing, as well as intelligent automated management.

Cloud Computing: Cloud computing is a service that provides on-demand access to computer resources without requiring the user to exert direct control over the resources. Large clouds often have a scattered function that is distributed over a number of locations, with each location acting as a data center in its own right. In order to achieve coherence and scale economies, cloud computing relies on the sharing of resources, which is a key feature of cloud computing. Cloud computing is increasing as a result of the abundance of hardware, networking, and computing resources that are easily accessible, as well as the widespread usage of hardware virtualization, service-oriented design, autonomic and utility computing, and other emerging technologies and techniques. By the year 2017, it is expected that Linux-based operating systems would power 90 percent of public cloud infrastructure worldwide. Cloud computing may be a function that is only available to a single company or to a group of businesses (public cloud). Cloud providers, by using a "pay-as-you-go" model, help clients in lowering capital expenditures; nevertheless, they also have the potential to result in unexpected operating charges for customers who are not well informed.

Scheduling (computing): In computer science and engineering, a schedule is the process of allocating resources to complete tasks on a schedule. Processors, network connections, and expansion cards are all examples of resources. Threads, processes, and data flows are just a few of the types of tasks we've covered thus far.

When it comes to scheduling, the mechanism known as the scheduler is in charge of things. Schedulers are often built with the goal of optimizing system usage and capacity, allowing multiple users to share system resources efficiently, or distributing resources in an efficient way in order to achieve a certain level of Quality-of-Service (QoS).

It is critical to the functioning of a computer system that the concept of scheduling be understood, and it is an integral part of the computer system's execution model. In order for a computer system to function properly, the idea of scheduling must be understood (CPU).

4.13 SUMMARY

Throughout the course of the chapter, we have discussed what a relevant literature review is and how to go about doing one. We went through all of the different types of literature reviews that may be done in our first class session in great depth. As a result of this conversation, we spoke about the essential structure of literature reviews in more detail. The information cycle is used as a guide to help you write a solid literature review, which we will demonstrate at the end of the text. Adaptive resource allocation in cloud systems is covered in depth in this section of the technique section, which is written from the standpoint of a system. There is a comprehensive overview of the many types of cloud computing services that are accessible.

How to Generate Research Ideas

CONTENTS

This chapter describes how to generate an idea to start research work. The scientific or engineering papers normally require novel ideas on either theoretical or practical aspects. Corresponding to the formulated problems, the novel idea should have a significant difference or improvement compared with ideas in the literature review. Then, the authors should be able to summarize this novel idea with simple but clear descriptions.

DOI: 10.1201/9781003139058-5

5.1   BE PATIENT

Johnson stresses that good ideas don't come from 'Eureka' moments but as the result of slow hunches: an interesting thought, a gut feeling, a small seed that is grown and nurtured into a good idea. The time this takes can vary from days to years. The important thing about a hunch is that it is not a fully formed idea, and may even turn out to lead nowhere in the short term. But by keeping that hunch consciously accessible rather than ignoring or forgetting it, and by colliding old hunches with new ones, a really great idea may emerge.

From a research perspective making notes of these hunches is key – do you always record your early thoughts or trust that you'll remember them when it comes to the analysis stage? And do you revisit these hunches throughout the analytical process to stop them from stagnating? The reality of research means that slow and in-depth analysis can feel like a luxury. But hunches can grow and develop across projects, clients and sectors, and each chance to revisit them could take the idea a little further.

5.2   COLLECT HUNCHES READY TO BE STITCHED TOGETHER LATER

How you record your hunches is an important part of the process of 'incubation' and 'collision'. I've found a combination of dedicated notebooks and blogging to be useful. My notebook is not a collection of meeting minutes and scrawled interview notes, but a place to record the unconnected sparks and interesting ideas I come across. It is now full of other people's thoughts that I've collected from conferences, books and of course research projects.

Blogging is another fun way of recording the thoughts that you stumble across. My blog is now a visual diary of interesting case studies, media innovations, and insight nuggets I've read, and I love looking back and finding thoughts that I had forgotten about. Recommendation tools like Stumbleupon are another great way to bookmark interesting thoughts and find other people's favorite items on the web.

An interesting tip that Johnson gives about collecting hunches is to avoid categorising them. The act of organisation can limit and channel thoughts too early in the idea generation process, while allowing them to mingle can facilitate their free connection. This has some quite interesting implications for qualitative analysis frameworks – where does the balance lie between free connection and thematic identification?

5.3 CONNECT YOUR HUNCHES WITH THE HUNCHES OF OTHERS

Good ideas rarely come from solitary pursuits. An analysis session or brainstorm is a great place to share hunches, but how often is this saved until the later stages of the research process rather than developed throughout?

We've just completed a piece of analysis for a homeware client, the success of which I believe was down to the collaborative process. We wanted a way that the entire research team could share and develop hunches from day one and we decided that the group blogging service Posterous would be great for this – it's free and easy to use. Throughout the project the research team shared their hunches and uploaded images and related articles. We were able to help develop one another's hunches and feed in new thoughts as the research progressed.

The approach allowed us to become cultural trendspotters, which was particularly fitting for this project. As we shared our discoveries, they inspired even more avenues for exploration and we ended up with over 70 blog posts and many more comments, creating a wealth of stimuli for our client and a strong foundation for identifying the key cultural trends in their category. It created better ideas that had been nurtured in many minds throughout the project, and sped up the analysis stage at the end.

5.4 DIVERSE MINDS

Bringing many minds together is important, but also crucial is the diversity of those minds – speaking to people with different perspectives. Johnson recommends freely publishing your ideas for all to use in a 'creative commons' approach, but at present this is at the edge of most people's comfort zones (not to mention the client confidentiality issues).

However, there is enormous advantage in involving broader stakeholders in the idea generation process. As a research team embedded in a media agency, this is where my team is fortunate. A few steps across the room and we are at the desks of our clients' media planners, strategists and econometricians. We have close relationships with their creative agencies and sometimes we can bring in media owner perspectives too.

This kind of diversity worked nicely when we used a blogging platform in our analysis. It turned out that the core four-person research team was only the start of it – our team extended to include people in our department who wanted to help develop our ideas, and went even further to include the planners, strategists and even our client.

Diversity of interests is another key way of colliding ideas, and is how I, as a researcher, can justify reading books about typography and design at work. "Have a lot of hobbies," Johnson advises. Diverse interests, he believes, were key to the success of Charles Darwin in developing his theory of evolution; and John Snow, the 19th-century doctor who worked out that cholera was carried in the water, not the air. Even the technology that became the worldwide web began as a hobby of its creator, Tim Berners-Lee.

5.5   MAKE SPACE FOR HUNCHES TO INCUBATE

Finally, good ideas come when you aren't forcing them. I remember hearing somewhere about the three "B's being great hubs of creative ideas: in the bath, on the bus and in bed." While research projects don't always leave space for relaxed timelines it's important to create some space for your mind to wander – even half a day for the hunches to incubate. Maybe go for a walk, or even just get away from the desk and sit somewhere else for a bit.

5.6   ACTIVELY LOOK FOR THE IDEA FITS YOU

This section is an attempt to provide some more specific advices to Ph.D. students in computer science. Cybersecurity and artificial intelligence are two of our major research interests. As a result of the examples I will provide, students in this specific field may find it more relatable. However, those suggestions should also easy to generalize to other practice areas such as networking, systems, and architecture. The thoughts expressed in this section are primarily based on my personal experiences and, as such, may be prejudiced and biased. Nonetheless, I'm hoping that some of you will find it beneficial.

For those of you who have never done any research before enrolling in a Ph.D. program, it can be intimidating to even consider where to begin. There are two extremes on a scale: (1) You are fortunate (or unfortunate) to be part of a highly creative group where many ideas are thrown at you – this is common when you work with a junior faculty member (of course with exceptions). (2) You are a member of a well-established group in which your adviser no longer provides students with concrete ideas to work on. Instead, they may provide a high-level direction along with a few relevant studies. That is, all you have to work with in order to generate a research idea.

If you fall into the first category, it is certainly beneficial to begin your first research assignment and follow through the entire procedure... except that you are not going through the complete process from beginning to end. In reality, you are skipping the most hardest part of any research endeavor, in my opinion: coming up with a strong study idea. Everything has a cost. Yes, you will receive an earlier publication, maybe a very good one, as a result of your advisor's idea selection and formulation (or a postdoc or senior grad student). However, you forego the opportunity to be schooled to generate your own ideas on your own, which is a vital talent for a Ph.D. I, too, am guilty as an advisor, for example, by undertaking the difficult work of identifying a vulnerability and then delegating the rest to the student.

If you fall into the second category, it could be a make or break issue. Either you pick out a decent concept to work on, or you waste the first one or two years of your Ph.D., realizing it isn't going anywhere and quitting. You want to begin the training process of seeking for a research proposal as soon as feasible in either sort of group (or anyplace in between). Otherwise, I consider it a severe shortcoming that may significantly harm you in the future when you graduate, such as having difficulty managing a research program independently as a professor in academia or researcher in industry. Here are a few pointers that I find useful:

5.6.1 Acquire the Ability to Read and Improve Your Taste

Ideas do not appear out of nowhere. One of the most prevalent methods for generating new ideas is to read other people's work and get inspired. Pay close attention to the relevant seminar classes, as this is where you will begin reading a large number of papers. Almost certainly, you will also be needed to create paper responses in which you will offer your thoughts, critiques, and any helpful thoughts. It can be difficult at first to read three–four papers per week for each class (I was taking two such classes in the same semester when I was a student). Maintain your composure. One widespread myth is that you must comprehend *all* the technical intricacies of a paper in order to consider the work completed. That is neither the primary objective nor an efficient use of your time! It is truly a process of learning to understand and critique research concepts in such seminars, e.g., what makes a paper good or bad? What makes a paper interesting? You are not have to read the entire document in order to answer these questions. There are numerous publications on how to read research papers that are really helpful. For instance, S. Keshav's "How to Read a Paper."

More importantly, determine which types of papers most interest you and why. Consider the cybersecurity field as an example; it is so vast that I am unlikely to capture all. In terms of study domains, any subject of computer science, such as operating systems, network protocols, or any software or hardware, has associated "game rules" and "security threats" that can be investigated. Additionally, human beings, who are frequently the weakest link, play a critical part in cybersecurity. They range in terms of study styles from novel assaults and exploitation techniques to studies of emerging systems or algorithms, as well as defenses and measures. Another dimension is the research tools employed in a publication, which may include manual analysis, reverse engineering, program analysis, formal methods, hardware-based system design, and data-driven approaches such as machine learning and artificial intelligence. Identifying your preferred types of papers will assist you in developing your own research taste and, ultimately, in narrowing your scope when developing a new research concept.

I was first drawn to the innovative defense that applies in state-of-the-art environments early when I first start research. They are innovative, sleek, and extremely satisfying, as they enable you to identify security holes that no one else sees. When I read these types of studies, I often wonder, "How did these people discover the flaws?" "What abilities are required to do this type of research?" This has intentionally or unconsciously led me to cultivate the attitude and abilities essential for pursuing a Ph.D. in this form of study. Given that my advisor was a MANET security expert at the time, I naturally concentrated on security issues in advanced 5G-enabled networks (e.g., VANET security). However, I did not have the opportunity to study any solid approaches at the time, such as program analysis, formal methods. As I neared the end of my bachelor's program, my research interests shifted correspondingly, as I recognized that fixing security challenges without adequate automated tools in my toolbox moving forward is neither truly sustainable nor scalable. As a result, I began studying machine learning/artificial intelligence. This has worked exceptionally well for me. Of all, everyone is unique, and you may always discover your own preferences and carve out your own route. Indeed, this is precisely the allure of academic liberty!

5.6.2 Recognize the Trends Associated with the Development of Research Ideas

Each paper has its own unique story, although their origins may frequently be divided into a few categories. The majority of these are drawn from my personal research experiences, but others are derived from the work of other researchers. For instance, Professor Philip Guo of UCSD wrote an excellent blog article describing different patterns. Below is another version, complete with specific examples. Take note that these patterns are not always orthogonal. They are merely mechanisms for realizing how an idea is generated. Once you've mastered a few of these patterns, coming up with fresh concepts will be a breeze (of course, you still need to triage the value of an idea before deciding to commit to it).

Pattern 1: Fill Out the Blank This is a straightforward pattern that I learned about during my undergraduate years. Conceptually, the concept is quite straightforward. Read a few articles on a topic, make notes about the differences between them in terms of assumptions, system guarantees/properties, approaches, techniques, and datasets, and then create a table (not necessarily 2-dimensional). Look for empty spaces; these are potential new research areas on which you might focus your efforts (in fact many good papers use such a table or figure to clearly distinguish themselves from related works). One example is in the field of adversarial machine learning, where many researchers initially concentrated on images, for example, how to disrupt a photograph of a cat such that it is misclassified as a banana. Eventually, more domains such as video, audio, and malware will be explored (e.g., how to fool a malware classifier by injecting meaningless instructions). Another straightforward example is that while static analysis has been used to discover some sorts of vulnerabilities automatically, no one has yet used dynamic analysis. You may then compare the advantages and disadvantages of static vs. dynamic analysis for particular types of vulnerabilities. Of course, there are additional sorts of static and dynamic analysis in practice. You can create a much finer-grained table, which will increase your chances of identifying the blanks. Similarly, if a particular sort of vulnerability has been researched, you may be able to work on another type.

For this pattern to work well, it's important to know the size of the room. There will be more blanks to fill the deeper you dig. To construct a table and convince yourself that a specific technique has not been tried out to solve an issue, you must be familiar with the many types of program analysis techniques. There are numerous types of vulnerabilities that you need to be aware of (there are a dozen of memory corruption vulnerability types alone).

There are normally two ways to draw out the dimensions. To begin, broaden your reading and search for distinctions between publications on comparable topics. They will come in helpful one day when you connect the dots, believe me. Another option is to study survey articles, which often summarize a space in a number of dimensions previously. In the field of cybersecurity, the IEEE Security and Privacy conference (a prestigious one) accepts and publishes a few papers in the form of Systemization of Knowledge each year (SoK). If you're interested in the subject, you should read them.

Pattern 2: Expansion This is the logical next step in the process of "fill out the blank." As previously noted, determining appropriate measurements for a place can be the most difficult stage. However, if you already have some thoughts in a space (for example, published a paper or two), you may be in a better position to notice dimensions that others do not.

Our ICCV 2021 paper "Rethinking the Backdoor Attacks" Triggers: A Frequency Perspective" can be an interesting example, as we expand the detection of deep learning backdoors to the frequency domain, thus finding a simple but effective way to detect existing backdoor triggers, presenting a new perspective for the attackers to develop novel attacks. While backdoor attacks have been thoroughly investigated in the image domain from both attackers' and defenders' sides, an analysis in the frequency domain has been missing thus far. So we look into how we can expand the backdoor attacks and defense from the frequency perspective. Therefore this paper comes up.

Pattern 3: Build a Sword then Find Palces to Adapt The high-level idea is that if you have unique expertise, technique, system, or even dataset (that no one else can easily replicate), you can take advantage of it and use it to look for interesting problems to solve (we are lucky to have so many practical problems in computer science). An interesting example I can relate to is Tajana S. Rosing's group's recent work on hyperdimensional computing. They developed and generalized hyperdimensional computing to a variety range of implementations, ranging from IoT to biology and energy control.

My Ph.D. group, ReDS lab at Virginia Tech has also been trying to generalize the utility learning model we proposed, thus implementing them for more generalized cases, including data quality management, active learning, etc. [250].

Even if this is, in my opinion, a great technique to conduct research, i.e., impactful and sustainable, it is not for everyone. To begin with, developing the knowledge, system, or infrastructure to the point where you can begin reaping the benefits can be incredibly time-consuming. Second, such projects may necessitate the vision, planning, and co-ordination of a team (sometimes beyond the ability of a single Ph.D. student). Finally, few groups usually dominate a space. It is quite tough to outperform them unless you have a distinct point of view. That being said, if you can identify an area where a lot of people are in need but no appropriate answer exists, it might be worth exploring.

Pattern 4: From Zero to Hero A study idea is frequently sparked by a minor observation. After some investigation, you can determine whether it can be expanded into a full-fledged idea worthy of publication. Now, deciding whether to pursue it and how much time you should spend digging before giving up can be difficult. In my experience, there are a few positive signals to watch for: (1) When you first saw it, the initial observation (however minor) was exciting and startling. (2) As you delve deeper, you find that the phenomenon is anchored in something fundamental and cannot be easily explained by well-known concepts (e.g., a novel design flaw that leads to security vulnerabilities). (3) The observation is unlikely to be a one-time occurrence; for example, there is a larger space behind you, and there are numerous additional similar scenarios that you can study.

I can again use our ICCV 21 paper as an example [279]; at the very beginning, we actually just start with the idea of what it looks like in the frequency domain. Then we observed the frequency artifacts that hold true across different existing triggers and datasets. Thus the generalized effect can thus earn for an explanation, and unified exploration then comes our paper.

Pattern 5: Reproduction of Prior Work The preceding pattern may have made you wonder, "How do I make these minor observations or discoveries in the first place?" One method is to try to replicate the results of a previously published paper. Believe it or not, what is published in a study may not be exactly what you notice when you try to replicate it. There are several causes for this: (1) Inadvertent errors committed by the authors, (2) some results not being 100% replicable by design, e.g., measurement of some Internet event that changes over time, and (3) skewed benchmarks or datasets chosen to benefit a method suggested in a study. If you can find significant differences or restrictions in previous work, it usually suggests there is room for development. Even if you are successful in reproducing the work exactly as planned, there may be additional insights or side discoveries that were not addressed in the publication along the road (there is only so much space in a paper).

An interesting example is the SHAP (SHapley Additive exPlanations), which currently became one of the most effective ways to explain datasets and models. The paper was a reproduction of the Shapley value from the 60s, which originally belongs to the economic domain.

Pattern 6: Industry, News, and More If you work in a practical field like cybersecurity, there must be a lot going on in the industry and in real life (outside of academia). Take advantage of opportunities to engage with industry professionals and learn about their pressing requirements and problem points. They are excellent resources for research ideas. Despite being more resourceful than academia, the industry has a distinct priority and perspective when it comes to tackling technical difficulties, for example, they are more interested in trustworthy solutions and less willing to invest in hazardous ones. The wonderful thing about academia is that we don't have to solve the problem completely in one shot, and it may be exploratory. In reality, you are in some ways responsible for defining a success metric/threshold. If you are solving a real problem in the industry for which there is no good solution yet, the threshold for a "successful" research project is significantly lowered.

Other patterns specific to cybersecurity research: (1) Adversarial research is a type of study in which two people compete against one other Because security is essentially adversarial, assaults and defenses are a continuous subject. You can always try to shatter a pre-existing defense or construct a defense against an attack. Indeed, I've frequently seen an unique assault paper followed by a defensive piece (which may or may not come from the same group). (2) Process automation. Many aspects of system security analysis, including as reverse engineering, vulnerability detection, bug triage, exploitation, and determining whether or not a patch has been implemented, have always needed some manual effort, at least in some contexts. Automating (even partially) such a procedure using techniques such as program analysis can have tremendous scientific value. This is a pattern that may extend beyond cybersecurity but is particularly common in system security.

5.6.3 Make it a Habit to Think about Research Ideas

The difficulty is that if you don't put it into practice, it will be meaningless. And if you don't have a good habit, you'll probably forget to do it. Here are a few pointers to help you build that good habit:

1. Recognize that the execution of a project is fundamentally different from the development and formulation of an idea. Do not become fully engrossed in your ongoing endeavor and isolate yourself from the outer world (many students make this mistake). Continue to read some papers on a regular basis, such as when a fresh batch of papers from a conference is released. The very least you can do is go through all of the paper titles. Read the abstracts of a few papers that look intriguing. Then, if they're actually*interesting to you, read them more attentively (this goes back to your research taste). Make a point of paying attention to the research ideas in these articles (not just the technical side of things).

2. Take paper evaluations seriously. Advisors frequently assign paper evaluations to students and then debate these papers with them. This is an excellent opportunity to understand "how the sausage is cooked." Normally, you will read only publications that have a high novelty and effect (also well written). During paper evaluations, however, you will be able to read rejected articles and understand why they were deemed inadequate.

3. Be inquisitive and have an open mind when it comes to the sorts of papers you could be interested in. My advice is to "read widely." We are at a position in practical computer science (e.g., systems, networking, security, software engineering) where each particular discipline has matured to the point that many brilliant ideas emerge from crossings of other domains. Even though my adviser was primarily interested in networking at the time, I continued to study articles on systems and program analysis, which helped me greatly when I became a professor.

4. Attend reading groups and seminars on a regular basis and ask questions. Participate in any discussion-heavy meetings, such as those held by your own research group. If you are afraid to do so (due to a lack of knowledge or experience), remember that your advisor is attempting to help everyone in the group (particularly the junior students), and no one will mock you for asking a "stupid" question or anything like that. If you truly have nothing to ask or add to a conversation, attempt to study the article that will be discussed ahead of time to get an edge. In reality, you may surely have a debate about the topics covered in this article, such as which pattern of thought resulted in the formation of the concept for a paper. Once you've done it once or twice and felt rewarded (being able to have a nice talk), you'll gradually grow more at ease. One thing I like is debating whether an idea is good or not (even if it is already published in a good conference). Some students take on the role of the attacker, looking for flaws and limits, while others strive to defend the work. This, like the paper review process, will give you an indication of how "defensible" a concept is.

5. Informally, chat to your labmates frequently, get to know them personally, and establish a good rapport. You will most likely spend far more time chatting to your classmates than you will with your adviser. So why not make an effort to create a memorable experience? It's great to be able to strike up a casual chat about a study topic, have a friendly argument over a paper, and bounce ideas off of others. One approach to create a welcoming environment is to speak with them on a regular basis, inquire about how their project is progressing, and offer your honest criticism. They will most likely reciprocate, which can get things started. Aside from that, it may be quite useful in instances when you are stuck for an extended period of time due to obstacles. Talking to others might provide you with a new viewpoint that can be beneficial.

5.7 CYBER SECURITY AGAINST BUFFER OVERFLOW ATTACKS

In chapter 1, we brifly discussed a case study of buffer overflow attack in telehealth systems, in this section, we will view this issue from a more general perspective. Buffer overflow is a type of software coding bug or vulnerability that hackers might use to gain unauthorized access to business systems. It is one of the most well-known software security flaws, although it is still very prevalent. This is due in part to the fact that buffer overflows can occur in a variety of ways, and the approaches employed to avoid them are frequently error-prone.

The software mistake focuses on buffers, which are consecutive pieces of computational memory that temporarily hold data as it is moved between places. Buffer overflow, also known as a buffer overrun, happens when the quantity of data in the buffer exceeds its storage limit. That excess data spills into nearby memory regions, corrupting or overwriting the data in those locations.

A buffer overflow attack occurs when an attacker exploits a code mistake to perform malicious operations and compromise the targeted system. The attacker modifies the application's execution route and overwrites portions of its memory, causing the program's execution path to be altered in order to destroy existing files or disclose data.

Buffer overflow attacks generally entail breaking programming languages and overwriting the limits of the buffers on which they exist. Most buffer overflows are triggered by a mix of memory manipulation and incorrect assumptions about the composition or quantity of data.

Typically, a buffer overflow vulnerability occurs when code:

1. Is reliant on external data to control its behavior

2. Is dependent on data properties that are enforced beyond its immediate scope

3. Is so complex that programmers are not able to predict its behavior accurately

As a result, almost all the worms used it to break into systems:

Internet Worm – Buffer overflow in fingerd

Code Red, Code Red II, etc., MS Index Service DLL

Sapphire (SQL Slammer), MS SQL Server

MS Blaster, MS DCOM RPC

Witty Worm, ISS Protocol Analysis Model in ICQ Instant Message Protocol

Sasser Worm

5.7.1 Buffer Overflow Exploits

The buffer overflow exploit techniques employed by a hacker are determined by the architecture and operating system of their target. However, the additional data they provide to a software will almost always contain malicious code that allows the attacker to do more operations and send new instructions to the application.

Injecting new code into a software, for example, may send it new instructions that grant the attacker access to the organization's IT infrastructure. If an attacker is aware of a program's memory layout, he or she may be able to purposefully enter data that cannot be held by the buffer. This will allow them to rewrite memory regions containing executable code with malicious code, allowing them to seize control of the application.

Attackers exploit a buffer overflow to corrupt the execution stack of a web application, run arbitrary code, and seize control of a system. Buffer overflow flaws can occur in both application servers and web servers, particularly in online applications that employ libraries such as graphics libraries. Buffer overflows may occur in bespoke web application code as well. This is more likely since they are subjected to less inspection by security teams, but they are less likely to be detected by hackers and are more difficult to exploit.

5.7.2 Buffer Overflow Consequences

The following are some of the most common consequences of a buffer overflow attack:

1. System crashes: Typically, a buffer overflow attack will cause the system to crash. It may also cause a lack of availability causing programs to enter an endless loop.

2. Loss of access control: A buffer overflow attack frequently involves the usage of arbitrary code, which is frequently outside the scope of software security regulations.

3. Additional security concerns: If a buffer overflow attack results in arbitrary code execution, the attacker may utilize it to exploit additional vulnerabilities and undermine other security services.

Especially, buffer overflow attack is serious for special purpose systems, e.g., routers, network base stations, wireless devices, aircrafts, and nuclear plants. For such critical or military applications, the hostile penetration by using buffer overflow will cause serious damages

Several forms of buffer overflow attacks are used by attackers to compromise the systems of companies. The most frequent are as follows:

1. **Stack-based** buffer overflows are the most prevalent type of buffer overflow attack. An application that has stored malicious code in a stack buffer is susceptible to an attack using a stack-based method. In this instance, the return pointer and its associated data are overwritten on the stack, including the transfer control.

2. **Heap-based** buffer overflows: It is harder to carry out a heap-based attack than one that involves the stack. This strategy entails overflowing the program's memory space such that the program's memory is longer than the memory it's using for runtime activities.

3. In a **format string** attack, a program takes in input data as a command or fails to properly verify input data. This helps the attacker carry out a number of different malicious activities, including executing code, reading stack memory, and triggering a segmentation fault in the program. This might lead to further behaviors that compromise the system's security and stability.

5.7.3 Why C/C++ are More Vulnerable to Buffer Overflows?

Buffer overflows are a threat to nearly all applications, web servers, and online application environments. With the exception of interpreter overflows, environments developed in interpreted languages, such as Java and Python, are immune to the assaults.

Buffer overflow attacks are generally the result of coding faults or problems in program development. As a result of the program failing to create correctly sized buffers and failing to check for overflow concerns, buffer overflow occurs. These concerns are especially severe in the computer language C/C++, which lacks built-in buffer overflow prevention.

This is not the only computer language that is vulnerable to buffer overflow attacks. A buffer overflow application written in Assembly, C,

C++, or Fortran is also especially susceptible and increases the likelihood of an attacker compromising a system. Applications developed in JavaScript or Perl, on the other hand, are usually less prone to buffer overflow attacks.

5.7.4 Buffer Overflow Attack Examples

A common buffer overflow scenario is when an attacker corrupts memory that has been injected with malicious code. They may either use the buffer overflow and nearby memory corruption to their advantage.

When code that depends on external data receives a 'gets()' method to read data in a stack buffer, a simple buffer overflow may occur. Code safety is therefore dependent on users inputting less than BUFSIZE characters. Here's how it could look:

```
"...

char buf[BUFSIZE];
gets(buf);
..."
```

Figure 5.1: An example of a buff overflow bug lies in codes

Other buffer overflow attacks employ user input to influence behavior and then add indirection via the memory function 'memcpy().' This lets you choose whether to accept the destination buffer, source buffer, and how many bytes to copy, and it uses the 'read()' command to fill the input buffer with 'memcpy()', which will make sure the number of bytes read equals the amount of bytes copied.

Another cause of buffer overflow is when data characteristics are not locally checked. The lccopy() method accepts a string and produces a heap-allocated copy with uppercase characters converted to lowercase. Because it expects 'str' to be less than 'BUFSIZE,' the function does not conduct bounds checking. An attacker can circumvent the code or alter the size assumption to overrun the buffer. Here's an example of this code:

Another type of buffer overflow is code that is too complicated to foresee. The image decoder libPNG, which is utilized by browsers such as Mozilla and Internet Explorer, is used in the example below. The code looks to be safe since it verifies the variable-length size, but it also performs a "png_ptr->mode" check, which complicates matters.

```
"...
char buf[64], in[MAX_SIZE];
printf("Enter buffer contents:\n");
read(0, in, MAX_SIZE-1);
printf("Bytes to copy:\n");
scanf("%d", &bytes);
memcpy(buf, in, bytes);
..."
```

Figure 5.2: An example of a buff overflow attack scenario

```
"char *lccopy(const char *str) {
  char buf[BUFSIZE];  char *p;

  strcpy(buf, str);
for (p = buf; *p; p++) {
   if (isupper(*p)) {
    *p = tolower(*p);
   }
  }
return strdup(buf);
}"
```

Figure 5.3: An example of a buff overflow attack utilizing data properties

This might lead to blind length checks in the 'png_crc_read()' function, demonstrating the significance of reducing code complexity in memory operations.

```
"if (!(png_ptr→mode & PNG_HAVE_PLTE)) {
  /* Should be an error, but we can cope with it */
  png_warning(png_ptr, "Missing PLTE before tRNS");}
else if (length > (png_uint_32)png_ptr→num_palette) {
  png_warning(png_ptr, "Incorrect tRNS chunk length");
  png_crc_finish(png_ptr, length);
  return;
}
...
png_crc_read(png_ptr, readbuf, (png_size_t)length);"
```

Figure 5.4: An example of a buff overflow attack due to complexity

5.7.5   How Can We Mitigate Buffer Overflows?

Application developers may avoid buffer overflows by including security protections into their development code, utilizing programming languages with built-in protection, and testing code on a regular basis to discover and correct problems.

Avoiding standard library functions that have not been bounds-checked, such as gets, scanf, and strcpy, is one of the most popular ways for preventing buffer overflows. Another popular technique is to avoid buffer overruns by enforcing bounds-checking at runtime. This validates that the data sent to a buffer is inside the proper bounds.

Modern operating systems now include runtime protection, which provides extra protection against buffer overflows. This includes typical safeguards such as:

1. Address Space Layout Randomization (ASLR): Buffer overflow attacks generally need knowledge of the location of executable code. ASLR travels at random across data area locations to randomize address spaces, making overflow attacks nearly impossible [292].

2. Data execution prevention: This approach stops an attack from running code in non-executable portions of memory by marking memory sections as executable or non-executable.

3. Overwrite protection for structured exception handling (SEHOP): Attackers may attempt to overwrite the structured exception handling (SEH), which is a built-in mechanism that controls hardware and software exceptions. They do this by using a stack-based overflow attack to rewrite the exception registration record, which is kept on the program's stack. SEHOP prevents malicious programs from attacking the SEH and utilizing its overwrite exploitation method.

The only way to prevent systems against compromise is to implement additional security measures around code and operating systems. When a buffer overflow vulnerability is found, it is critical to fix the program as soon as possible and make it available to all users.

5.8 SUMMARY

We wrote this chapter to provide advice on the fundamentals of acquiring and developing fresh ideas for your study. We hope you find it useful. A tremendous deal of information was given in the instructions and examples. In order to finish the technique part, we conducted a research on buffer overflow attacks in the context of information security to bring it all together.

III

Bring Your Idea to the Reality

How to Design Algorithms

CONTENTS

This chapter describes how to design the algorithms to solve the research problems. An algorithm is normally an abstracted method used mostly in science and engineering research areas. The algorithm can be used to evaluate the cost and the possibility to solve a problem. In this chapter, we will list specific examples to show how to design an algorithm in several research domains. Then, how to summarize and formulate such algorithms will also be given since making algorithms understandable are also important in writing articles for science and engineering.

6.1 OVERVIEW

Algorithm design is a field of discrete mathematics and computer science concerned with the study, development, and implementation of sequential and asynchronous algorithms. While there are no professions with the title algorithm designer, most graduate-level computer science employment includes a significant amount of algorithm theory and research. Algorithms are utilized in every discipline that deals with quantifiable quantities, as well as many fields that do not. An algorithm is just a series of instructions; a recipe, like a set of driving instructions, is an algorithm.

Creating the right algorithm for a particular application is never a simple task. Taking a problem and drawing a solution from the ether necessitates a big creative endeavor. This is far more difficult than altering or adjusting someone else's concept to make it a bit better. The range of options available in algorithm design is vast, leaving you with enough leeway to hang yourself.

6.2 THE IMPORTANCE OF ALGORITHMS IN COMPUTER SCIENCE

The reason algorithms are used so often in computer science is that computers can be programmed to execute each instruction in a sequence, allowing programmers to instruct computers how to render 3-D graphics, display text and perform various operations on numbers. The first uses of computers were to perform basic arithmetic operations on huge volumes of numbers, sometimes requiring several months to return an answer that would take a few seconds or minutes on today's hardware. Computer scientists at the time didn't realize that algorithms could be used to program computers to make photo-editing and design applications, video games and automated financial trading software.

These sophisticated programs that are often used to process unquantifiable data are constructed from hundreds or thousands of short functions that are themselves constructed of hundreds or thousands of processor instructions. The smallest unit of a computer program is an instruction, which is a simple operation performed on the bits contained in a processor register. The operations that can be performed on the bits of data depend on the processor architecture, and they typically involve switching certain bits from zero to one, shifting bits to the left or right and other similar, simple transformations of base-two, or binary, numbers. For example, to multiply a base-two number by two, all of the bits in a register are shifted to the left, similar to the way every digit in a base-10 number is shifted to the left when it's multiplied by 10: 15 becomes 150, 150 becomes 1500, and so on.

6.3 HOW PEOPLE BENEFIT FROM ALGORITHMS

High-level programming languages like C, C++, Java, and Python allow programmers to write extremely complicated programs with relatively little code. For example, a C++ program that executes a linear search algorithm can check every element in an array with just two or three lines of code, but the same sequence of instructions written in Assembly language might require 20 or 30 lines of code.

The most common algorithms in programming are sorting and searching functions, and there are always efforts being made to make them more efficient. One of the most important concepts in computer science is the question of P versus NP, or whether the set of polynomial-time algorithms is the same as the set of non-deterministic polynomial-time algorithms, according to the Clay Mathematics Institute. If they're the same, then computer scientists could solve problems that would take millions of years to solve using currently known algorithms. Most people think P and NP are not equal.

When only one instruction can be executed at a time, an algorithm must be performed sequentially, but quantum computing could make today's technology obsolete, according to Scientific American. If you have a graduate-level interest in discrete mathematics and computer science, consider going into algorithm design.

6.4 ALGORITHMS DESIGN TECHNIQUES

An algorithm is a technique that may be used to solve a specific issue in a finite number of steps with a certain amount of input. The algorithms can be categorized in a number of different ways. They are as follows:

1. Implementation Method

2. Design Method

3. Other Classifications

The different algorithms used in each categorization technique are explained in detail in this section. When it comes to this form of categorization, there are basically three primary categories into which an algorithm might be classified. They are as follows:

1. **Recursion or Iteration:** Rather than using loops and/or data structures such as stacks and queues to solve any problem like iterative algorithms do, recursive algorithms call themselves again and over until the base condition is reached. Every recursive solution may be implemented as an iterative solution, and vice versa for every iterative solution.

   Example: The Tower of Hanoi issue is implemented in a recursive manner, but the Stock Span problem is solved repeatedly in this example.

2. **Exact or Approximate:** Either the exact algorithm or the exact search algorithm are used to describe algorithms that are capable of discovering the best answer to any issue. It is necessary to apply an approximation approach for any issues in which it is not feasible to discover the most optimal solution. Approximate algorithms are the types of algorithms that discover the solution to a problem by averaging the outcomes of several subproblems together.

   Example: Approximation algorithms are employed in the solution of NP-Hard problems. Sorting algorithms are the same as the same as the precise methods.

3. **Serial or Parallel or Distributed Algorithms:** Serial algorithms are those in which one instruction is performed at a time, whereas parallel algorithms are those in which the problem is divided into subproblems and the subproblems are processed on separate processors. Dispersed algorithms are those that are distributed across several machines and are used to implement parallel algorithms.

There are five primary categories into which an algorithm may be classified in this sort of categorization, according to the design approaches perspective. They are as follows:

1. **Greedy Method:** A choice is taken at each phase of the greedy approach to pick the local optimum without considering the repercussions of that decision in the future.

   Example: Fractional Knapsack, Activity Selection.

2. **Divide and Conquer:** A method known as Divide and Conquer

is breaking a problem down into smaller subproblems, solving them recursively, and then recombining the subproblems to arrive at a final solution.

Example: Merge sort, Quicksort.

3. **Dynamic Programming:** It is comparable to the strategy of divide and conquer when it comes to Dynamic Programming. What distinguishes this approach from others is that, if we encounter recursive function calls with the same outcome as the first, we attempt to store the result in a data structure in the form of a table and retrieve the results from the table. As a result, the total complexity of time is decreased. The term "dynamic" refers to the fact that we decide on the fly whether to invoke a function or get information from a table.

Example: 0–1 Knapsack, subset-sum problem.

4. **Linear Programming:** It is possible to have inequalities in terms of inputs and to maximize or minimize some linear functions of inputs when using Linear Programming.

Example: Maximum flow of Directed Graph

5. **Reduction (Transform and Conquer):** We solve a difficult problem by converting it into another problem for which we already have an optimal solution using this technique. Essentially, the objective is to develop a reduction algorithm whose complexity is not dominated by the complexity of the resultant reduced algorithms, which is a difficult task.

Example: When searching for the median in a list, the first step is to sort the list and then look for the middle element in the sorted list. This is known as the selection algorithm. These approaches are sometimes referred to as change and conquer techniques.

In addition to categorizing algorithms into the major categories listed above, algorithms may be categorized into additional broad categories such as those listed below.

1. **Randomized Algorithms:** Randomized algorithms are algorithms that make decisions based on chance in order to provide speedier answers [284].

Example: Randomized Quicksort Algorithm.

2. **Classification by complexity:** An algorithm that is classed according to the amount of time it takes to find a solution to any issue, regardless of the quantity of the input. The term for this type of study is temporal complexity analysis.

   Example: Some algorithms run in $O(n)$ time, whereas others run in exponential time.

3. **Classification by Research Area:** Each discipline of computer science has its own set of challenges that require efficient algorithms [275].

   Example: Sorting Algorithm, Searching Algorithm, Machine Learning etc.

4. **Branch and Bound Enumeration and Backtracking:** These are mostly employed in the field of Artificial Intelligence.

6.5   QUESTIONS FOR YOURSELF

The key to algorithm design (or any other problem-solving task) is to proceed by asking yourself a sequence of questions to guide your thought process. What if we do this? What if we do that? Should you get stuck on the problem, the best thing to do is move onto the next question. In any group brainstorming session, the most useful person in the room is the one who keeps asking, "Why can't we do it this way?" not the person who later tells them why. Because eventually, she will stumble on an approach that can't be shot down.

Towards this end, we provide below a sequence of questions to guide your search for the right algorithm for your problem. To use it effectively, you must not only ask the questions but answer them. The key is working through the answers carefully by writing them down in a log. The correct answer to, "Can I do it this way?" is never "no," but "no, because ...." By clearly articulating your reasoning as to why something doesn't work, you can check if it really holds up or whether you have just glossed over a possibility that you didn't want to think hard enough about. You will be surprised how often the reason you can't find a convincing explanation for something is that your conclusion is wrong.

Towards this end, we provide below a sequence of questions to guide your search for the right algorithm for your problem. To use it effectively, you must not only ask the questions but answer them. The key is working through the answers carefully by writing them down in a log. The correct answer to, "Can I do it this way?" is never "no," but "no, because ...." By clearly articulating your reasoning as to why something doesn't work, you can check if it really holds up or whether you have just glossed over a possibility that you didn't want to think hard enough about. You will be surprised how often the reason you can't find a convincing explanation for something is that your conclusion is wrong.

When faced with a design problem, too many people freeze up in their thinking. After reading or hearing the problem, they sit down and realize that they don't know what to do next. They stare into space, then panic, and finally end up settling for the first thing that comes to mind. Avoid this fate. Follow the sequence of questions provided below and in most of the catalog problem sections. We'll tell you what to do next!

Obviously, the more experience you have with algorithm design techniques such as dynamic programming, graph algorithms, intractability, and data structures, the more successful you will be at working through the list of questions. Part I of this book has been designed to strengthen this technical background. However, it pays to work through these questions regardless of how strong your technical skills are. The earliest and most important questions on the list focus on obtaining a detailed understanding of the problem and do not require specific expertise.

6.6   THE USEFUL LIST OF QUESTIONS

This list of questions was inspired by a passage in that wonderful book about the space program The Right Stuff [257]. It concerned the radio transmissions from test pilots just before their planes crashed. One might have expected that they would panic, so that ground control would hear the pilot yelling Ahhhhhhhhhh –, terminated only by the sound of smacking into a mountain. Instead, the pilots ran through a list of what their possible actions could be. I've tried the flaps. I've checked the engine. Still got two wings. I've reset the –. They had "the Right Stuff." Because of this, they sometimes managed to miss the mountain.

I hope this book and list will provide you with "the Right Stuff" to be an algorithm designer. And I hope it prevents you from smacking into any mountains along the way.

1. Do I really understand the problem?

    (a) What exactly does the input consist of?

    (b) What exactly are the desired results or output?

    (c) Can I construct an example input small enough to solve by hand? What happens when I try to solve it?

    (d) How important is it to my application that I always find an exact, optimal answer? Can I settle for something that is usually pretty good?

    (e) How large will a typical instance of my problem be? Will I be working on 10 items? 1,000 items? 1,000,000 items?

    (f) How important is speed in my application? Must the problem be solved within one second? One minute? One hour? One day?

    (g) How much time and effort can I invest in implementing my algorithm? Will I be limited to simple algorithms that can be coded up in a day, or do I have the freedom to experiment with a couple of approaches and see which is best?

    (h) Am I trying to solve a numerical problem? A graph algorithm problem? A geometric problem? A string problem? A set problem? Might my problem be formulated in more than one way? Which formulation seems easiest?

2. Can I find a simple algorithm or heuristic for the problem?

    (a) Can I find an algorithm to solve my problem correctly by searching through all subsets or arrangements and picking the best one?

        i. If so, why am I sure that this algorithm always gives the correct answer?

        ii. How do I measure the quality of a solution once I construct it?

        iii. Does this simple, slow solution run in polynomial or exponential time? Is my problem small enough that this brute-force solution will suffice?

        iv. If I can't find a slow, guaranteed correct algorithm, why am I certain that my problem is sufficiently well-defined to have a correct solution?

(b) Can I solve my problem by repeatedly trying some simple rule, like picking the biggest item first? The smallest item first? A random item first?

    i. If so, on what types of inputs does this heuristic work well? Do these correspond to the data that might arise in my application?

    ii. On what types of inputs does this heuristic work badly? If no such examples can be found, can I show that it always works well?

    iii. How fast does my heuristic come up with an answer? Does it have a simple implementation?

3. Are there special cases of the problem that I know how to solve exactly?

(a) Can I solve the problem efficiently when I ignore some of the input parameters?

(b) What happens when I set some of the input parameters to trivial values, such as 0 or 1? Does the problem become easier to solve?

(c) Can I simplify the problem to the point where I can solve it efficiently? Is the problem now trivial or still interesting?

(d) Once I know how to solve a certain special case, why can't this be generalized to a wider class of inputs?

(e) Is my problem a special case of a more general problem in the catalog?

4. Which of the standard algorithm design paradigms are most relevant to my problem?

(a) Is there a set of items that can be sorted by size or some key? Does this sorted order make it easier to find the answer?

(b) Is there a way to split the problem in two smaller problems, perhaps by doing a binary search? How about partitioning the elements into big and small, or left and right? Does this suggest a divide-and-conquer algorithm?

(c) Do the input objects or desired solution have a natural left-to-right order, such as characters in a string, elements of a permutation, or the leaves of a tree? If so, can I use dynamic programming to exploit this order?

(d) Are there certain operations being repeatedly done on the same data, such as searching it for some element, or finding the largest/smallest remaining element? If so, can I use a data structure to speed up these queries? What about a dictionary/hash table or a heap/priority queue?

(e) Can I use random sampling to select which object to pick next? What about constructing many random configurations and picking the best one? Can I use some kind of directed randomness like simulated annealing in order to zoom in on the best solution?

(f) Can I formulate my problem as a linear program? How about an integer program?

(g) Does my problem seem something like satisfiability, the traveling salesman problem, or some other NP-complete problem? If so, might the problem be NP-complete and thus not have an efficient algorithm?

5. Am I still stumped?

(a) Am I willing to spend money to hire an expert to tell me what to do? If so, check out the professional consulting services online.

(b) Why don't I go back to the beginning and work through these questions again? Did any of my answers change during my latest trip through the list?

Problem-solving is not a science, but part art and part skill. It is one of the skills most worth developing. My favorite book on problem-solving remains Polya's How to Solve It [161], which features a catalog of problem-solving techniques that are fascinating to browse through, both before and after you have a problem.

6.7 INTRODUCTION TO HETEROGENEOUS MEMORY ARCHITECTURE

Memory is a device or system in computing that stores information for immediate use in a computer or associated computer hardware and digital electronic devices [123]. The term memory is sometimes identical with the terms primary storage or main memory [94]. The term "store" is an ancient synonym for "memory."

When compared to slower but larger capacity storage, computer memory runs at a rapid speed. If necessary, the contents of the computer memory can be moved to storage; one popular method is to use a memory management technique known as virtual memory [182].

In this section, we will take the chance to give a brief introduction to the heterogeneous memory architectures.

6.7.1 Introduction and Basic Concepts

Modern memory is implemented as semiconductor memory, in which data is stored within memory cells constructed from MOS transistors on an integrated circuit. There are two types of semiconductor memory: volatile and non-volatile. Flash memory and ROM, PROM, EPROM, and EEPROM memory are examples of non-volatile memory. Primary storage, which is generally dynamic random-access memory (DRAM), and rapid CPU cache memory, which is typically static random-access memory (SRAM) that is quick but energy-consuming, with lower memory areal density than DRAM, are examples of volatile memory [183].

The majority of semiconductor memory is arranged into memory cells or bistable flip-flops, each of which stores one bit (0 or 1) [156]. Flash memory organization comprises single-bit memory cells as well as multi-level cells that can store several bits per cell. Memory cells are organized into words of a specific length, such as 1, 2, 4, 8, 16, 32, 64, or 128 bits. Each word may be accessed using a binary address of N bits, allowing 2N words to be stored in memory [184].

For Chip Multiprocessor (CMP) systems, low power consumption and short-latency memory access are the two most important design goals. Nowadays, the development of current CMP systems is substantially hindered by the daunting memory wall and power wall issues [200]. To bridge the ever-widening processor-memory speed gap, traditional computing systems widely adopted hardware caches. Caches benefitting from the temporal and spatial locality have effectively facilitated the layered memory hierarchy. Nonetheless, caches also present notorious problems to CMP systems, such as lack of hard guarantee of predictability and high penalties in cache misses. For example, caches consume up to 43% of the overall power in the ARM920T processor [149].

Therefore, how to develop alternative power-efficient techniques to replace the current hardware-managed cache memory is challenging [50]. Scratch Pad Memory (SPM), a software-controlled on-chip memory, has been widely employed by key manufacturers due to two major advantages over the cache memory [2, 3]. First, SPM does not have the comparator and tag SRAM since it is accessed by direct addressing. Therefore, the complex decode operations are not performed to support the runtime address mapping for references. This property of caches can save a large amount of energy. It has been shown that an SPM consumes 34% less chip area and 40% less energy consumption than a cache memory does [184]. Second, SPM generally guarantees single-cycle access latency, whereas accesses to cache may suffer from capacity, compulsory, and conflict misses that incur very long latency [179]. Given the advantages in size, power consumption, and predictability, SPM has been widely used in CMP systems, such as Motorola M-core MMC221, IBM CELL [183], TI TMS370CX7X, and NVIDIA G80. Based on the software management characteristics of SPM, how to manage SPM and perform data allocation with the help of compilers becomes the most critical task.

A hybrid SPM architecture must resolve how to reduce energy consumption, memory access latency, and the number of write operations to MRAM. To take advantage of the benefits of each type of memory, we must strategically allocate data on each memory module so that the total memory access cost can be minimized [138]. Recall that SPMs are software-controllable, which means programmers or compilers can manage the datum on them. Traditional hybrid memory data management strategies, such as data placement and migration [198, 210], are unsuitable for hybrid SPMs since they are mainly designed for hardware caches and are unaware of write activities. Fortunately, embedded system applications can fully take advantage of compiler-analyzable data access patterns, offering efficient data allocation mechanisms for hybrid SPM architecture. For instance, there are practical products that adopted hybrid memory architecture, for instance, Micron's HMC (Hybrid Memory Cube) controller.

In the context of data allocation for hybrid on-chip memory, Sha et al. [102] employed the multi-dimensional dynamic programming (MDPDA) method to reduce write activities and energy consumption. However, this method will consume a significant amount of time and space [300]. Based on this observation, we use a genetic algorithm to allocate data on different memory units for CPMs with our novel hybrid SPM comprising SRAM and MRAM.

The following section will review interesting solutions on data allocation for the CMP systems, which solves data allocation over different memory units.

6.7.2 Overview of Scratchpad Memory Management

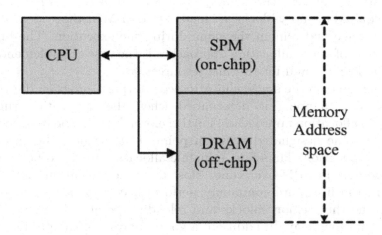

Figure 6.1: A typical scratchpad memory

Scratchpad Memory (SPM) is a software-controlled on-chip memory that has been envisioned as a promising alternative to hardware caches in both uniprocessor and multiprocessor embedded systems with tight energy and timing budgets due to its superiority in timing predictability, area and power consumption, and guarantee of single-cycle access latency. Figure 6.1 shows a typical processor with a scratchpad memory, in which the SPM is implemented by direct address mapping. Particularly, the access address is always in a predetermined memory space range [69]. To efficiently use the SPM, a scratchpad memory management unit (SMMU) is regularly introduced so that the programmers or compilers can explicitly manage the data allocation on it [75, 78].

Since this benefit is achieved at the cost of interference from the programmer or compiler, the development of sophisticated mechanisms is a must to SPM management, improving the overall system performance. This paper aims to address the data allocation problem of the CMP embedded systems (but not just limited to CMP systems, it can also be easily applied to uniprocessor embedded systems) based on the proposal of a heterogeneous architecture associated with an array of novel scheduling algorithms. The goal is to reduce the memory access cost and extend the wear-out leveling of the on-chip systems.

Depending on when the data allocation decision is made, existing work can be categorized into static data allocation and dynamic data allocation. In static data allocation scenarios, the application program and data allocation decision analysis are made at compile-time (offline). The required memory blocks are loaded into SPM at the system initialization stage and remain the same during the execution. The biggest advantage of static allocation approaches is the ease of implementation and the low demand for runtime resources.

Compared to the static allocation counterpart, program data/code to memory mapping is determined when the application runs in dynamic allocation approaches. Furthermore, data can be reloaded into SPM at some designated program points to guarantee the execution of the application. Therefore, dynamic allocation needs to be aware of the contents in SPM over time. Most dynamic allocation approaches used in the literature commonly perform a compile-time analysis to determine the memory blocks and reloading points, therefore, amortizing runtime delay. In addition, a good analysis of the profiled trace file or historical information of program execution is effectively beneficial to making better mapping decisions. However, the most obvious shortcoming of dynamic allocation is the inexorable high cost of data mapping at runtime. To reduce this overhead, previous work depends on either pre-extracting part of the program that doesn't need runtime information [61, 68] or performing a compile-time analysis to find out the potential allocation sites [21].

Udayakumaran et al. [236] proposed a heuristic algorithm to allocate data for an SPM, with major consideration of stack and global variables. Dominguez et al. [18] applied a dynamic data allocation method on heap data for embedded systems with SPMs. Three types of program object are considered in their allocation method: global variables, stack variables, and program code. They divided a program into multiple regions, where each program region is associated with a time stamp. According to the order of timestamps, they then utilized a heuristic algorithm to determine the data allocation for each program region.

In [102, 103, 104], Sha et al. proposed a multi-dimensional dynamic programming (MDPDA) strategy for the hybrid SPM architecture. Their method can achieve optimal allocation for each program region. Compared with their approach, this paper has several different aspects:

First, while their targeted hybrid architecture only consists of an NVM and SRAM, this paper investigates the features of MRAM and Z-RAM, and we proposed a more complicated architecture to attack the on-chip memory access problem. Second, [102, 103] focused on single processor platforms with hybrid SPM. However, we step further to investigate multicore embedded systems where each core is attached with a hybrid on-chip memory.

6.7.3   Basics of the System Model

HARDWARE MODEL: The figure below exhibits the architecture of a target CMP system with hybrid SPMs. Each core is tightly coupled with an on-chip SPM which is composed of an SRAM, an MRAM, and a Z-RAM [122]. We call a core accesses the SPM owned by itself as local access, while accessing an SPM held by another core is referred to as remote access [43]. Generally, remote access is supported by an on-chip interconnect. All cores access the off-chip main memory (usually a DRAM device) through a shared bus. CELL processor [196] is an example that adopts this architecture. There is a multi-channel ring structure in a CELL processor to allow communication between any two cores without intervention from other cores [119]. Consequently, we can safely assume that the data transfer cost between cores is constant. Generally, accessing the local SPM is faster and dissipates less energy than fetching data from a remote SPM, while accessing the off-chip main memory incurs the longest latency and consumes the most energy.

In order to make sure a hit for an access to the memory modules on the heterogeneous memory, we need to move the data from the memory unit holding this data preliminarily. However, this movement will inevitably incur much higher overhead, since it needs to access a remote SPM or the main memory. In this case, the data transfer overhead is composed of two major parts: reading the memory module of a remote SPM or main memory owning the data and writing the data to the target memory module.

CHROMOSOME MODEL A chromosome for the data allocation problem is a set of defined parameters that is able to represent a solution. The parameters here are the data blocks and the size of each memory module, including all on-chip memory modules and the off-chip main memory. Therefore, we define a gene in a chromosome as a pair of these two parameters. That is, a chromosome represents an allocation scheme. There are numerous ways to represent a

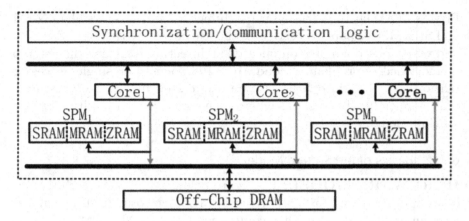

Figure 6.2: System architecture. An n-core with hybrid on-chip SPMs and an off-chip DRAM main memory. Core1 accesses data in SPM1 is referred to as local access, while accessing data in other cores is regarded as remote access. All accesses to shared main memory utilize the on-chip interconnect.

chromosome. Intuitively, we can use a matrix to represent a chromosome, where the rows indicate the main memory and all on-chip memory units of an SPM in each processor core. The columns indicate data allocation on the corresponding memories. For example, Figure 6.3 shows two randomly generated chromosomes, A and B. These two chromosomes are constructed in matrix structure according to the size of each memory unit, where C_1S, C_1M, C_1Z, C_2S, C_2M, C_2Z, and MM represent SPM1's SRAM, SPM1's MRAM, SPM1's ZRAM, SPM2's SRAM, SPM2's MRAM, SPM2's ZRAM, and the main memory, respectively. Each row of data given in the chromosome matrix is a gene sequence, which represents the data allocation on the corresponding memory module.

However, this form of a chromosome is inconvenient to perform genetic operations, particularly for crossover, because it is hard to maintain the space constraint of each memory module. Hence, we modify the chromosome and organize it as a list structure where each gene in the list is defined as a data item and a memory unit pair: (d, MT). Each gene cell shows that the data item d is allocated to the memory unit MT. In this method, all the memory units are numbered uniquely. Suppose that the target CMP system has N cores, where each core has an on-chip heterogeneous memory configured from MRAM and SRAM;

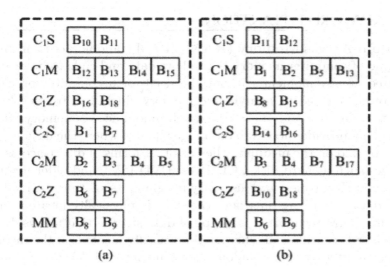

Figure 6.3: Two chromosomes in matrix structure. (a) Chromosome C1. (b) Chromosome C2.

we need at most $2 \times N + 1$ numbers to label these memory units. For simplicity, we use numbers $3 \times i - 2$, $3 \times i - 1$, and $3 \times i (1 \leq i \leq N)$ to represent the SRAM, MRAM, and ZRAM of the SPM associated with core i, respectively. Number $3 \times N + 1$ represents the main memory. Two chromosomes in this structure are shown in Figure 6.4, and they are transformed from the chromosomes A and B in Figure 6.3, respectively. Figure 6.4 uses 1, 2, 3, 4, 5, 6, and 7 to correspondingly represent SPM1's SRAM, SPM1's MRAM, SPM1's ZRAM, and SPM2's SRAM, SPM2's MRAM, SPM2's ZRAM, and the main memory. For example, the gene (B1, 4) represents data B1 is allocated to SPM2's SRAM.

$(B_1, 4) \to (B_2, 5) \to (B_3, 5) \to (B_4, 2) \to (B_5, 5) \to (B_6, 6) \to (B_7, 6) \to (B_8, 7) \to (B_9, 7)$
$\to (B_{10}, 1) \to (B_{11}, 1) \to (B_{12}, 2) \to (B_{13}, 2) \to (B_{14}, 2) \to (B_{15}, 2) \to (B_{16}, 3) \to (B_{17}, 4) \to (B_{18}, 3)$

(a)

$(B_1, 2) \to (B_2, 2) \to (B_3, 5) \to (B_4, 5) \to (B_5, 2) \to (B_6, 7) \to (B_7, 5) \to (B_8, 3) \to (B_9, 7)$
$\to (B_{10}, 6) \to (B_{11}, 1) \to (B_{12}, 1) \to (B_{13}, 2) \to (B_{14}, 4) \to (B_{15}, 3) \to (B_{16}, 4) \to (B_{17}, 5) \to (B_{18}, 6)$

(b)

Figure 6.4: Change the above chromosomes into list structure, C1 $\to$ C3, C2 $\to$ C4. (a) Chromosome C3. (b) Chromosome C4

6.8   KEYWORD EXPLANATION

Random-Access Memory (RAM): RAM (random-access memory) is a kind of computer memory that allows data and code to be read and updated at any moment without the need for a computer processor. It is often referred to as dynamic memory since it is frequently utilized to store program and user data. Random-access memory (RAM) technology provides access to data regardless of where the data is physically located on the medium, whereas other forms of direct-access data storage (such as hard disks, CD-RWs, DVD-RWs, and older magnetic tapes and drum memory) use varying amounts of time to read and write data depending on where the data is physically located on the medium. RAM technology is a type of data storage that allows data to be accessed regardless of where it is physically located on the medium. In a computer system, random-access memory (RAM) is a kind of memory that may be used to store data.

RAM is equipped with multiplexing and demultiplexing circuitry, which enables it to link data lines to the targeted storage in order to read or write an item to that storage space. RAM devices are classified as "8-bit" or "16-bit" devices, and when several RAM devices are used, more than one data storage unit is often accessible by the same address, which is referred to as "multiple RAM device access."

A contemporary technology that makes use of integrated circuits (ICs) incorporating MOS memory cells, random-access memory (RAM) is known as random-access memory (RAM). It has been feasible to create both dynamic random-access memory (DRAM) modules and nonvolatile random-access memory (NVRAM) modules in recent years (NVRAM). Write operations are not allowed in certain kinds of nonvolatile memory, such as flash memory and magnetic tape, despite the fact that RAM has the capacity of performing random reads. The majority of ROM kinds, as well as the NOR-Flash type of flash memory, which is a form of nonvolatile memory, are discussed in this section of the manual.

For storing random data, there are many different kinds of semiconductor memories available, the most common of which being static random-access memory (SRAM) and dynamic random-access memory (DRAM), both of which have become more popular (DRAM). The first commercial application of semiconductor RAM happened in 1978, when Toshiba incorporated DRAM memory cells into the Toscal BC-1411 electronic calculator, which was launched the same year IBM developed the SP95 SRAM chip for their System/360 Model 95 computer. This was the first time that MOS transistors were used in the development of commercial MOS memory, and commercial MOS memory has since since served as the basis for all commercial semiconductor memory technology. It was the Intel 1103 DRAM integrated circuit that was introduced to the market in October 1970, making it the world's first commercially available DRAM IC. Synchronous dynamic random-access memory (SDRAM) was first made commercially available in 1992, thanks to the introduction of the KM48SL2000 chipset by Samsung.

Memory Management: Memory management is a kind of resource management that is used in computer memory, and it is referred to as such in the literature. Memory management is required if you wish to offer dynamic memory allocations to applications as and when they are required. The ability to recover memory when it is no longer required is also essential. Modern computer systems are capable of doing a large number of processes at the same time.

There have been a variety of various techniques used in attempt to improve the efficacy of memory management systems. When virtual memory systems are used, the memory addresses used by a process are separated from the actual physical addresses, allowing for process separation as well as an expansion of the virtual address space beyond the amount of RAM that is physically available. Virtual memory systems are used to separate the memory addresses used by processes from the actual physical addresses. The quality of virtual memory management has the potential to have a substantial impact on the overall performance of a computer system.

Dynamic memory allocation: To fulfill the allocation request, it is necessary to locate a block of free memory that is big enough to handle it. As part of the system's effort to fulfill its memory requirements, memory chunks (also known as the heap or free storage) are allocated from a vast pool of memory. Despite the fact that every heap has at least one portion that is now in use, there will be "free" (unused) RAM available for future allocations in the event that the heap is resized.

The fragmentation produced by smaller gaps in allocated memory blocks, which interferes with the proper allocation of memory blocks, is one of the many problems that must be addressed in order to successfully execute the suggestions of the proposal. When the allocator provides information on the allocations, it is feasible for individual allocations of modest size to increase in size as a result of the information given. This is often accomplished by breaking down large tasks into smaller parts. The memory management system must keep track of all pending allocations in order to avoid overlapping and guarantee that no memory is ever "lost." This is necessary in order to ensure that no memory is ever 'lost' (i.e., that there are no "memory leaks").

6.9 SUMMARY

While working on your projects, you may have encountered issues that you needed to solve. The aim of this chapter was to explain how you could create algorithms to solve such problems. The types of algorithms were briefly discussed from a number of viewpoints, and we gave a brief summary of them. Also included is an algorithm design guide in the form of a checklist with items to think about before formalizing your algorithm. After that, we addressed the basics of heterogeneous memory architecture as well as the problem of data allocation in distributed systems in the methods section.

How to Do Experiments

CONTENTS

This chapter describes how to experiment with the algorithms designed for solving the problems. The experimentation in scientific and engineering research must be able to cope with the designed algorithms to prove the effectiveness. Also, the experimentation should be concise and clear to avoid too many technical details of implementation which are not preferred by the science and engineering research papers. Therefore, carefully defining the scenario with the research challenge is very important. In this chapter, some examples will be given to show how to choose the scenario and perform the research experimentations.

DOI: 10.1201/9781003139058-7

7.1 THE IMPORTANCE OF EXPERIMENTS IN COMPUTER SCIENCE

Experiments are essential in science. However, the relevance of experiments in computer science is diverse and uncertain. Until the 1980s, little thought was given to the importance of experiments in computer science. As the profession shifted toward experimental computer science, many technically, conceptually, and empirically focused perspectives on experiments arose. As a result of such arguments, experiments and experiment language are used in several ways in today's computer science areas. This chapter breakdowns computer experimentation and provides five conceptualizations of experiments in computer science: feasibility experiment, trial experiment, field experiment, comparison experiment, and controlled experiment. This chapter aiming at three goals: to clarify experiment terminology in computer science, contribute to disciplinary self-knowledge of computer science and enhance understanding of experiments in modern science in general due to computer prominence in other areas.

7.2 EXPERIMENTATION IN COMPUTER SCIENCE

Views of computing as an empirical or experimental science have widespread acceptance among computing researchers. The words empirical and experimental, however, are not always employed consistently. The word "empirical" is commonly used in the sciences to refer to research that depends on observation-based collecting of primary data. The phrase "empirical research" is used to distinguish it from theoretical and analytical research. In many disciplines of science, the term "experimental" is more specific than "empirical" and refers to a type of study in which controlled experiments are performed to test ideas. However, in the realm of computers, the term "experimental" has come to denote a far broader variety of things.

When Feldman and Sutherland [56] issued their paper "Rejuvenating Experimental Computer Science," the importance of experimentation in computing became a hot subject. According to the study, colleges and the federal government of the United States should acknowledge and promote experimental computer science. Denning [148] agreed with the Feldman committee, writing that no scientific field can be fruitful in the long run if its experimenters just construct components. Denning was also a member of the ACM Executive Committee, which agreed with the Feldman committee that experimental computer science was undervalued at the time [45].

Many authoritative people in computing have urged computer scientists to experiment more. Given that much of the encouragement came from other areas, it's worth taking a look at the computer side of the tale. What, in particular, do computer scientists from various backgrounds imply by "experimental computer science?" This section initially provides the background of the experimental science discussion through four perspectives: empirical dimensions of computers, experimentation subjects, experimental activities, and diverse terminological and categorization perspectives. Second, this part presents critical perspectives on computer experiments as provided in computing literature.

7.2.1 Empirical Dimensions

All reports of experiments in computing, from controlled experiments to experimental algorithmics, fall under the umbrella term of empirical work. Computing and empirical research have been linked in the literature in a variety of ways, one of which is mentioned here. Computing and computers, for example, are study topics. Second, they are research instruments. Third, they might be both at the same time.

One frequent method to discuss computing and experimentation is to consider computers and the phenomena that surround them to be study subjects. There is a substantial corpus of experimental work on computers, programming languages, interfaces, users, and algorithms, to mention a few topics. Some experiments are carried out in a highly controlled environment, whilst some writers refer to their exploratory work as "experimental." Viewing computing, computers, and the phenomena that surround them as a subject of inquiry opens the door to a number of perspectives on experimentation, and this paper examines that element of computing experiments.

Another frequent approach to addressing experimentation in computing is to see computers as research instruments in other areas. Computing and computers as instruments for experiments (simulations) in various disciplines have a long history. Stibitz [223] stated in his introduction to the renowned Moore School lectures of 1946 that digital computers are an extraordinary laboratory where "the components of every experiment are precisely separated." According to Stibitz, computers provide infinite accuracy and an infinite supply of research instruments. Later, the first modern computers were utilized for practical sciences such as ballistics computations [89], warfare [8], meteorology, and quantum physics [146]. Progress in modern research is so reliant on computers that many writers have labeled the growing reliance as "algorithmization" of sciences [52], "the age of computer simulation" [255], and even a "info-computational" worldview [49]. Virtual experiments, simulations, heuristic models, and neural networks are just a few of the tools that computing has provided to other sciences. Viewing computer as a tool of study offers a distinct picture of experimentation than viewing computing as a subject of inquiry.

Models of various types are also prevalent in the world of computers. Specifications, program texts, and programming languages can all be thought of as models [150]. The experiment is an important component of validating models or evaluating the model's fit to the reality. However, when computer models are utilized as tools, it is important to consider which field is being investigated. As an example, Colburn [38] employed computational models in genetics. Is the programmer a geneticist or a computer scientist? In many computational disciplines, collaborative effort helps both computing and the field in which it is used. In other words, computers may be both a tool and a subject of study. This study, on the other hand, does not focus on the instrumental element of computing, but rather on research into computing for the sake of research into computing.

7.2.2 Subjects and Topics

Another way to describe the context of computer experimentation is to look at its subjects and topics. Because there are already a plethora of debates concerning experimental computer science, examples may be drawn straight from the literature. Denning [46] mentioned research on memory rules in time sharing and research on queuing networks in his overview of computer science experiments. Freeman [60] provided instances of a robot competition, data-intensive supercomputing research, and future network architecture research. Feldman and Sutherland [56] incorporated sophisticated computer applications. Gustedt et al. [95] emphasized research on grid computing, parallel computing, large-scale distributed systems, and several other large-scale computing initiatives. Software engineering and high-end computers were suggested by Basili and Zelkowitz [10]. Nature, according to several writers ranging from Chaitin to Zuse [16], calculates. In the end, the subject itself is unimportant. Any subject may be researched scientifically, and many can be researched experimentally.

7.2.3 Activities

One may also look at what activities are covered by the phrase "experimental computer science." Exploration (page 498), building and testing (page 499), hypothesis testing, demonstration, and modeling were all terms used in the original "rejuvenating" report [56] (page 500). Denning included the following: modeling, simulation, measurement, validation, prototyping, testing, performance analysis, and comparisons [47]. Other discussion participants included measuring, testing, hypothesizing, observing, gathering data, categorizing, and sustaining or rejecting theories [83]. Denning [46] cited performance analysis as a classic example of experimental computer science – the design, validation, and empirical assessment of computer systems. Belady [11] described his experimental computer science as involving the construction of prototypes, observation, organization of observations, and formalization of observations into models. All of the tasks listed above are essential to science, although they are essential to various types of science.

Denning et al. [48] highlighted modeling as one of the three pillars of computing in their renowned study "Computing as a discipline" at the end of the 1980s. Experiments had a part in that report that was similar to their role in natural sciences. Denning et al. described the scientific computing work cycle in four steps: (1) form a hypothesis, (2) create a model and make a prediction, (3) plan an experiment and collect data, and (4) analyze findings. Freeman [60] abandoned the hypothesis and argued for a perspective of computer experimentation based on a cycle of observation, measurement, and result analysis. Gelernter [87] emphasized the generalizability of results, explicitly mentioning the deductive and inductive phases of research, and argued that computing is a science insofar as its combination of theoretical foundations and experiments allows for the formulation and verification of general statements.

The cycle of test-driven development has one unique formulation of an experiment-like method in computing – one with automated and repeated experiments, which is elaborated in Figure 7.1. Each cycle of software development in test-driven development begins with the creation of a test for a new software feature. The method is then repeated by running all of the tests and seeing the previously added test fail, creating code that implements the desired feature, then running the tests again to ensure that the newly written code indeed implements the desired functionality. In other words, the programmer begins with a specific functionality need, creates an automated experiment to test that capability, and then implements code that passes all new and prior tests.

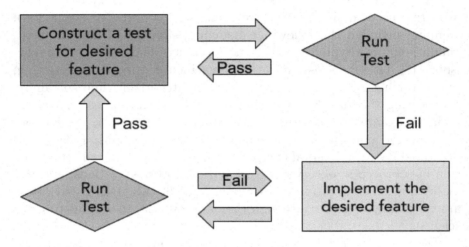

Figure 7.1: Cycle of work in a test-driven development/experiment

There is a rich history of discussions on experimental methods in the field of software engineering, including highly influential accounts like that of Basili, Selby, and Hutchens [256], though terminology in those discussions is frequently used differently than what the stalwart proponents of experimental computer science advocated. Zelkowitz and Wallace [276] classified "experimental approaches" in software engineering into three types: observational methods (which collect data throughout the project), historical methods (which collect data from previously completed projects), and controlled methods (which attempt to increase the statistical validity of results by providing multiple instances of observations). They mentioned project monitoring, case study, assertion, and field research as observational approaches [276]. They cited literature searches, legacy data, lessons learned, and static analysis as historical techniques. They mentioned repeated experiments, synthetic environment experiments, dynamic analysis, and simulation as controlled approaches. It is worth noting that Zelkowitz and Wallace [276] referred to their models and techniques as "experimental," rather than "empirical." They claimed that their categories encompassed the previously published taxonomies, such as Kitchenham's [115] nine variations of quantitative and qualitative experiments and Basili's [9] six kinds. Again, the explanations of experimentation in software engineering are all fundamental to science, albeit in different ways.

On a larger level, one component of the scientific process that computer scientists excel at is debugging. Unlike Dijkstra, who referred to debugging as "putting the cart before the horse," Morrison and Snodgrass referred to debugging as "one of the purest kinds of empirical investigation." There have been several attempts to define debugging as a "science of debugging" [228]. Hacking [96] recognized "debugging" as a crucial ingredient in modern experimentation in one of his pioneering works in the philosophy of experimentation – though its meaning in the context that Hacking addressed differs from its meaning in computers. Other current interpretations of the scientific process involve debugging, albeit under various names, throughout the scientific research cycle. The literature on the philosophy of engineering expands on this element of study, for example, through parameter variation: the repeated assessment of a device's performance while systematically altering the device's parameters of its operating circumstances [237].

7.3 FIVE PERSPECTIVES ON EXPERIMENTATION IN COMPUTER SCIENCE

This section presents five different uses of the term "experiment," each relatively common in the computer science literature. Here, we describe how the experiment is used in standard works and how it has been used in the literature. This section aims to give an overview of how you might scale your experiments when you are working on your projects.

7.3.1 Feasibility

For starters, the word "experiment" is loosely used in many publications that report on and explain new methods and instruments. Typically, it is unknown in such writings whether job t can be automated efficiently, reliably, realistically, or cost-effectively, or by fulfilling some other basic criteria. A demonstration of experimental (untested, freshly developed) technology demonstrates that it is possible. Combining the words "demonstration" and "experimental" in the same sentence may seem to be a forced union of two mutually incompatible ideas.

Nonetheless, as the following examples show, the term "experiment" is often used synonymously with "demonstration," "proof of concept," or "feasibility proof" in the computer science literature.

When it comes to big software systems, Plaice [160] stated in ACM Computing Surveys that we frequently don't know what these tools will provide until they are actually utilized. It is a scientist's meticulous definition of what must be done and careful execution that makes an experiment, he added. In experimental computer science, Feitelson [55] defined the demonstration of feasibility as one of the three prevalent viewpoints. Demonstration of feasibility experiments in practical computer science are substantially separated from theoretical computer science, according to Feitelson's analysis [55].

7.3.2 Trial

Experimentation in computing refers to more than just proving feasibility. When doing the trial experiment, certain preset variables are used in order to assess the system's different features A new system's performance or ability to fulfill requirements isn't known in most of these investigations. (Test or experiment) A trial (or test, or experiment) is intended to assess the system's characteristics (or test, or experiment with them). Most of the time, these tests are performed in a laboratory, but they may also be undertaken in the field with some restrictions.

When it comes to the four different types of experiments described by Gustedt and colleagues [95], emulation, benchmarking and simulation fall under the category of trial experiments since they allow for the greatest abstraction. Emulation is the process of running a real program in a model environment, simulation is the process of running a model application with restricted functionality in a model environment, and benchmarking is the process of evaluating a model application in a real environment [95]. In software engineering, "toy" and "serious" differences are established [57].

7.3.3 Field

It is also used to refer to a system's performance as measured by a set of metrics in the third frequent use of the word "experiment." This is due to the fact that a field experiment moves the system out of a lab. A system's ability to meet its stated purpose and needs in its sociotechnical context of usage is not known, as is the case in most such research. In a live environment, the system is evaluated for factors such as performance, user-friendliness, and robustness Gustedt et al. [95] used the phrase "in situ experiments" to describe actual programs running on real hardware.

Different examples of field experiments are used in the computer science discussions. An example of a field experiment is a robot automobile racing [60]. DARPA's Grand Challenge pits autonomous cars against one other in a race to find their way across a variety of terrains and situations. Large numbers of variables and poor control in live settings are typical drawbacks of field experiments. Field experiments, however, provide greater control than case studies or surveys since they are frequently quasi-experiments or experiments with restricted controls [155].

7.3.4 Comparison

Fourth, the word "experiment" is used to describe comparisons of solutions. There are many branches of computing research that are concerned with finding the "best" solution to a specific problem [58] or developing a new way to do things "better" in one way or another. Reports on these research often do not state if system A outperforms system B given data set d and parameters p, or state that it has not been shown. When A(d, p) and B(d, p) are compared, the new system wins on a number of criteria. The term "horse racing papers" was coined by C. Johnson [10]. Several types of experimental computer science, according to Fletcher [58], are particularly suited to this kind of study (Fletcher referred to [88, 234]).

Comparison experiments can be biased in a variety of ways, despite the fact that they seem to be "objective" from numerous angles [55, 15]. The blinding concept, for example, is frequently overlooked in such studies [58]. For his or her own system, the researcher should not be able to positively choose B, d, C, and p "All too frequently, the experiment is a poor example favoring the proposed technology over alternatives," stated A. Zelkowitz and Wallace [276, 277]. Another example where standard tests, input data, and anticipated outcomes are used to evaluate rival solutions is in the area of computer science (e.g., [238]). When designing a comparison experiment, do consider those blind spots, thus providing readers with more comparable results.

7.3.5 Controlled

The controlled experiment is the fifth-frequent use of the word "experiment." In many areas of science, the controlled experiment is the gold standard of scientific research, particularly when researchers are trying to eliminate confusing factors. It also allows for generalization and prediction. It is frequently employed in circumstances when it is not known whether two or more variables are linked or if x affects y.

By "experiment" in many computer science arguments, the author means "controlled experiment" either directly or implicitly, although not necessarily for the same reason. Their idea was that controlled trials would generate greater generalizability and better-justified claims about goods. Morrison and Snodgrass [151] hoped to see software development outcomes more generalizable than they had been in the past. Because of their increasing user involvement, Schorr [220] argues that software and systems have become too big for other types of approaches. Due to their ability to provide probabilistic information about causation and improve confidence in what technical inputs produced the change, Curtis [40] and Pfleeger [159] highlighted controlled experiments' importance in software engineering. In the field of applied computer science, Feitelson [55] advocated assessments under controlled circumstances. In deep learning or computer vision literatures, we can always see the use of term ablation study, which can also be interpreted as a version of controlled experiment to evaluate each functionalities' contribution and necessity.

7.4 MACHINE LEARNING EXPERIMENTAL PIPELINES

The route and structure of machine learning (ML) projects may at first resemble those of software development projects, but in reality, they are more like those of scientific research. Successive trials may provide valuable results, lead to a dead-end, or inspire entirely new directions of study, but they all contribute to the success of a project. A number of mini-experiments is also included in each experiment.

In order to use machine learning or employ someone to do so, it's important to understand how practitioners of the ML experimental pipeline operate.

On the other hand, a software development project begins with the query, "How can we create X?" and ends when it is completed [64, 65, 153]. The definition of X is usually refined along the process because

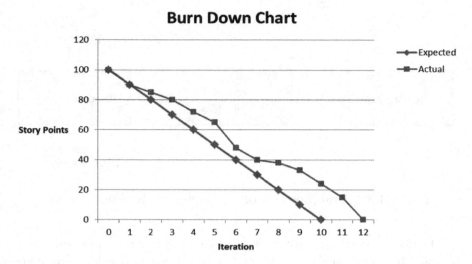

Figure 7.2: Agile burn down charts

it was too ambiguous and incomplete. The requirements, design, and development phases of a successful project, on the other hand, result in something that is recognizably similar to what was requested. On joyful software projects, the progress is gradual and follows a non-predetermined route, but it is made purposefully. It is for this reason why Agile's burndown charts are so prevalent nowadays. You can see how expected uncertainties alter a baseline route.

On the other hand, ML projects might start with the query: what can we build? Three possible results may be achieved while developing a machine learning model and data science in general:

1. Good enough results have been discovered to release or utilize.

2. Financial, time, and computational constraints restrict future development.

3. This causes efforts to be diverted or abandoned.

7.4.1 How a Machine Learning Model is Built

This whole process is accomplished by creating a model (or models) that tells us something insightful about the data being analyzed. Typically, this involves taking in new inputs and generating predictions as a result of them.

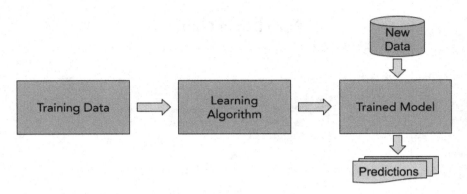

Figure 7.3: General pipelines of developing a ML model (models)

To do so, computers are instructed to analyze data and train themselves. More specifically, we enter training data into a learning algorithm, which generates a model that has been trained to tell us important things about data comparable to the training set.

The data science effort required to create the ML model may be separated into three stages:

1. The process of analyzing data to determine how it should be used is known as exploratory data analysis.

2. Assembling data, preparing it for analysis, running the training algorithm, and evaluating the results.

3. Results will be evaluated and, possibly, implemented.

Many times, this process reaches the stage where deployment is being considered. Early on in the evaluation process, opportunities for further exploration and improvement are identified for further investigation and improvement. A model's performance against new data will be continuously evaluated, however, even after it has been successfully deployed. Processes are really cycles. And the trained model it produces is really a series of trained models reflecting the best hypotheses.

This section simply provides an initial understanding of the machine learning process: get some data, run a training algorithm, and then produce a model. However, in some respects, the original description was accurate. Input data is fed into an algorithm, which creates a model, and then the algorithm makes predictions on its own.

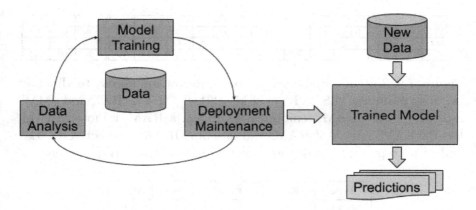

Figure 7.4: ML projects' experimental pipelines

However, this process diagram is fundamentally misleading in one important respect: machine learning development is a cycle, not a process, according to the diagram. I believe that the cycle is actually a cycle of cycles. The fact that practitioners prefer to work in small increments isn't the only reason why. Because machine learning (ML) development is primarily an empirical activity, feedback from each experimental step is critical for the next; this is the reason for the slow pace.

7.5 AN ADAPTIVE GENETIC ALGORITHM FOR MEMORY ALLOCATION

In the previous chapter, we draw an overview of the heterogeneous memory systems and data allocation problem. In this chapter, we will use the technical section to explain a genetic algorithm for memory allocation [184].

The objective of our algorithm is to minimize memory access latency, energy consumption, and the number of write operations to MRAM for CMP systems with the hybrid SPM consisting of SRAM, MRAM, and Z-RAM [35]. In this section, we present an example to illustrate the rationale behind the proposed algorithm.

We normalize latency and energy consumption of memory access to MRAM, SRAM, Z-RAM, and off-chip main memory for demonstration purposes, as the Figure below shows. In this Figure, the columns of "LS", "RS", "LM", "RM", "LZ", "RZ", and "MM" represent the memory access cost to local SRAM, remote SRAM, local MRAM, remote MRAM, local Z-RAM, remote Z-RAM, and off-chip DRAM,

Op	LS		RS		LM		RM		LZ		RZ		MM	
	La	En	La	En	La	En	La	En	La	En	La	En	La	En
Read	1	0.1	2	0.18	5	0.36	10	0.85	3	0.34	8	0.76	60	6.2
Write	1	0.1	3	0.25	10	0.98	20	2.1	5	0.44	12	1.08	60	6.2

Figure 7.5: Latency and energy consumption for access to different memory modules. "LS", "RS", "LM", "RM", "LZ", "RZ", and "MM" represent local SRAM, remote SRAM, local MRAM, remote MRAM, local Z-RAM, remote Z-RAM, and off-chip DRAM, respectively. "La" and "En" represent latency and energy consumption, respectively

Type	SRAM	MRAM	ZRAM	Main
SRAM	3	12	7	62
MRAM	11	20	15	70
ZRAM	9	18	13	68
Main	61	70	65	0

Figure 7.6: Latency of moving data between different memory modules

respectively. "La" and "En" represent latency and energy consumption, respectively. During the execution of an application, data can be allocated to any memory module and moved back and forth among all memory modules in SPMs.

We assume data moving latency and energy consumption between different memory modules are given in the following Figures. In these two Figures, the column of "Type" indicates different types of memory, and other columns represent latency and energy consumption of data movement between different memory modules. For example, the column of "SRAM" represents the cost of moving data from other kinds of memory modules to SRAM.

Type	SRAM	MRAM	ZRAM	Main
SRAM	0.28	1.16	0.62	6.38
MRAM	0.95	1.83	1.29	7.05
ZRAM	0.86	1.74	1.20	6.96
Main	6.30	7.18	6.64	0

Figure 7.7: Energy consumption of moving data between different memory modules

Data		B_1	B_2	B_3	B_4	B_5	B_6	B_7	B_8	B_9	B_{10}	B_{11}	B_{12}	B_{13}	B_{14}	B_{15}	B_{16}	B_{17}	B_{18}
C1	R	18	17	14	10	14	10	12	10	10	12	14	7	6	5	8	3	17	1
	W	1	2	0	4	5	6	4	8	7	8	11	12	13	14	15	16	0	18
C2	R	0	0	2	5	0	3	0	0	0	10	8	12	13	1	15	16	17	1
	W	0	0	3	0	0	0	3	0	2	9	5	7	6	18	0	3	4	18

Figure 7.8: The number of data accesses for each core. The column of "Data" refers to the 18 data blocks, the columns of "R" and "W" represent the number of reads and writes to the corresponding data block, respectively

We assume the target system has two cores, and each of them equips with a hybrid SPM consisting of SRAM, MRAM, and Z-RAM. The off-chip shared memory is a DRAM. In order to demonstrate the viability of our data allocation strategy, we assume a simple program that has 18 data blocks obtained from a program, namely B_1, B_2, . . . , and $B_1 8$. Initially, only data block $B_1 8$ is stored in the core2's SRAM, and all others blocks are stored in the off-chip DRAM. In order to illustrate the example, we assume the number of accesses for each data by each core is given in Figure below. In this figure, the column of "DATA" indicates the data blocks used in this example. The rows of "Read" and "Write" represent the number of reads and writes to each data block incurred by each core.

7.5.1 An Adaptive Genetic Solution

In this section, we will discuss the details of the adaptive genetic algorithm. Typically, a genetic algorithm involves three significant steps: initialization, evaluation of fitness function, and genetic operations [6, 23]. First, we formally define the problem of data allocation in a CMP system. Then, we present each step of the genetic algorithm by using the example illustrated above.

The cost optimization problem of memory access incurred by data allocation in a CMP with P processors (each of these processors is integrated with an SPM which consists of an SRAM and an MRAM) can be defined as Given the number of data N, the initial data allocation on the on-chip memory units of all processor cores and the off-chip main memory, the capacity of each core's SRAM and MRAM, the number of cores P, the number of reading and writing references to each data of each core, the cost of each memory unit access, and the cost of moving data between different memory units, how to allocate each data to the hybrid memory units of each core so that the total memory access cost can be minimized and the write activities on MRAMs can be reduced? In this problem, we assume each core can access the off-chip main memory, the SRAM and MRAM in its local SPM, and every remote SPM with a different cost. The cost of access to each memory unit is given in Figure 7.5.

The objective function of the target problem is described as given the number of local reads NLR, local writes NLW, remote reads NRR, remote writes NRW, the cost of local read CLR, local write CLW, remote read CRR, remote write CRW, and the cost of data movement CMove exhibited in Tables 2 and 3, the cost of memory access (CM) for a specific data can be formulated as Equation below:

$$CM = N_{LR} \times C_{LR} + N_{LW} \times C_{LW} + N_{RR} \times C_{RR} + N_{RW} \times C_{RW} + C_{Move}$$
$$(7.1)$$

The population size PopSize (PS) usually depends on the proposed problem and is determined experimentally [25]. To accelerate the process of data allocation and the implementation of genetic operations, we will use the greedy algorithm in [63] to generate the initial population. A whole population will be generated from these initial individuals by randomly swapping the memory positions of genes.

In general genetic algorithms, the fitness function is typically obtained from the objective function that needs to be optimized. The fitness of an individual u is regarded to be better than the fitness of another individual v if the solution corresponding to u is closer to an optimal solution than v. According to Darwin's principle of survival of the fittest, the individual with a greater fitness value will have higher likelihood to survive in the next generation than the counterpart with a lower fitness value. We define the fitness function as Equation below:

$$FT(i) = M - Total\_Cost(i) \qquad (7.2)$$

where M represents maximum total cost have observed by this generation and $FT(i)$ represents the fitness value of chromosome i. $Total\_Cost(i)$ is the total cost of memory access to the chromosome i. Essentially, it equals to the total memory access cost of each gene (data) in this chromosome. We calculate the total cost by using Equation:

$$Total\_Cost(i) = \sum_{N}^{j=1} CM(j), \qquad (7.3)$$

for chromosome i. where N is the number of data items and $CM(j)$ is the memory access cost of data j that is defined as Equation 7.1.

7.5.2   Genetic Algorithm Operations

Generally, the genetic operations include selection, crossover, and mutation. We describe each of them as follows.

SELECTION: The selection process is carried out to form a new population, through strategically choosing some chromosomes from the old population with respect to the fitness value of each individual. It is utilized to enhance the overall quality of the population. Based on the natural selection rule, many methods are exploited to select the fittest chromosomes, such as roulette wheel selection, Boltzman selection, rank selection, and elitism, etc. In our genetic algorithm, we will use a rank based roulette wheel selection scheme with elitism to select chromosomes. In this method, an imaginary wheel with total 360 degrees is applied, on which all chromosomes in the population are placed, and each of them occupied a slot size according to the value of the corresponding fitness function.

Let PS denote the population size and A_i represent the angle of the sector occupied by the i th ranked chromosome. The chromosome-to-sector mapping is consistent to the fitness of each chromosome, and the 1st ranked chromosome has the highest fitness value, therefore allocating to the sector 1 with the largest angle A1. The (PS)th ranked chromosome has the lowest fitness value and is allocated to the sector $PS-1$ with smallest angle APS . Equations below hold for the angles:

$$\rho = \frac{A_i}{A_{i+1}} \tag{7.4}$$

$$A_1 = \frac{1-\rho}{1-\rho^{PS}} \tag{7.5}$$

$$A_i = \frac{(1-\rho)}{1-\rho^{PS}} \times \rho^{i-1} \tag{7.6}$$

where $Ai < 1$, $\rho < 1$, and $0 \leq i < PS$. Therefore, the fitter an individual is, the more area of it will be assigned on the wheel, and thus the more possible that it will be selected when the biased roulette wheel is spun. The algorithm to implement it is shown as Algorithm 1 (Figure 7.9):

Crossover is a crucial step after selection. Generally, it is employed to more broadly explore the search space. We can find the individual with higher fitness function with this operation. Conventionally, crossover operation includes signal point crossover, two point crossover, and uniform crossover. The rationale is that the "good" characteristics of the parents should be well preserved and passed down to children.

Algorithm 1 Algorithm for Genetic Selection

Input: An old population Old_{Pop} and the size of the population PS.

Output: A selected chromosome k.

1: Define the total fitness $SumFit$ as the sum of fitness values of all individuals in the current population;
2: **for** $i = 1 \rightarrow PS$ **do**
3: $\quad SumFit = SumFit + Old_{Pop}(i).FT$;
4: **end for**
5: Generate a random number $RanN$ between 1 to $SumFit$;
6: **for** $k = 1 \rightarrow PS$ **do**
7: $\quad$ **if** $\sum_{i=1}^{k} Old_{Pop}(i).FT \geq RanN$ **then**
8: $\quad\quad$ break;
9: $\quad$ **end if**
10: **end for**
11: **return** chromosome k;

Figure 7.9: Algorithm for genetic selection

However, the rational selection may lead to the local optimal problem. To avoid this problem, the crossover operations are carried out with a specific probability, which is often referred to as crossover rate, denoted by PC. We randomly select pairs of chromosomes as parents to generate new individuals. In this section, we will use an adaptive cycle crossover strategy to perform the crossover operation. The basic idea of cycle crossover works as follows:

$$PC = \frac{\varrho_c(FT_{max} - FT_{bestC})}{FT_{max} - FT_{avg}} \qquad (7.7)$$

where FT_{max} is the maximal fitness value in the current population, FTbestC is the fitness value of the parent with higher fitness value between the two crossover parents, FTavg is the average fitness value of the current population, and ϱ_c is a positive constant less than 1.

We start at the first allele of parent 1 and copy the gene to the first position of the child. Then, we look at the allele at the same position in parent 2. We cannot copy this gene to the first position of the child because it has been occupied. We will go to the position with the same gene in the parent 1 and suppose it is at the position i. We copy the gene in parent 2 to the position i of the child. We then apply the same operation on the gene in position i of parent 2. The cycle is repeated

---

Algorithm 2 Adaptive Cycle Crossover Algorithm

Input: Two parent chromosomes *P1* and *P2*.
Output: A new chromosome.
 1: Assume the length of each chromosome is *L*.
 2: **while** Child chromosome has empty position **do**
 3:   **for** $i = 1 \rightarrow L$ **do**
 4:     **if** Gene *i* in *P1* has not been copied to the child chromosome **then**
 5:       Keep the gene and break;
 6:     **end if**
 7:   **end for**
 8:   **if** The memory unit associated with gene *i* is full **then**
 9:     Adaptively search an available position from neighboring memory units;
10:   **else**
11:     Copy gene *i* to the same position of the child;
12:   **end if**
13:   Get a gene *Ge* at position *i* in *P2*;
14:   **while** *Ge* has already existed in the child **do**
15:     Locate the gene *Ge* in *P1*, suppose its position is *j*;
16:     Copy the gene *Ge* to the position *j* of the child;
17:     Get a new gene *Ge* at position *j* in *P2*;
18:   **end while**
19:   Apply the same process on *P2* to copy genes to the child chromosome;
20: **end while**
21: **return** The child chromosome;

Figure 7.10: Adaptive cycle crossover algorithm

until we arrive at a gene in parent 2 which has already been in the child. The cycle started from parent 1 is complete. The next cycle will be taken from parent 2. This crossover mechanism enables the child to efficiently inherit the characteristics from both parents. As elaborated in Algorithm 2 (Figure 7.10).

After the crossover operation, a genetic mutation will be performed to recover some good features eliminated by the crossover and prevent the premature convergence to a local optima. It is archived by randomly flipping bits of a chromosome. Similar to the crossover, it is happened in a certain specific probability that is called mutation rate. We define it to be a tunable parameter given in Equation:

$$PM = \frac{\varrho_m(FT_{max} - FT_{bestM})}{FT_{max} - FT_{avg}} \tag{7.8}$$

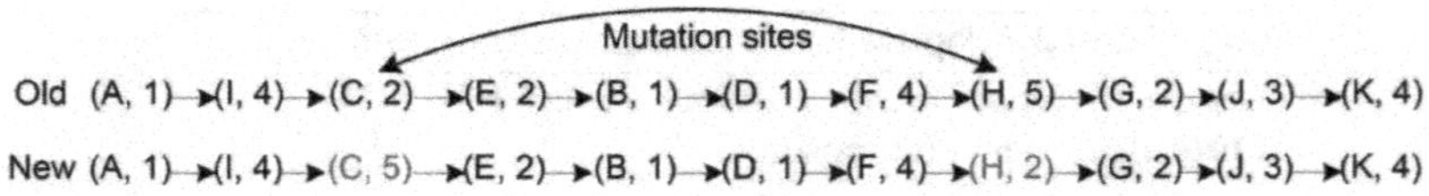

Mutation sites

Old (A, 1)→(I, 4)→(C, 2)→(E, 2)→(B, 1)→(D, 1)→(F, 4)→(H, 5)→(G, 2)→(J, 3)→(K, 4)

New (A, 1)→(I, 4)→(C, 5)→(E, 2)→(B, 1)→(D, 1)→(F, 4)→(H, 2)→(G, 2)→(J, 3)→(K, 4)

Figure 7.11: An example of mutation between gene (C, 2) and (H, 5).

where FT_{bestM} is the fitness value of the chromosome to be mutated and ϱ_m is a positive constant less than 1. The probability of a mutation is much lower than that of a crossover. For every new chromosome generated by the crossover operation, we perform the genetic mutation on it with a probability of PM. Since the gene in this research is defined as a data item and a memory unit pair, the mutation operation can be performed by swapping either the data or the memory units of the selected genes. However, since the datum are independent of each other, these two mutation methods are equal. We will thus swap the number of memory units of two genes to achieve the mutation Figure 7.11. For example, Figure 7.12 illustrate the result of our genetic mutation for a chromosome.

The whole procedure of our AGADA algorithm is described by Algorithm below. First, we need to generate the initial population. In this procedure, a number of chromosomes will be generated randomly. These chromosomes are random permutations of pairs of data and all memory units of a CMP system (line 1). After the initialization, the fitness value of each individual will be calculated according to Equation 7.3 (line 2). Then, a search process will be iteratively applied to determine the best solution for the data allocation problem until a termination condition is reached. The termination criterion includes two conditions: 1) the number of new generations exceeds a predefined maximum number of iterations, 2) after a certain number of search (typically 500 or even more), a better solution is still unreachable. In each generation, the crossover and mutation operation will be carried out in terms of the predefined crossover rate PC and mutation rate PM (line 6–8). Finally, based on the new population, the fitness value of each individual will be calculated and the selection operation will be employed to generate a new population (line 10).

Input: A set of data items, a CMP system with P processor cores, each core has a hybrid SPM. Any SPM_i has a SRAM with size of SS_i and a MRAM with size of SM_i.

Output: A data allocation.

1: Generate initial population;
2: $New_{PoP} \leftarrow \emptyset$;
3: Determine the fitness of each individual;
4: **while** Termination criterion is not met **do**
5:    **for** $i = 0 \rightarrow PS$ **do**
6:       Randomly select two chromosomes i and j from current population;
7:       Optionally apply the crossover operation on chromosomes i and j with probability PC;
8:       Optionally apply the mutation operation on the new chromosome with probability PM;
9:    **end for**
10:   Evaluate all individuals and perform selection;
11: **end while**
12: **return** The best allocation has obtained;

Figure 7.12: Adaptive genetic algorithm for data allocation

7.6 SUMMARY

In this chapter, we looked at a number of alternative methods of classifying various types of computer science experiments in general terms. Additionally, a section on the basic pipeline of experiments in machine learning is provided, and this part is expanded on in great depth. Afterwards, in the methodology section, we went through the adaptive evolutionary method for resolving the memory allocation problem in heterogeneous memory systems that we had covered before in the previous chapter.

How to Write a Paper

CONTENTS

This chapter describes how to finish the writing part for scientific or engineering research papers. In fact, the papers are formulated with all the previous chapter's contents from the introduction section until the experimentation. In this section, the examples of how to select the prepared materials to build a research article will be given. The students will learn how to organize the basic logic of writing a scientific and engineering article and understand how to write a paper independently.

8.1 RESEARCH YOU TOPIC

As you conduct research, try to make your paper's subject more and more narrow. You can't defend an argument about a super broad subject. However, the more refined your topic, the easier it'll be to pose a clear argument and defend it with well-researched evidence. It's easy to drift off course, especially in the early research stages. If you feel like you're going off-topic, reread the prompt to help get yourself back on track [3].

For instance, you might start with a general subject, like British decorative arts. Then, as you read, you home in on transferware and pottery. Ultimately, you focus on 1 potter in the 1780s who invented a way to mass-produce patterned tableware.

If you need to analyze a piece of literature, your task is to pull the work apart into literary elements and explain how the author uses those parts to make their point.

If you're writing a paper for a class, start by checking your syllabus and textbook's references. Look for books, articles, and other scholarly works related to your paper's topic. Then, like following a trail of clues, check those works' references for additional relevant sources.

Authoritative, credible sources include scholarly articles (especially those other authors reference), government websites, scientific studies, and reputable news bureaus. Additionally, check your sources' dates, and make sure the information you gather is up to date.

Evaluate how other scholars have approached your topic. Identify authoritative sources or works that are accepted as the most important accounts of the subject matter. Additionally, look for debates among scholars, and ask yourself who presents the strongest evidence for their case.

You'll most likely need to include a bibliography or works cited page, so keep your sources organized. List your sources, format them according to your assigned style guide (such as MLA or Chicago), and write 2 or 3 summary sentences below each one.

As you learn more about your topic, develop a working thesis, or a concise statement that presents an argument. A thesis isn't just a fact or opinion; rather, it's a specific, defensible claim. While you may tweak it during the writing process, your thesis is the foundation of your entire paper's structure.

Imagine you're a lawyer in a trial and are presenting a case to a jury. Think of your readers as the jurors; your opening statement is your thesis and you'll present evidence to the jury to make your case.

A thesis should be specific rather than vague, such as: "Josiah Spode's improved formula for bone china enabled the mass production of transfer-printed wares, which expanded the global market for British pottery."

8.2 DRAFTING YOUR ESSAY

Create an outline to map out your paper's structure. Use Roman numerals (I., II., III., and so on) and letters or bullet points to organize your outline. Start with your introduction, write out your thesis, and jot down your key pieces of evidence that you'll use to defend your argument. Then sketch out the body paragraphs and conclusion.

Your outline is your paper's skeleton. After making the outline, all you'll need to do is fill in the details.

For easy reference, include your sources where they fit into your outline, like this: III. Spode vs. Wedgewood on Mass Production A. Spode: Perfected chemical formula with aims for fast production and distribution (Travis, 2002, 43) B. Wedgewood: Courted high-priced luxury market; lower emphasis on mass production (Himmelweit, 2001, 71) C. Therefore: Wedgewood, unlike Spode, delayed the expansion of the pottery market.

Present your thesis and argument in the introduction. Start with an attention-grabbing sentence to draw in your audience and introduce the topic. Then present your thesis to let them know what you'll be arguing. For the remainder of the introduction, map out the evidence you'll use to make your case.

For instance, your opening line could be, "Overlooked in the present, manufacturers of British pottery in the eighteenth and nineteenth centuries played crucial roles in England's Industrial Revolution."

After presenting your thesis, lay out your evidence, like this: "An examination of Spode's innovative production and distribution techniques will demonstrate the importance of his contributions to the industry and Industrial Revolution at large."

Some people prefer to write the introduction first and use it to structure the rest of the paper. However, others like to write the body, then fill in the introduction. Do whichever seems natural to you. If you write the intro first, keep in mind you can tweak it later to reflect your finished paper's layout.

Build your argument in the body paragraphs. First, set the context for your readers, especially if the topic is obscure. Then, in around 3 to 5 body paragraphs, focus on a specific element or piece of evidence that supports your thesis. Each idea should flow to the next so the reader can easily follow your logic. For a paper on British pottery in the Industrial Revolution, for instance, you'd first explain what the products are, how they're made, and what the market was like at the time.

After setting the context, you'd include a section on Josiah Spode's company and what he did to make pottery easier to manufacture and distribute. Next, discuss how targeting middle class consumers increased demand and expanded the pottery industry globally. Then, you could explain how Spode differed from competitors like Wedgewood, who continued to court aristocratic consumers instead of expanding the market to the middle class. The right number of sections or paragraphs depends on your assignment. In general, shoot for 3 to 5, but check your prompt for your assigned length.

Address a counterargument to strengthen your case. While it's not always necessary, addressing a counterargument can help make your argument more convincing. After layout out your evidence, mention a contrasting view on the topic. Then explain why that differing perspective is incorrect and why your claim is more plausible.

If you bring up a counterargument, make sure it's a strong claim that's worth entertaining instead of ones that's weak and easily dismissed. Suppose, for instance, you're arguing for the benefits of adding fluoride to toothpaste and city water. You could bring up a study that suggested fluoride produced harmful health effects, then explain how its testing methods were flawed.

Summarize your argument in the conclusion. Think of your paper's structure as "Tell them what you'll tell them. Tell them. Tell them what you told them." After the paper's body, remind the reader of your thesis and the steps you've taken to defend it.

Sum up your argument, but don't simply rewrite your introduction using slightly different wording. To make your conclusion more memorable, you could also connect your thesis to a broader topic or theme to make it more relatable to your reader. For example, if you've discussed the role of nationalism in World War I, you could conclude by mentioning nationalism's reemergence in contemporary foreign affairs.

8.3 GENERAL PAPER STRUCTURE IN COMPUTER SCIENCE

On the Internet, you can find a variety of information on what should be considered to include in a scientific article. This section outlines some of the most important topics concerning the subject. These concerns also apply to writing a master's or Ph.D. thesis. However, the standards for the contribution vary substantially between different types of publications, as does the number of pages you are permitted to produce (often around 100 pages for a thesis and only approximately 8–10 pages for a full research paper submitting to a conference or a journal).

8.3.1 Title

Find a succinct and precise title for your work that corresponds closely to the content. It is worthwhile to devote time to this task because the title will be the part of the document that is referred to (in case it gets published). Normally, suppose you find yourself fall into a situation where too many aspects you need to consider when developing the paper title. In that case, you can revisit this task after you have the specific outline of the paper is developed or the paper is done written. The reason is that after you have a clear mind of the structure of the paper, then you will have a better understanding of which part of the aspect is more emphasized in the article; thus, you can shed some light in the title to represent that.

8.3.2 Abstract

One of the most significant portions of the article is the abstract. You only have a few seconds to pique the reader's curiosity. A poor abstract may already push you to the rejection side of the reviewer's decision-making process.

Establish the context and relevance of your study in your abstract, justify the problem, briefly discuss the solution, and present the results of your work. To keep your abstract short, use one (short) sentence for each of the above-stated topic components. Overall, this should be a brief summary of your paper's entire content, including outcomes. In a few phrases, the reader should understand the main point of your paper. As a result, choose the most important finding and include it in the abstract, such as "Results reveal that our algorithm improves performance by 23% relative to state of the art method." Consider your abstract to be a personal challenge for each of your papers.

It's okay to make a quick draft of the abstract before deciding the outline of the paper. Writing the abstract ahead of time actually aids you in focusing your paper. However, once you've finished the paper, go back and reread the abstract. After that, you will most likely rewrite it to improve it.

8.3.3 Main Body Structure

Generally, a standard structure of research papers' main body in computer science contains the following elements, some of the elements can be combined into separate sections, and some should hold themselves and be written independently:

1. **Introduction:** presents the paper's context and demonstrates why your study is relevant

2. **State of the art/Backgrounds:** describes the current state of the art in your paper's field and frequently leads to problem motivation

3. **Problem formulation & motivation:** precisely identifies the issue addressed by the paper This section is sometimes included in the introduction.

4. **Solution:** explains how you solved the problem.

5. **Related work:** succinctly highlights the work of others in the same field of your paper, for example, addressing the same topic or having a comparable solution to a potentially different problem Furthermore, compare the relevant work to your own work, noting what is similar and where the contrasts are. Please keep in mind that slandering the work of others in order to claim that you do it better is unethical. Compare your work objectively/neutrally against the work of others – and be honest!

6. **Proof/Evaluation/Discussion:** You must demonstrate that your solution actually solves the problem. This will look different depending on the paper. Theoretical papers often include a

formal/mathematical proof, whereas empirical publications typically present an examination (quantitative and qualitative) of a prototype implementation. However, you should be the most knowledgeable about how to demonstrate your work.

7. **Conclusion:** finishes the paper by emphasizing your primary message once again. In contrast to the abstract, you might expand on the fact that the reader now knows what your work is about.

8. **Future work:** State your thoughts on what you believe could be done in the future to improve on the stated situation. You may also include additional problem areas that you discovered that will be studied in the future. This area is optional, although it may help others uncover interesting new research challenges.

These components do not have to have their own section, and some of them, such as state of the art and problem motivation, may be integrated as part of the introduction, especially for shorter papers. However, the topics stated above should be considered to include in your paper because they are frequently required to understand your work and contribution, and a conference or journal reviewer will search for them.

The topic of whether related work should be included at the conclusion or alongside the state of the art section must be addressed separately for each paper. It sometimes fits better at the start and sometimes at the end. Suppose I don't need to expand on the similar work section's content. In that case, I usually retain it towards the end because it allows for a better comparison of your own and related work, which is difficult to do before the reader knows the content of your paper.

Try to be as detailed as possible with section headers and avoid using generic titles whenever feasible, e.g., "The MY-Framework-Name" is far better than just "Solution" because it gives your solution a name. Some parts, such as "Related Work" or "Conclusion," will, of course, be labeled in that manner for better illustration.

8.4 EFFECTIVELY USE TABLES AND FIGURES TO BETTER ELABORATE YOUR IDEAS

Research papers are frequently based on large volumes of data that may be summarized and readily understood using tables and graphs.

Data must be presented to the reader in a visually appealing manner when writing a research report. The data in figures and tables, on the other hand, should not be a duplicate of the material found in the text. There are numerous ways to present data in tables and figures, all of which are defined by a few simple criteria. The usefulness of tables and figures in preparing a research paper cannot be overstated. How do you know if a table or figure is required? The general guideline is that if you can't present your material in one or two phrases, you should use a table.

8.4.1 Using Tables

Tables may be simply constructed in tools like Excel or Latex. Tables and figures in scientific articles are excellent tools for presenting data and making comparisons. Understanding your reader and the pieces that make a table is required for effective data presentation in research articles. The legend, column titles, and body are all components of a table. Tables, like academic writing, must be structured in such a way that readers can easily grasp them. Disorganized or otherwise unclear tables will cause the reader to lose interest in your work. Here are some important remarks for you when you consider adding a table:

1. Tables should have a **clear, descriptive title** that serves as the table's "subject sentence." Depending on the discipline, the titles might be long or short.

2. **Column Titles:** The purpose of these title headings is to make the table easier to read. The reader's attention is drawn sequentially from the headline to the column title. A solid set of column headings will help the reader understand what the table is about immediately.

3. **Table Body:** This is the primary section of the table that contains numerical or textual data. Construct your table so that the items read from top to bottom rather than across.

Figure 8.1 depicts some simple suggestions and strategies for designing your table.

Tables are also a really good way to illustrate the difference or the improvement of your work compared to the state-of-the-art methods. Here I use an example from our recent work [250] where we list out all

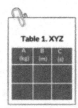

- A clear, descriptive, and concise title placed above the table.
- A good set of column titles (with units/unit symbols wherever applicable) that allow the reader to grasp the context of the table.
- Data should read from top to bottom.

Figure 8.1: Simple tips and tricks for table designing

the interesting properties when designing a data management tool for nowadays machine learning environment.

Figures and tables should be placed in the center of the page. It should be correctly cited and numbered as it appears in the text. Tables should also be separated from the text. Text wrapping should be avoided. In certain journals, tables, and figures are published after the references.

8.4.2 Using Figures

Figures can take many different shapes, including bar graphs, frequency histograms, scatterplots, drawings, maps, and so on. Always keep your reader in mind while utilizing figures in a research report. What is the simplest figure for your reader to grasp? How can you deliver the information in the simplest and most effective way possible? A photograph, for example, may be the greatest choice if you want your reader to grasp spatial relationships. Here we list some important factors you might find helpful when deciding to include a figure in your paper:

1. **Figure captions:** Figures should be numbered and captioned with descriptive titles or captions. The captions should be brief enough to be understood at a glance. Captions are placed beneath the figure and are justified to the left.

2. **Image itself:** Choose an image that is straightforward and easy to understand. Consider the image's size, resolution, and general visual appeal.

Method Type	Multi-purpose	Task-Driven	Model-Agnostic	Est. Utility
Traditional	✗	✗	✗	✗
Data Cleaning	✗	○	○	✗
Perm-Shapley [19]	✓	✓	✓	✗
TMC-Shapley [16]	✓	✓	✓	✗
G-Shapley [16]	✓	✓	✗	✗
KNN-Shapley [20]	✗	✗	✓	✗
Least Core [18]	✓	✓	✓	✗
Leave-one-out [10]	✓	✓	✓	✗
Infl. Func. [10]	✗	✓	✗	✗
TracIn [11]	✗	✓	✗	✗
DATASIFTER	✓	✓	✓	✓

Table 1: Summary of the differences between previous works with our methods (DATASIFTER). ○ means only some of the techniques in the type satisfy the property.

Figure 8.2: A good example of using table to present comparison of the related works

3. **Additional Information:** Illustrations and tables in manuscripts are numbered separately. Include any legends or other information that the reader will need to comprehend your figure.

Below in Figure 8.3, we include the simple tips for figure designing:
Interesting figures not only helps you to illustrate your idea it also helps to draw the readers' attention in the best way. Here, we use an example from the paper above to show what a good figure in a research paper might look like:
Figure 8.4 illustrates the whole process of the framework proposed in that work. We make the figure clear and comprehensive, which helps the readers understand what each element in the proposed framework is responsible for and draws the readers' attention in the first place when they pass through the paper.

8.4.3 Common Errors When Using Tables and Figures

Understanding the common flaws that render data presentation inefficient is required for good data presentation in research articles. Using the incorrect type of figure for the data is one of the most prevalent blunders. For example, using a scatterplot instead of a bar graph to represent hydration levels is a mistake. Another common error is for

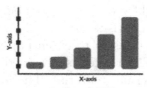

Y-axis
X-axis
Figure 1. ABC
• A clear, descriptive, and concise caption placed below the figure.
• A high-quality image with good resolution and appropriate size.
• Can include bar graphs, histograms, maps, scatter plots, etc.

Figure 8.3: Simple tips and tricks for figure designing

Patched Data
Clean Samples
Backdoor Data Detection
Poisoned Model
Poisoned Model Detection
Patched Data
Ensemble of Models
Attack Invalidation

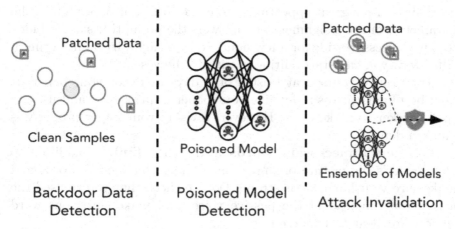

Figure 8.4: A good example of using figures to illustrate the difference between related works

authors to italicize the table number. Keep in mind that just the table title should be italicized. Another typical blunder is forgetting to properly attribute the table. If the table or figure is from another source, simply write Note. "Adapted from..." is written beneath the table. This should help to avoid any plagiarism issues.

The use of tables and figures in research papers is critical for the readability of the article. The reader is provided the opportunity to comprehend data through visual material. These components should be addressed when writing a research paper as part of good research writing. If the data is too complex or extensive, APA research papers, MLA research papers, and other manuscripts require visual material. The relevance of tables and graphs is emphasized by the primary goal of writing, which is to be understood.

8.5 REVISE YOUR PAPER

Ensure your paper is well-organized and includes transitions. After finishing your first draft, give it a read and look for big-picture organizational issues. Make sure each sentence and paragraph flow well to the next. You may have to rewrite a paragraph or swap sections around, but taking the time for revisions is important if you want to hand in your best work.

This is also a great opportunity to make sure your paper fulfills the parameters of the assignment and answers the prompt! It's a good idea to put your essay aside for a few hours (or overnight, if you have time). That way, you can start editing it with fresh eyes.

Try to give yourself at least 2 or 3 days to revise your paper. It may be tempting to simply give your paper a quick read and use the spell-checker to make edits. However, revising your paper properly is more in-depth.

Cut out unnecessary words and other fluff. In addition to your paper's big-picture organization, zoom in on specific words and make sure your language is strong. Double check that you've used the active voice instead of the passive voice, and make sure your word choices are clear and concrete.

The passive voice, such as "The door was opened by me," feels hesitant and wordy. On the other hand, the active voice, or "I opened the door," feels strong and concise. Each word in your paper should do a specific job. Try to avoid including extra words just to fill up blank space on a page or sound fancy. For instance, "The author uses pathos to appeal to readers' emotions" is better than "The author utilizes pathos to make an appeal to the emotional core of those who read the passage."

Proofread for spelling, grammatical, and formatting errors. After you've revised your paper's organization and content, fix any typos and grammar issues. Again, it's helpful to put your paper aside for a while so you can proofread it with fresh eyes.

Read your essay out loud to help ensure you catch every error. As you read, check for flow as well and, if necessary, tweak any spots that sound awkward.

Ask a friend, relative, or teacher to read your work before you submit it. Have 1 or 2 people assess your draft's organization, persuasiveness, spelling, and grammar. New readers can help you find any mistakes and unclear spots that you may have overlooked.

It's wise to get feedback from one person who's familiar with your topic and another who's not. The person who knows about the topic can help ensure you've nailed all the details. The person who's unfamiliar with the topic can help make sure your writing is clear and easy to understand.

8.6 SET UP YOUR PERSONAL DEEP LEARNING ENVIRONMENT – SELECTION OF THE HARDWARE

Building up your own deep learning environment can actually happen in cases where you are at the phase of self-founded or the case your lab is planning to upgrade to a new set of environments. Having those machines operated on your own is actually way better than having a cloud server in terms of security, privacy, and long-term costs. This section will first introduce how and what you should be interested in when selecting your new hardware for the environment. In the next chapter's technical section, we will finally elaborate on how you should accordingly set up your basic software environment.

8.6.1 GPUs

GPUs are at the heart of deep learning model training. When it comes to deep learning algorithms, GPUs are the fastest because they have hundreds or thousands of simple cores that are extremely efficient at matrix multiplication. Deep learning GPUs are available from Nvidia, which is the most reliable brand in the industry. This software library allows GPUs to be interfaced with by most deep learning frameworks.

Tensor cores are the most cost-effective GPUs. In order to train models with half-precision or mix precision, tensor cores perform special matrix math.

Because of this, larger batch sizes, faster training and bigger models are now possible. As part of the Nvidia RTX GPU family, Tenor cores are included in the GPU models. Depending on the type of models you plan to train, your GPU will require different amounts of memory.

A GPU with less memory is sufficient if you only plan on training small models for embedded devices. In order to train larger models, such as GPT from the NLP domain, I would recommend getting as much memory as you can afford.

You guessed it ... larger batch sizes, faster training, and larger models are all made possible with more GPU memory. If you're planning on using more than one GPU, you'll need either blower fans or liquid cooling.

Because they are designed to remove heat from the case, blower fans are essential when running multiple GPUs. System overheating can occur if you do not have blower-style fans. Nvidia RTX 2080 TI is a good choice if you're looking for an affordable option. In addition, it comes with 11GB of VRam.

8.6.2 CPUs

The CPUs are primarily used in Deep Learning to load data into memory. To train your models, you can use more threads on a single CPU. As a result, the GPU doesn't have to wait too long to load data.

For reinforcement learning problems, CPUs are crucial because the majority of computation will take place in your learning environment, which is almost certainly powered by a CPU. Using a GPU to speed up training large neural networks with reinforcement learning is a must. Check to see if your CPU is compatible with the number of GPUs you plan on having if you only plan on doing deep learning.

When choosing a CPU, you might want to ask yourself these questions:

1. In what way do you plan to use reinforcement learning? If you want faster training, choose a high-end CPU that performs well on benchmarks.

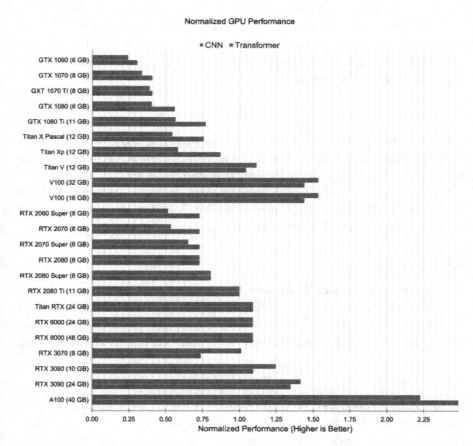

Figure 8.5: Top-tier GPUs' performances on DL tasks

2. Do you only wish to engage in deep learning techniques? Then you can get away with a cheaper CPU, but more threads would help with data loading.

3. What about a multi-GPU setup? Verify that your CPU can handle the number of GPUs you want to run at the same time.

Intel's i9–10920X, with 12 cores and 24 threads, is a good choice for a decent CPU. In addition, it has a clock speed of up to 4.8 GHz and supports up to four graphics processing units. The Intel i9–10920X is a powerful CPU that can perform both deep learning and reinforcement learning tasks simultaneously.

8.6.3 RAMs

Thinking that you need the fastest RAM with the highest clock rate is a big mistake. Linus Tech Tips explains that high RAM clock speeds are a marketing ploy. It is better to spend your money elsewhere if you want to see a significant improvement in your training. What's important is the RAM's memory capacity. Aim for a minimum of the same amount of RAM as your GPU's memory.

8.6.4 Motherboard

Check the number of PCIe slots on the motherboard you're considering before making a purchase decision. The PCIe slots should also be large enough for the GPUs. In general, a GPU occupies two PCIe slots. The motherboard should be compatible with your CPU and RAM as well.

8.6.5 Storage

Data loading speed can be improved by using a faster storage device, such as a Solid State Drive (SSD). SSDs are more expensive than standard hard drives, so it makes sense to buy a smaller SSD for the operating system and a larger standard disk hard drive as a secondary storage device. If you want to train faster, you can transfer the data you need to your SSD.

8.6.6 Power Supply Unit

You'll need a Power Supply Unit (PSU) that has enough wattage to power your entire system. Multiply by 110 percent the amount of power needed for the CPU and GPU PCIe connectors must be available on your Power Supply Unit (PSU).

8.6.7 Cooling

As a matter of fact, you'll need a CPU cooler. Consider a water cooling setup to reduce fan noise. Consider liquid cooling for your GPUs as well if you have the budget. As a result, it would be incredibly quiet. For multi-GPU setups if you plan to use air cooling, make sure you have blower-style cooling.

8.6.8 Case

Cases come in all shapes and sizes, so long as your parts fit inside. I'd recommend getting a case with good airflow, thus your colling systems and work at their best status.

8.6.9 Final Checking List Before Your Shoping

Use **PC Part Picker**[1] when building your rig. It has a feature where it checks for part compatibility so you don't totally screw up your build. It's not perfect though, because it alerted me that my parts don't fit in my case but everything fits perfectly, so use it as a compass while building.

Why would I build my own machine, you ask? The cloud is an option, but it's not the only one. It's a yes, all right. But building your own machine has its advantages, including cost savings in the long run.

Building your own deep learning rig may be worthwhile for these three reasons:

1. Cost savings are the number one benefit. As long as you're regularly using it to train, building your own GPU can save you money over time! A v100 costs around $3 an hour or about $2100 a month to rent. A machine can be built for that price, and it can be kept indefinitely.

2. As a matter of fact, your own hardware is faster than the cloud itself. Virtualization causes slow IO between instances and GPUs in the cloud. According to Bizon-Tech, cloud computing is more expensive than buying your own personal computer [283].

---

[1]https://pcpartpicker.com/

3. Owning your own rig allows you to use it as a productivity machine for other tasks. As a result, you might be able to train DNNs at the highest settings and have more than ten tabs open in Chrome!

4. Here's a little something extra: Every time I train a model, I don't have to worry about how much money I'll spend. The fact that I was required to pay for each training session made me hesitant to try new things because I knew it would cost me money. Due to my own machine, I was able to experiment more and perfect the art of deep learning faster than if I had relied on cloud computing. Google Colab and Kaggle kernels are two other free GPU-enabled options, but there is a time limit on how long you can train, which limits my choices of models and problems. However, I strongly recommend that most people who are just getting started with deep learning use them.

8.7 SUMMARY

This chapter went through the fundamental structure of computer science papers in depth, as well as how to effectively include figures and tables into your work. Furthermore, we provide extensive guidelines for machine learning or deep learning beginners on how to select a hardware setup for experiments in our methodology section, which may be found here.

IV

Put Your Work Out and Make
Impacts

Paper Submission and Publication

CONTENTS

This chapter describes the common routine of how to select and submit a scientific paper to the right place. Also, how a scientific paper is published from the submission will also be introduced. Since there are several main categories of scientific papers including conference papers, journal papers, etc., some examples will be introduced to illustrate how the submission should be made and how the publication process is like.

9.1 CHOOSING WHERE TO SUBMIT YOUR PAPER

It can be tempting to begin writing a paper before giving much thought to where it might be published. However, choosing a journal or conference to target before you begin to prepare your paper will enable you to tailor your writing to the journal's audience and format your paper according to its specific guidelines, which you may find on the journal's website.

Here are the top ten factors to consider when choosing where to submit your paper:

1. **Peer review:** Does the journal or conference provide a peer review service? Peer review is considered a stamp of quality from the research community.

2. **Relevance:** Does the journal or conference publish other papers similar to the one you are preparing? Does it publish theoretical, experimental or applied research?

3. **Reputation:** Does the journal or conference have a strong reputation in your field? Where do your peers publish?

4. **Scope:** Is the journal or conference broad in its scope or is it a specialist journal read mainly by a particular community?

5. **Timeliness:** Is fast publication important to you? Have you checked the publication times for the journal or conference?

6. **Cost:** Will the journal or conference charge you for publishing your paper? Will your institution cover the publication charge if there is one? Will you be charged for extra pages/colour figures/supplementary data?

7. **Language:** Most international journals or conferences publish papers written in English. Will you need to have your paper checked by a native English speaker?

8. **Citation:** Is the journal or conference likely to be cited by other researchers working in your field?

9. **Indexing:** Is the journal or conference indexed in the major online databases such as ISI Web of Science?

10. **Appearance:** Does the journal or conference publish papers in a format that is suitable for your work?

Here are some usful rankings that you might find helpful: Computer Science Conference Ranking [1], Computer Science Journal Ranking [2].

Following Jeremy Fox interesting blog post [59]. Here are my thoughts on where to submit your paper. In a nutshell, I think times are changing. If you are in a strong position, you can bet for the model you think is best. But if you are not settled yet, I think is wise to have a compromise between publishing some old school papers based on journals prestige, but also make your bet by submitting other manuscripts to faster and open access Journals. That way you can defend your position in a variety of situations.

Aim as high as you reasonably can. Agreed, but "high" is a vague term. Impact factor is not a reliable measure and "prestige" is difficult to asses. I think like Jan, that the difference is between the 3 top interdisciplinary journals, the top journals of your field, and then everything else. Within this categories, I don't worry anymore about the journal in terms of "high impact".

Don't just go by journal prestige; consider "fit". I do think fit is important, but not in terms of people finding your paper (despite lots of researchers keep using TOC's of a few well-known journals), but because having a type of journal (or reader) in mind helps you frame your article. For example, I'd expect different things from the same title in Am Nat, than in Ecology.

How likely is the journal to send your paper out for external review? I liked Ethan's advice on the importance of the speed of the process. By maximizing your chances of being sent to review, not only you can accumulate citations faster but also it reduce the amount of frustration.

Is the journal open access? Ideally, Yes, is very important for me. In reality, well, my projects rarely have the money to pay for it, so I end up not making them open.

Does the journal evaluate papers only on technical soundness? I think this is a model that will substitute all low tier journals. I'm writing mainly three types of papers. Papers that I hope can make a great advance on Ecology and that I would like to see in a top journal. Papers that has an specific niche, and where I want to target people working on this niche. And good papers that I think can make its moderate contribution, and I want them out there fast for people to read. This papers are ideal for open access and evaluated on technical soundness.

Is the journal part of a review cascade? Again, completely agree with Ethan. In fact, I would love a model where papers are valued on technical soundness and then there is an "editors choice" or something like that.

Is it a society journal? I value supporting Societies. But most important: Is the publisher making profit? Is Copyright retained to the author? Society journals or other organisational journals (i.e., PLOS) has the great advantage from my point of view that revert the benefits to the community, and usually they require a licence to publish, but not a copyright transfer. It's important for me to avoid as much as possible making a business of science.

Publish in a diversity of journals: If you want to increase your readership, increase the spectrum of journals you publish. Publish in general ecology Journals, in more specialised journals, Plos ONE stile. That would help you gain experience with the system too.

Listen to your feelings: Is there any journal you like (rationally or irrationally) specially? Forget the pros and cons. Publishing is hard, and its also important to fulfil your whims.

9.1.1 Why Preferring Conferences?

Conference publication is more preferred to journal publication in certain areas of computer science, at least for experimentalists. This was the recommendation (a memo) of the Computer Research Association (CRA) in 1999. The CRA memo asserts that conference publication is superior to journal publication in computer science. According to the memo, the typical conference submission receives four to five evaluations, whereas the typical journal submission receives only two to three evaluations.

Computing researchers are right to view conferences as an important archival venue and use acceptance rate as an indicator of future impact. Papers in highly selective conferences, with acceptance rates of 30% or less, should continue to be treated as first-class research contributions with impact comparable to, or better than, journal papers. This distinguishes computer science from other academic fields where only journal publication carries real weight. There are two main reasons to publish in the proceedings of selective conferences:

1. Conferences are more timely than journals.

2. Conferences have higher standards of novelty. Journals often only require 20–30% of the material to be new, compared to an earlier conference version.

Conference selectivity serves two purposes: pick the best submitted papers and signal prospective authors and readers about conference quality. Is there a connection between conference acceptance rate and impact factor, where impact is measured by the number of citations received? The answer is positive, up to some threshold. Adopting the right selectivity level helps attract better submissions and more citations. With respect to ACM-wide data, that acceptance rates of 15-20% seem optimal for generating the highest number of future citations for both the proceedings as a whole and the top papers submitted. Conferences rejecting 85% or more of their submissions risk discouraging overall submissions and inadvertently filtering out high-impact research.

9.1.2 Why Preferring Journals?

Many universities evaluate faculty on the basis of journal publications because, in most scientific fields, journals have higher standards than conferences. Journals may have longer page limits and journal reviews tend to be more detailed. Many times, conference committees enlist inexperienced graduate students as reviewers of papers in order to meet the quota for reviews. Because conference papers are limited in length, and because a large number of papers must be reviewed within a short time, the quality of reviews of conference papers is generally low. In contrast, for journals, because there are usually no page limits, authors can explain their ideas completely. Editors can choose qualified reviewers carefully. Reviewers can take adequate time to write thorough reviews.

By polishing a manuscript for journal publication, the author minimizes the number of errors and improves the clarity of the exposition. Thus, journal papers are more likely to be correct and readable than conference papers. Journals are more widely distributed through libraries than conference proceedings, which go out of print quickly. In all disciplines, the criteria for quality include innovation, thoroughness, and clarity, appraised through rigorous peer review. Across disciplines, there are common standards for the evaluation and documentation of publicly presented scholarly work. According to some authors, computer science is not sufficiently different from other engineering disciplines to warrant evaluation on completely different grounds. The evaluation of the scholarship of academic computer scientists should continue to emphasize publications in rigorously refereed, archival scientific journals.

The "conferences vs journal" debate is far from over and was recently relaunched in Communications of the ACM. Studying the metadata of the ACM Digital Library, we can tell that papers in low-acceptance-rate conferences have higher impact than in high-acceptance-rate conferences within ACM. Highly selective conferences – those that accept 30% or less of submissions – are cited at a rate comparable to or greater than ACM jounals.

Unlike every other academic field, computer science uses conferences rather than journals as the main publication venue. This has led to a great growth in the number of low level conferences. Some call such conferences "refereed conferences" but we all know this is just an attempt to mollify promotion and tenure committees. The reviewing process performed by program committees is done under extreme time and workload pressures, and it does not rise to the level of careful refereeing. Only a small fraction of conference papers are followed up by journal papers.

9.2 HOW TO SUBMIT A RESEARCH PAPER TO A JOURNAL OR CONFERENCE

In the later stages of your studies, one of the important things you will need to do is to submit one or more papers to research journals or conferences for possible publication. You should do this as soon as your dissertation adviser tells you that your research is ready for publication, but not before! If you are co-authoring a paper with your adviser, then he or she may be handling the submission details as the senior co-author. If so, ask your adviser to use the submission process to teach you how it is done, so you will be able to do this yourself in the future. However, if you are submitting a paper as the sole or senior author, then you will need know how to handle this process yourself. Over the years, there have been advanced graduate students who could have benefited from some general advice about the submission process. This letter has been written in the hope that you will navigate the publication process smoothly.

Remember that any papers based on your dissertation research should include a grateful acknowledgment – either in the introductory section, as a footnote, or at the end. State that this work is part of your doctoral dissertation at Louisiana State University and thank your adviser. Your acknowledgment of the role of your doctoral adviser may help to insure that a journal editor takes your work seriously, since it has at least passed the scrutiny of your adviser. If other researchers have helped, thank them too. Most researchers are generous about sharing their ideas, but they will surely notice and remember if you fail to acknowledge them. This is good advice to remember for the future as well.

You should give careful thought to your paper's introduction. The introduction to your paper should explain clearly what your main results are and why they are interesting or important. The introduction should tell your audience how your researchl work is related to recent research in the area. It is very important to properly reference these works. A referee for your paper may be chosen from among the researchers whose work you cite. You would like the introduction to motivate readers to read more. Read the introductions from leading researchers in your area to give you ideas about what you should include in your introduction.

Ask your adviser read your entire paper and listen carefully to his or her suggestions. It takes much experience to know how to write well for a research journal. It is likely that you will need to go through several thorough revisions before your adviser is pleased with your writing. Expect this to happen and learn from the process. It will benefit you for years to come.

It is important that your paper be sent to referees with current expertise in the field of your research. With this in mind, the first thing to do is to ask your adviser to suggest a suitable journal and a suitable editor to whom to send your paper. Your adviser may know that a certain journal is an active venue for publication in your field. Before you and your adviser make a final choice of the journal to which you will submit your paper, you may be well-advised to check the backlog of the journals that you are considering. Especially during the early years of your career, you may have a practical need to get several papers into print without very long delays.

Many journals have websites, which you should visit to read their instructions for authors. For example the AMS Journals use this page: Information for Authors. You will note that some editors favor electronic submission, some favor paper, and some want both. You will probably find a list of members of the journal's editorial board, as one finds at List of Transactions Editors for example. Be sure to discuss with your adviser which editor would be the best one to receive your submission. You may also find a page listing style files for that journal which you can download: Authors Package for Transactions. Other journals provide similar information. For example, here is a link for the Backlog Information for the Journal of the AMS. A number of journals or conferences accept submission of articles from listings which authors can place at the arXiv.org. Once you have selected a journal or conference, check the requirements for publication in that journal, with regard to style, type and length of papers published, etc., to make sure you get these things right.

9.3 HOW TO WRITE REBUTTALS AND REPLIES?

Publishing work can be hard and requires a lot of work. And the only way to have your ideas being published and having a great impact on others is to polish your work and aiming for better versions of your work. Reviews from conferences or journals can be a great opinion on your work that can instruct you to better polish your work. However, sometimes you may also be facing some reviewers that give you wired opinions without fully understand the background or the details of your work; thus, their opinion can be annoying and may also impede your work from publishing. Thus, writing a decent rebuttal for conferences or replies for journals is quite an important procedure for you and the reviewers. It's also an important way for you to exchange ideas and pave the confusion raised by the reviewers. Thus you can acquire better ideas on how you may improve your work.

Most manuscripts have to be revised at least once before they are accepted. This holds true despite the fact that, for the most part, authors and researchers exert a great deal of effort and diligence towards drafting their manuscript. The anticipation period for most authors, as they await feedback from a journal, is marked by an unpredictable concoction of excitement and anxiety.

Regardless of the author's expectations or subsequent reactions to reviewer comments, authors are required to follow certain protocol with respect to responding to such feedback. During this stage of publication, authors tend to be faced with the problem of how to write a rebuttal letter.

For journals, once the author receives a decision for acceptance with major or minor revisions, he/she has to revise the manuscript based on the peer reviewer comments. The revised manuscript is then submitted to the committee along with a point-by-point response to the reviewer comments. A cover letter for a revised manuscript should be sent to the editor along with the author's responses to the reviewer comments. This letter is often called the response letter or the rebuttal letter.

The rebuttal/response letter is more common in top-tier conferences. Normally, multiple rounds of reviews are included, thus allowing the authors to provide a rebuttal to the preliminary reviews returned from the reviewers.

Thus, it is important to compose a good response letter, no matter it is for a journal or a conference. A response letter or rebuttal letter can be written in two ways:

1. You write a cover letter and attach a separate document in which you have addressed the reviewer comments.

2. Alternatively, your rebuttal letter can be divided into two sections: an introductory part addressed to the journal editor and a second part containing detailed responses to the reviewer comments.

Begin the letter by mentioning the manuscript title and id. Include a small paragraph thanking the reviewers for their valuable time and useful contribution. Mention that you appreciate the inputs they have given and that their inputs will definitely help improve your manuscript. Rebuttal letters that thank the referees set a positive tone right from the beginning.

If you are including your responses in a separate document, add a paragraph that broadly summarizes the major changes that you have made in the manuscript based on the reviewers' comments. Mention that you have attached a document containing point-by-point responses to the reviewers' comments. If you are including the detailed responses in the same letter, mention that the next section contains your responses.

Addressing reviewer comments can be a difficult task, especially, if there are many comments and the comments are long. Here are a few things to keep in mind when addressing reviewer comments:

1. **Address each and every point raised by the editor and reviewers:** Copy every single comment in your rebuttal letter and write your reply immediately after each point in a clear and concise manner. Make sure that not a single point raised by the reviewers/editor goes unanswered. Even if you do not agree with a point or have not made the change suggested, please mention that and provide a reason for your decision.

2. **Provide point-by-point responses:** Number the reviewers' points and respond to them sequentially. Highlight the corresponding changes in the manuscript or refer to the line numbers in the original and revised manuscripts. Consider setting the reviewer comments in bold to distinguish them from your responses. This makes it easier for the editor/reviewer to follow what you have done.

3. **Categorize the reviewers' comments:** If there are too many comments, it would help if you separate the comments into categories. For example, all the comments related to methodology could be grouped together, all related to language could be under one category, etc. If you decide to do that, make sure you add a sentence such as "I have separated my responses to the reviewers' comments according to several categories in order to achieve an integrated approach in my responses."

4. **If comments are in the form of paragraphs, split them into points:** If the reviewers' comments are in the form of large paragraphs, divide them into separate points so that you can address them individually. If you are not sure of what a particular comment means, begin your response by explaining what you have understood from the comment.

5. **In case you feel the reviewer has misunderstood something, clarify politely:** Reviewers are experts who have extensive knowledge of their field; therefore, if you feel that a reviewer has misunderstood certain parts, it is likely to be due to lack of clarity in your presentation. In such cases, point out the misunderstanding politely and provide the necessary clarification. For instance, you could write: "I am sorry that this part was not clear in the original manuscript. I should have explained that. . . . I have revised the contents of this part."

6. **If you cannot address a point, give a reason:** If you cannot address any of the reviewers' concerns, explain why you cannot do it, for instance, if the reviewer has asked you to provide additional data or conduct additional experiments, which you feel are not necessary. Avoid giving personal reasons like lack of funds or lack of time as reasons. Do not show a negative attitude. Be respectful in your reply. First, thank the reviewer for his/her in-depth analysis and useful comments. Then, explain where you

feel you cannot completely agree with the reviewer's suggestion. Your answer should be clear and logical and should be backed by evidence.

7. **When adding new data or figures, mention their location in the manuscript:** If you have included new data, tables, figures, etc., indicate where you have added the information: mention page numbers, figure panels, etc. If required, attach supplementary material so that the reviewer/editor has everything that he/she needs and does not have to go searching for the material.

8. **Maintain a polite and respectful tone throughout:** Remember that the reviewers have spent a lot of time and effort in evaluating your manuscript. Even if some of the comments appear to be negative, do not take them personally. The reviewers are critiquing your work, not you, and their inputs are valuable additions to your work. Be polite and respectful in your tone even if you feel that some of the comments are unfavorable or unreasonable. Sometimes some reviewers may have conflicting views. But remember that each of them will read your rebuttal letter, so it is best to be equally polite to all the reviewers. The tone of the cover letter is very important.

9. **Conclude the letter appropriately:** Be careful of how you end the rebuttal letter. A concluding sentence such as the following may sound overly conceited: "Since all the corrections have been made, we hope the manuscript will now be accepted without any further changes." A straightforward but polite ending would be "We look forward to hearing from you regarding our submission. We would be glad to respond to any further questions and comments that you may have." Such an ending are formal, polite, and reflects a willingness to make further changes if required.

9.4 SET UP YOUR DEEP LEARNING ENVIRONMENT – SOFTWARE LEVEL

In the previous chapter, we have discussed what you might want to consider when selecting the hardware for your deep learning setup. In this chapter, we will discuss the standard process of building the software environment for your hardware.

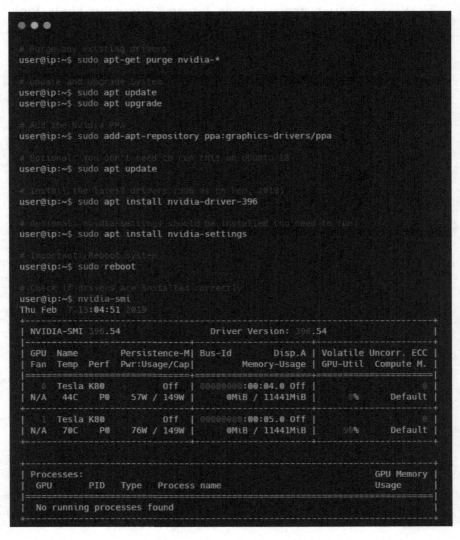

Figure 9.1: Installing your GPU drive

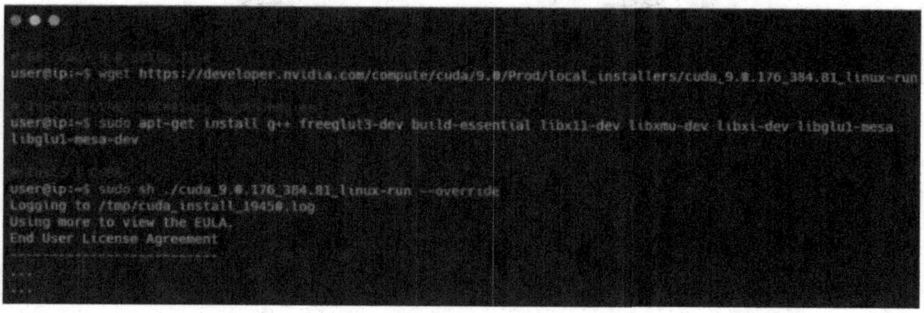

Figure 9.2: Installing CUDA

9.4.1 Install Graphics Drivers

The first step in this process is to ensure that your GPU's graphics drivers are properly installed. We will proceed on the assumption that you are utilizing an NVIDIA GPU. The textbfnvidia-smi command from the terminal is the most reliable approach to determine whether or not the drivers have been installed. In the event that the command does not function properly, we will need to install the GPU drivers. Further details are illustrated in Figure 9.1.

9.4.2 Install CUDA

The NVIDIA CUDA Toolkit is a development environment that allows developers to create apps and programs that take advantage of NVIDIA GPUs to their full potential. Parallel computing on GPUs is made possible by CUDA packages, which provide drop-in acceleration across a wide range of disciplines such as linear algebra, image and video processing, deep learning, and graph analytics. You may get the necessary setup file from the official NVIDIA CUDA page if you are using an Ubuntu-based machine. At the time of writing this article, CUDA 11 is available, although it is still considered to be in its early stages. Because of this, we will be utilizing the old CUDA 9.0 version, which can be downloaded from the legacy releases page. If you are working on a server, it is preferable to utilize the terminal and download the setup file directly, followed by the following instructions to configure CUDA. Further details are illustrated in Figure 9.2.

Then, the final step is thus to reboot your device and test if CUDA is installed correctly. Further details are illustrated in Figure 9.3.

Figure 9.3: Reboot and check the cuda

9.4.3 Install cuDNN

On GPUs, Deep neural networks are implemented using the NVIDIA CUDA Deep Neural Network library (cuDNN), which is a GPU-accelerated collection of primitives. With the cuDNN library, you may get finely tailored implementations of typical neural network procedures such as forward and backward convolutional networks as well as pooling, normalization, and activation layers. Deep learning practitioners may rely on cuDNN, which is a GPU-accelerated deep learning framework that accelerates frequently used deep learning frameworks. It is possible to download cuDNN from the official website, but you will need to create an NVIDIA account in order to do so. If you were to use your educational email address to create an account, it would normally not be a problem. You will be provided with a download link for cuDNN, which you can then use in the terminal to download the application directly to your computer's hard drive. Further details are illustrated in Figure 9.4.

The majority of the dependencies for our GPU configuration are taken care of in this manner.

9.4.4 Install and Manage Deep Learning Frameworks

Before we get our hands over the deep learning frameworks, we normally install Anaconda first. Anaconda enables us to play around with different environments and coding APIs. Directly go to the official web set of Anaconda can help lead you to the download link of the Anaconda that works for your environment. At the time I am writing this chapter, Anaconda is provided with Python 3.9, which is quite a newer version of Python. You might find a lot of trouble with newer versions of Python when you play around with codes download from existing projects. However, this would not be an issue, as you can always set

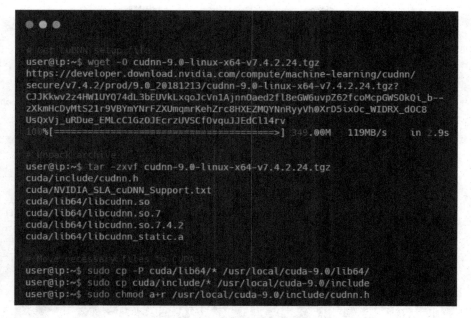

Figure 9.4: Install cuDNN

a new Python environment after you have the AAnaconda in your machine.

In the event that our Python deep learning frameworks are not already installed, we must now install and configure them. We generally make extensive use of keras and tensorflow, and the instructions that follow will assist us in installing them in our environment. Further details can be found in Figure 9.5.

Till here, your deep learning environment should be ready to go. You can download some projects to your machine and get your hands dirty to test if your machine is 100 % functional and all the training is indeed utilizing the GPUs. An example can be found in Figure 9.6.

9.5 SUMMARY

It was discussed in detail in this chapter how to go about determining where to submit your work for publication. In the end, the goal is to maximize your academic impact and, as a consequence, to help you in obtaining access to more resources. The technique section, which builds on the previous chapter, includes instructions on how to set up a deep learning environment on a computer using software, which we expanded on in the previous chapter.

```
user@ip:~$ conda install tensorflow
user@ip:~$ conda install tensorflow-gpu
user@ip:~$ conda install keras

The following NEW packages will be INSTALLED:

  keras              pkgs/main/linux-64::keras-2.2.4-0
  ...
  ...
  keras-base         pkgs/main/linux-64::keras-base-2.2.4-py36_0

Proceed ([y]/n)? y

Preparing transaction: done
Verifying transaction: done
Executing transaction: done
```

Figure 9.5: Install deep learning framworks

```
user@ip:~$ ipython
Python 3.6.5 |Anaconda, Inc.| (default, Apr 29 2018, 16:14:56)
Type 'copyright', 'credits' or 'license' for more information
IPython 6.4.0 -- An enhanced Interactive Python. Type '?' for help.

In [1]: import tensorflow as tf

In [2]: tf.test.gpu_device_name()
2019-02-07 13:23:56.934537: I tensorflow/core/platform/cpu_feature_guard.cc:141]
Your CPU supports instructions that this TensorFlow binary was not compiled
to use: SSE4.1 SSE4.2 AVX AVX2 FMA
...
...
2019-02-07 13:24:02.615422: I tensorflow/core/common_runtime/gpu/gpu_device.cc:1084]
Created TensorFlow device (/device:GPU:0 with 10761 MB memory) -> physical GPU
(device: 0, name: Tesla K80, pci bus id: 0000:00:04.0, compute capability: 3.7)
2019-02-07 13:24:02.803649: I tensorflow/core/common_runtime/gpu/gpu_device.cc:1084]
Created TensorFlow device (/device:GPU:1 with 10761 MB memory) -> physical GPU
(device: 1, name: Tesla K80, pci bus id: 0000:00:05.0, compute capability: 3.7)
Out[2]: '/device:GPU:0'

In [3]: tf.test.is_built_with_cuda()
Out[3]: True

In [5]: tf.list_devices()
Out[5]:
[_DeviceAttributes(/job:localhost/replica:0/task:0/device:CPU:0, CPU, 268435456),
 _DeviceAttributes(/job:localhost/replica:0/task:0/device:GPU:0, GPU, 11284542260),
 _DeviceAttributes(/job:localhost/replica:0/task:0/device:GPU:1, GPU, 11284542260)]

In [6]: import keras
Using TensorFlow backend.

In [7]:
Do you really want to exit ([y]/n)? y
```

Figure 9.6: Test deep learning framworks

Reference and Research Impact

CONTENTS

This chapter describes how to select proper references for improving the research impact of submitted papers. Selecting references for a scientific paper is very important to help reviewers or readers to better understand the background information, research motivation, and more importantly, the importance of the contribution. Selection proper references are also important for improving the research impact since good research papers should always have improvements compared with the state-of-the-art published papers.

DOI: 10.1201/9781003139058-10

10.1 INTRODUCTION

References are a list of sources chosen by the writers to represent the finest materials related to the research topic. They serve as the cornerstone for every research article. Although they are usually produced towards the conclusion of the article-writing process, they are highly significant. They set the stage for the hypothesis and serve to establish the need for the research investigation. Authors utilize references to inform readers about the procedures used to conduct the study and to persuade them that the methodology employed is suitable. References aid in providing a suitable context through which the study findings should be seen and evaluated. This message will go through the purpose of citations, how to choose reputable sources for referencing, and the significance of correctness while composing the reference list.

10.2 PURPOSE OF CITING REFERENCES

As previously said, references assist writers in explaining the purpose for the study and providing insights on methodology. They also lend credence to the interpretations proposed, hypotheses formed, and inferences drawn. References that are properly chosen contribute to the scientific reputation of the paper. In addition, editors go through reference lists to choose reviewers. References allow peer reviewers to evaluate research work more effectively and efficiently. References are used by readers to double-check the details of a method that has been mentioned. Reference lists are also a collection of resources on the issue being referred, and students and other readers utilize them to find related material to help them comprehend it better. Individual scientists are also given credit when their work is mentioned in reference lists.

10.3 ORGANIZATION OF REFERENCES

While planning the research, writing the protocol, and even conducting the study, investigators conduct a comprehensive search for relevant literature. After the results have been evaluated and interpreted, a new round of literature searches is conducted to hunt for relevant evidence that may have been created during the intervening period. They are unable to cite all of the content that has been read in the text. They must distinguish between the most appropriate and relevant materials and those that are just tangentially linked. Because of the limitations on the number of references that may be listed, even all relevant sources cannot be cited. In fact, the authors are compelled to choose only a few items from a large pool of relevant content. The initial element of reference organization is the selection, which includes the writers citing the most credible and appropriate sources from this pool of highly relevant content.

The second level of organizing is determining which sources or references belong to certain sections of the article. The objective of each part of a research article is explicitly defined by the IMRaD format: The introduction section provides background information to allow readers to judge the need for conducting the research study, the methodology section describes how the study was conducted, the results section provides the study findings, and the discussion section provides a forum to describe the interpretation and implications of the study findings. With the exception of the results section, various claims in these parts must be backed by references. The references listed in the methodology section, among other things, assist explain the laboratory procedures and diagnostic criteria utilized in the study, as well as sample size estimation methods. Although some information addressing methodological concerns may need to be used in the 'Discussion' part to support specific aspects of approach, this is typically straightforward to decide. However, there is a significant overlap between references listed in the introduction part to offer background information and those referenced in the discussion section to compare the study findings with observations made in previously published papers. Although there is no rule against referencing the same study in two separate parts or even in the same section of the article, this is usually done only in extreme cases and only for highly relevant content.

10.4 CITATION AND REFERENCE FORMATS

There are numerous methods for citing sources. The Council of Science Editors (CSE) specifies three methods for documenting the cited content. All of these systems need the inclusion of a reference list at the conclusion of the research article. This list contains all of the information that readers need to locate the source. The three systems are roughly classified as citation-name, citation-sequence, and name-year. The sources in the reference list at the conclusion of the article are organized alphabetically by the first author's last name in the citation-name system. The source is cited by utilizing the reference list number, which is inserted at the appropriate sentence. The sources in the reference list at the end of the article are ordered in the order in which they occur in the text in the citation-sequence system. The source is cited in the article using the reference list number and placed at the appropriate sentence in the text. The sources in the name-year system are listed alphabetically in the reference list at the conclusion of the research paper. In contrast to the other two methods, the sources in the reference list are not numbered, and sources are referenced by stating the author's last name and year of publication in parenthesis. A variety of reference and citation forms and styles are used. These formats include the Vancouver, Harvard, APA (American Psychological Association), ASA (American Sociological Society), MLA (Modern Language Association), Chicago, and many others. The Vancouver system (an example of a citation sequence format employing a sequential numbering system) and the Harvard system (an example of a name-publication year system) are the most often found. These two forms both have advantages and disadvantages. The Vancouver method is widely used in medical and physical science and is seen to be simpler and easier to utilize, particularly when reviewing manuscript versions. The Harvard method, on the other hand, which is mostly utilized in humanities and social science literature, honors individual scientists' contributions by guaranteeing that their names appear in the primary text. The debate about the advantages and disadvantages of one system over another, on the other hand, is of little importance because the author does not have a say in the matter. He must adhere to the format or style recommended by the journal to which he has decided to submit the paper. It is not out of place to emphasize here that authors must carefully study the journal's instructions for citing references and keep in mind the needs of particular publications, which is summarized in Table below.

Parameters	Variations
In-text citation of reference numbers.	The appropriate reference numbers are given in Arabic. Some journals, however, use plain text, while others use superscript. The reference number can be cited directly, in parentheses, or in square brackets. In addition, some journals want the reference number to be inserted after a punctuation mark, whilst others urge writers to do the reverse.
Authors' names appear in the reference list.	Journals differ in their guidelines on the number of authors' names to be included when citing a source with multiple authors. Journals urge that "et al." be included after the names of two, three, or four authors.
Journal details	Some journals that use Harvard style need a shortened name of the journal, while others require the entire journal name. In addition to the journal name, volume number, and page numbers, certain journals need the issue number to be supplied in parenthesis. Most journals need the beginning and last page numbers of an article mentioned. For some, simply giving the article's initial page number is sufficient. Some journals demand that the journal's name be put in italics.

10.5 AUTHORS' RESPONSIBILITIES

It is the writers' obligation to correctly credit the most relevant and acceptable sources. As Annesley explains, accuracy has two components: one, the article should precisely and truthfully quote, report, or paraphrase what the source has stated, and two, the reference list should accurately provide the various elements of the source such as authors' names, article title and journal name, volume number, year of publication, and page numbers. The first component of accuracy means that the author has discovered and studied every source referenced in the work, has comprehended what has been stated, and has then genuinely re-stated or reported what has been written in the original source. Errors in supplying source elements are connected with unfavorable outcomes. Many writers utilize citation management software tools (also known as reference managers) such as EndNote, Mendeley, Zotero, and RefWorks to guarantee that their reference list is correct and error-free.

We here summarizes the possible outcomes or consequences of errors in citing various of source in the reference:

1. The Editor cannot find the sources specified in the reference list. Might begin to mistrust the work's integrity and trustworthiness, reducing the odds of the piece being approved for publication.

2. The Editor is unable to invite peer reviewers using the incorrect reference list.

3. Reviewers are unable to identify the source or verify the validity of remarks ascribed to sources. This has a negative impact on the review process's efficiency and efficacy.

4. Readers cannot utilize references to learn more about the technique or to better understand the mentioned work.

5. References are not correctly connected in electronic databases. The source's authors are not given the credit they deserve.

10.6 TASKS RELATED TO REFERENCES

These tasks involve selecting sources for citation, inserting the citation into the document text, and creating the reference list. The following are some general guidelines:

10.6.1 Choosing References for Citation

1. Authors must choose the most relevant and acceptable references from the collected content. Every reference in a research paper should be accurate and offer value to the paper.

2. Although review articles can help readers understand a body of original work, they may not properly reflect the original work, and the linked remark may represent the reviewer's viewpoint. As a result, authors should choose to credit direct references to primary research materials.

3. The recommendations set by the Journal are quite important.

Authors should follow the guidelines for the amount of references that can be mentioned in a research publication.

4. Authors should verify that they are referencing reliable sources as references by assessing the dependability of the facts given, analysis done, interpretation offered, and arguments made in the source papers. Before being published, articles in reputable peer-reviewed journals are subjected to a multi-tiered editorial- and peer-review procedure. It is preferable to reference papers published in these journals.

5. It is preferable to avoid utilizing conference abstracts as references because they are rarely submitted to a rigorous peer-review procedure. Furthermore, they only give limited information, and it is unclear if the abstract is a good representation of the entire data set.

6. Authors must refrain from using self-citation.

7. Personal communications may be permitted only if they give vital information that is not available from a public source and if the individual consents. If personal conversations are referenced, the person's name and the date of the message should be included in parenthesis in the text.

8. Articles that have been approved but have not yet been published should be labeled as "in press."

9. Information from papers that have been submitted but have not yet been approved may be mentioned as "unpublished observations" in the text. This can only be done after obtaining formal permission from the source.

10. The writers may opt not to include a reference for assertions and facts that the readers are likely to be familiar with.

11. Given the abundance of scientific content available online, it is not unexpected that web-based sources are regularly cited as references. They provide some unusual problems. For example, a single mistake in transcribing the URL (Uniform Resource Locator) might make it difficult for readers to find the resource content. This does not occur in the case of printed resources, as the source

may be located using other components in the reference or citation. The second concern is the transience of webpage information and even entire websites. 15 Their absence might be attributed to a failure to preserve old connections or the closure of the entity responsible for the website. Regardless of these difficulties, it is not appropriate for writers to avoid referencing important and reputable internet information, nor is it appropriate for journal editors to urge authors to do so. The solution might be to archive the mentioned URL on the journal servers, use permanent URLs (PURLs), or use Internet archiving services to ensure that such material is available on an ongoing basis. 16 Most journals now encourage writers to provide the date the referenced webpage was viewed in the reference list.

12. Nowadays, many articles include material from a tertiary source that anybody may edit (for example, Wikipedia). This is a contentious subject that presents a variety of problems. Proponents of utilizing Wikipedia-like sites as references compare their accuracy to that of an encyclopedia and say that there is a need to realize that learning modes are shifting increasingly towards online sources. It is also stated that because Wikipedia is accessible to everyone and is maintained by so many people, content put on the website is continuously scrutinized. Those who disagree argue that tertiary sources do not meet the ICMJE requirements of directing readers to original research sources wherever feasible, and that Wikipedia pages are continuously changing, making it impossible for readers to evaluate the authenticity of referenced information. It may be appropriate to advise authors to use tertiary sources as references only when a primary, permanent, peer-reviewed alternate source is unavailable.

10.6.2   Inducting Citations in the Text

1. Authors can use their own words to summarize content (statistics, information, or opinion) from other publications. When the referred source is cited using the same words, phrases, or sentences as in the original article (verbatim), double-inverted commas ("——— ") should be used.

2. It is critical to follow the guidelines governing how citations

should be referenced. These are specified in the "Instructions to authors" section of the magazine. They may encourage authors to include reference numbers in the text in various ways, such as superscripted numerals, parentheses, square brackets, or plain numbers, and so on.

3. Unless otherwise specified in the journal rules, the reference number or citation should be added immediately after the information from the source is given. As a result, a citation may appear in the midst or at the conclusion of a sentence.

4. When reporting numerous facts in a sentence, it is best to utilize multiple citations and position them immediately after stating the relevant information. For example, instead of stating that "Multiple studies have reported that factors such as parental illiteracy, low socioeconomic status, and the lack of written instructions in doctors' prescriptions, instructions in local language on the drug label, and calibrated spoons are associated with dosing errors while administering medicines at home (a–h)," it would be preferable to state that "Multiple studies have reported that factors such as parental illiteracy, low socioeconomic status, and the lack of written instructions in doctors' prescription." Multiple studies have found that factors such as parental illiteracy (a), low socioeconomic status (b), and the lack of written instructions in doctors' prescriptions (a, c), instructions in local language on the drug label (b–d), and calibrated spoons (d–h) are associated with dosing errors when administering medications at home.

5. If two or more references are needed to support a claim, they might be presented in chronological sequence. If two references are from the same year, they can be sorted alphabetically by the first author's last name.

10.6.3   Preparing the Reference List

1. When compiling the individual items in the reference list, it is also important to carefully follow the journal's instructions about the structure of referring, usage of punctuation, italic text, abbreviated names of journals, issue number of the journal, and so on.

2. Parts of the manuscript text are relocated as the article is written, updated, and edited. As a result, the reference numbers must be updated with each edition. The reference management software may be quite useful in ensuring that such modifications are carried out accurately. The authors should submit the paper only after ensuring that each citation has a matching reference and that each reference is cited correctly in the text.

10.7   MACHINE LEARNING AND ADVERSARIAL LEARNING – THE BUG OF MLS

Machine learning, by which computers can be trained to recognize patterns in information and generate increasingly accurate predictions over time, has experienced a significant growth in popularity in recent years. As a key enabler of artificial intelligence (AI), machine learning is used in a wide range of applications, from simple spam filters to more complex technologies such as speech recognition, facial recognition, robotics, and self-driving cars. Machine learning is also used in a wide range of applications, from simple to complex.

While machine learning models have a wide range of potential benefits, they may also be susceptible to manipulation. This type of danger is referred described as "adversarial machine learning" by cybersecurity experts because artificial intelligence systems can be tricked (by attackers or "adversaries") into generating erroneous judgments [163, 174, 177, 205]. For example, providing a machine-learning model with incorrect or misrepresentative data while it is training, or adding deliberately prepared data to mislead an already trained model into making errors, are examples of adversarial attacks.

The University of California, Berkeley Professor of Computer Science, David Wagner, says that machine learning has great potential and holds the promise of making our lives better in a variety of ways. "But it also introduces a new risk that was not previously present, and we do not yet have a handle on that," he says.

The security of some machine learning models that are already in use in real applications may be jeopardized. A few tiny stickers placed on the ground in an intersection, for example, caused a self-driving car to make an aberrant judgment and go into the opposing lane of traffic, according to the researchers who tested their method.

Furthermore, making imperceptible changes to an image can fool a medical imaging system into incorrectly classifying a benign mole as malignant with 100 percent confidence, and placing a few pieces of tape can fool a computer vision system into incorrectly classifying a stop sign as a speed limit sign.

Even though most of the discussion around artificial intelligence has centered on the concerns of bias (since real-world data sets used to train the algorithms may reflect existing human preconceptions), adversarial machine learning poses a distinct set of challenges. Due to the widespread adoption of machine learning in industries such as business and transportation, as well as the military and other areas, adversarial assaults might be used for everything from insurance fraud to the firing of drone strikes on unintended targets.

For policymakers, corporate executives, and other stakeholders who may be engaged in the creation of machine learning systems but are unaware of the possibility that these systems might be controlled or corrupted, the following is a quick explanation of adversarial machine learning. This article concludes with a list of other resources that you may use to further your research.

10.7.1   Overview on ML Models

Machine learning models are computer programs that, in most situations, are meant to learn to detect patterns in data as they are being fed new data to process. Machine-learning algorithms known as 'classifiers' may be taught how to respond to diverse inputs with the assistance of people who provide "training data." These models are meant to become increasingly accurate over time as a result of repeated exposure to training data.

Using a machine learning model to learn about blue items, for example, and classifying them as "blue" in advance, the classifier can begin to learn about the features that distinguish blue objects from other colors. In the course of time, the model "learns" to determine if any other subsequent image is blue, with a degree of confidence that ranges from 0 percent to 100%. The greater the amount of data that is put into a machine-learning system, the better it learns — and the more accurate its predictions become, at least theoretically. However, this learning process, particularly in "deep" neural networks, may be unexpected and unpredictably slow [293].

10.7.2 Overview of DNNs

A neural network is a sort of machine learning model that is loosely based on the biology of the human brain and is used to learn new things. Deep neural networks are made up of a large number of decision-making layers that function in a sequential manner. Deep neural networks have been increasingly popular in recent years, and their use has resulted in significant improvements in the efficacy of machine learning [177, 278, 282, 283].

However, the computations that computers do within deep neural networks are extremely complicated, and they change at a breakneck pace as the "deep learning" process takes shape. If a neural network has a high number of layers, the computations that lead to a particular choice may be incomprehensible to humans: neither the process itself nor the logic of the decision-making can be viewed in real time or evaluated after the fact [142].

The classification parameters used by a machine-learning system may be different from those that can be intuitively comprehended by humans [225], resulting in what seems to be a "black box" In addition, even minor changes to the data might have a significant influence on the choice made by the neural network, despite their tiny magnitude [111]. It is because of this vulnerability that these systems are susceptible to manipulation, even through purposeful "adversarial attacks."

10.7.3 Adversarial Attacks on DNNs

In the realm of computer security, the word "adversary" is used to describe individuals or computers who may attempt to enter or damage a computer network or software, or both. When it comes to disrupting a machine learning model, adversaries might employ a number of assault tactics, either during the training process (known as a "poisoning" attack) or after the classifier has already been trained (referred to as a "evasion" attack).

Poisoning: Attacks on machine-learning systems that take place during the training phase are commonly referred to as "poisoning" or "contaminating," respectively. The adversary sends improperly labeled data to a classifier in certain situations, leading the system to make biased or erroneous choices in the future. Poisoning attacks necessitate the presence of some level of control over training data on the part of the opponent. Some examples can be found in Figure 10.1.

BadNets--GTSRB Trojan WM--PubFig Trojan SQ--PubFig L0 Invisible--Cifar10 L2 Invisible--Cifar10

Figure 10.1: Examples of backdoored samples in the training set

It can be difficult for humans to determine whether data has been poisoned since some of the poisoned data might be extremely subtle, according to Dawn Song, Professor of Computer Science at the University of California, Berkeley. According to our study, a 'back-door assault,' in which the model is accurate for most regular inputs, but can be trained to react incorrectly on particular sorts of inputs, can be used to deceive the user. It is extremely difficult to determine whether a model has acquired such behaviors, as well as what kind of inputs would cause a model to act in an inappropriate manner. As a result, "it is extremely difficult to detect."

A poisoning attack may employ a "boy who cried wolf" strategy, in which an adversary submits data during the training phase that is mistakenly classified as innocuous when it is in fact harmful, in order to deceive the system. The idea is that an attacker will gradually introduce instances that will cause some type of misclassification of input data and result in an incorrect result, according to Doug Tygar, Professor of Computer Science and Information Management at the University of California, Berkeley, in a presentation given last year. "Adversaries can be patient in laying the groundwork for their attacks, and they can change their tactics as needed."

Poisoning a Chatbot as an Example: In 2016, Microsoft released "Tay," a Twitter chat bot that was built to learn how to engage in discussion by interacting with other users on a consistent basis over time. While Microsoft intended for Tay to participate in "casual and light-hearted dialogue," internet trolls realized that the system's filters were insufficient and began feeding obscene and insulting tweets into Tay's machine learning algorithm, causing the computer to become more intelligent. The more these individuals interacted with Tay's tweets, the more insulting Tay's messages got. After only 16 hours of operation, Microsoft decided to shut down the artificial intelligence bot.

Evasion Attacks: These assaults often occur after a machine learning system has been trained; they occur while the model is estimating

"panda"
57.7% confidence

"gibbon"
99.3% confidence

Figure 10.2: Examples of the evasion attack

the likelihood of an unknown data input being used as input. Due to the fact that researchers (or adversaries) do not always know in advance which data changes would "break" a machine learning model, the majority of these assaults are built through trial and error. A classic example is illustrated in Figure 10.2.

For example, if attackers wanted to test the limits of a machine learning model meant to filter out spam emails, they might experiment with different email messages to determine which ones made it through the filtering system. If a model has been trained to screen for specific words (such as "Viagra") but to make exceptions for emails that contain a certain number of other words, an attacker could craft an email that contains enough extraneous words to "tip" the algorithm (i.e., to move it from being classified as "spam" to "not spam"), allowing the email to pass through the filter and reach the recipient.

It is possible that certain assaults are meant to compromise the integrity of a machine learning model, causing it to output an erroneous result or to generate a specific conclusion that has been predetermined by the perpetrator. Other adversarial assaults might be directed towards a system's secrecy, causing an AI-based model to divulge private or sensitive information. Using a language processing model that had been trained with a huge amount of emails, some of which contained sensitive personal information, Professor Dawn Song and her colleagues proved that they could extract social security numbers from a big volume of emails.

Exemplifications that are adversarial in nature have the potential to be harmful [30]. As stated in Practical Black-Box Attacks on Deep Learning Systems Using Adversarial Examples, attackers might, for example, target autonomous cars by using stickers or paint to produce an adversarial stop sign that the vehicle would perceive as a 'yield' or other sign.

According to new research from UC Berkeley, OpenAI, and Pennsylvania State University, Adversarial Attacks on Neural Network Policies, as well as research from the University of Nevada at Reno, Vulnerability of Deep Reinforcement Learning to Policy Induction Attacks, reinforcement learning agents can be manipulated by adversarial examples [261]. DQN, TRPO, and A3C are among the RL algorithms that have been shown to be sensitive to adversarial inputs, according to the findings of the study. These can result in reduced performance even in the face of pertubations that are too slight to be detected by a human, such as leading an agent to move a pong paddle down when it should be up or interfering with its ability to detect opponents in the Seaquest video game series.

The study of AI safety generally conjures up images of some of the most challenging challenges in the field: how can we assure that powerful reinforcement learning agents that are substantially more intelligent than human beings behave in the manner intended by their creators?

Indeed, we can see from adversarial instances that even the most simple contemporary algorithms, whether for supervised or reinforcement learning, may already act in unexpected ways that we did not anticipate [175].

10.7.4   Existing Defenses for Poisoning Attacks

Existing defense methods can be roughly divided into four categories, namely backdoor detection, backdoor invalidation, trigger invalidation, and trigger detection. We will analyze each category's limitation in 5G-enabled IIoT systems and reinforce the motivation to introduce an attack and model agnostic trigger detection framework specially designed for 5G-enabled IIoT edge-deployed DNN applications.

Backdoor detection. The most common backdoor defense direction is to verify if a deep learning model has an injected backdoor. [239] proposed to reconstruct the potential trigger for each class and then verify whether a model is poisoned by checking whether there exists a label with anomalous trigger reconstruction. Reccent works build upon the idea of [239] and attempt to improve it via using GANs [20], adopting new regularization terms [93], utilizing Generative Distribution Modeling [162], and adopting Artificial Brain Stimulation [143].

These detection methods require details of the DNN model, thus running the evaluations to detect the backdoor's existence. However, most of the IIoT deployed DNNs are bought or run by third parties, where details, i.e., model architecture, training coefficients, weights, etc., are not reported, therefore, making the proposed backdoor detection methods unfavorable in IIoT edges. Even if some edges use public DNNs to provide model details for such defenses, these detection methods often incur high temporal costs for large models. At the core, they require solving a large number of optimization problems, even supported with 5G clouds. The time-consuming issue gets even worse in the 5G-enabled mobile edge setting. In contrast to one-time training of centralized DNNs, 5G-enabled edge-deployed DNNs often require continual fine-tuning to adjust to the changing environment. The attacker can insert new triggers every time the model is fine-tuned, which, in turn, necessitates the constant operation of the backdoor detector. Hence, deploying the existing detectors, which are already expensive for a single process, will be even more costly for the edge setting. Most importantly, these defenses assume that there is only one target label for all malicious samples (i.e., single-target attack). The detection becomes infeasible when the adversary injects poisoned samples with multiple different target labels (e.g., all-to-all case introduced in [91]). They also assume the trigger has a small size and simple pattern and does not apply to complex triggers such as global patterns.

Backdoor Invalidation. This direction is to remove the potential backdoor from the model directly without any detection. [137] proposed to use pruning and fine-tuning to mitigate the backdoor. Yi et al. [172] proposed to use fine-tuning with intense pre-processes inputs to invalidate the backdoor. However, these approaches also require knowledge of the target DNN models. Meanwhile, they may reduce the accuracy over clean samples, thus interfering with the main functionality of a DNN. Moreover, this kind of defense is adopted without knowledge of the attack activities' existence; thus, they might inducing unnecessary overhead for clean models.

Trigger invalidation. This direction is to directly invalidate the effects of the triggers from the test samples. [129] proposed to adopt common image transformations to pre-process input such that the backdoor model will give correct results for both benign and malicious samples. However, this simple approach can only handle simple triggers but fail to defeat complex ones (e.g., global patterns) as shown in previous work [280]. Like the backdoor invalidation techniques, this kind of defense is also conducted in a manner agnostic to the attack's existence. Hence, it can incur extra overhead for clean samples and degrade model performance.

Trigger detection. This direction focuses on detecting the samples that contain triggers. This type of defense directly detects the attack's existence, and therefore it will not incur unnecessary model performance degradation when there is no attack activity. Moreover, it is often cost-effective, thus suitable for performing continual backdoor monitoring at the edge. [18] discovered that normal and poisoned data yield different features in the last hidden layer's activations. [235] proposed to classify benign and malicious samples based on their signatures on the covariance matrix's Eigen spectrum. However, these detection works require the knowledge of the poisoned model, thereby becoming inapplicable when the model details are covered as in most IIoT edges. A recent work [51] by Du et al. adopted the autoencoder to model normal data and then detected abnormal training samples by filtering out samples with large reconstruction loss. This method does not require the knowledge of poisoned model parameters and thus is directly comparable with our proposed detector.

10.7.5 Existing Defenses for Evasion Attacks

Traditional approaches for improving the robustness of machine learning models, such as weight decay and dropout, do not typically provide a viable protection against hostile instances in practice. So far, only two techniques have shown to be effective in providing a considerable defense.

Adversarial Training: When we produce a large number of adversarial instances and actively teach the model not to be deceived by each of them, we are using a brute force approach called adversarial training [128]. Uncovering an open-source implementation of adversarial training is made possible by the cleverhans library, and its use is demonstrated in the accompanying tutorial.

Defensive Distillation: This is an approach in which we train the model to produce probabilities for different classes rather than making hard judgments about which class to output. The probabilities are provided by a previous model that was trained on the identical problem using hard class labels and provided the probabilities. An adversary would generally attempt to attack smoothed surfaces in the directions in which they are attempting to exploit them, making it more difficult for them to identify hostile input adjustments that result in erroneous categorization of the model. In Distilling the Knowledge in a Neural Network, distillation was first described as a technique for model compression, in which a tiny model is trained to resemble a big model in order to save on computing resources.

But even the most sophisticated customized algorithms may be readily defeated by increasing the processing power available to the attacker.

A failed defense – "gradient masking": As an illustration of how a straightforward defense might fail, consider the reasons why a technique known as "gradient masking" does not function properly.

The phrase "gradient masking" was first used in Practical Black-Box Attacks on Deep Learning Systems Using Adversarial Examples, which was published in 2012. a whole family of unsuccessful security techniques that function by attempting to deny the attacker access to a beneficial gradient.

The gradient of the model is used by the majority of adversarial example building approaches to launch an assault. They examine an image of an airplane, determine which direction in picture space increases the likelihood of the "cat" class, and then offer a little push (in other words, disrupt the input) in that direction until the probability of the "cat" class increases [173, 281]. The new, updated picture is misidentified as a cat by the public.

Instead of using the gradient, what if there was no gradient at all, and an infinitesimal adjustment to the picture had no effect on the model's outcome? This appears to give some protection because the attacker is unsure which direction to "push" the picture, as shown in Figure 10.3.

We may easily conceive several very simple solutions to get rid of the gradient that are not difficult to envisage. Example: The majority of image classification models have two operating modes: one in which they output only the identification of the most probable class and another in which they provide probabilities for the most likely class. If the model's output is "99.9 percent airplane, 0.1 percent cat," then a little, insignificant change in the input results in a small, insignificant change in the output, and the gradient informs us which modifications will enhance the likelihood of the "cat" classification class. If we run the model in a mode where the output is just "airplane," then a little, insignificant change in the input will have no effect on the output at all, and the gradient will tell us nothing about the model.

Running the model in "most likely class" mode rather than "probability mode" will allow us to assess how effectively our model can

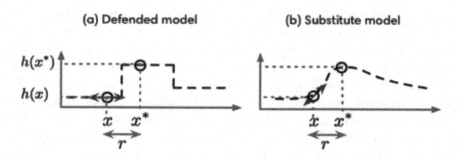

Figure 10.3: Illustration of the defended model through gradient masking

defend itself against hostile instances. Because the attacker no longer knows where to look for inputs that will be categorized as cats, we may be able to mount a defense against him. Unfortunately, any image that was formerly categorized as a cat is still classed as a cat in the present day. The attacker will be able to predict which points are adversarial instances, but those points will still be misclassified even if the attacker is correct. We haven't made the model more resilient; instead, we have just made it more difficult for the attacker to figure out where the weaknesses in the model's defense are.

What's more, it turns out that the attacker has developed a highly effective technique for determining where the weak points in the defense are located. The attacker can train their own model, which can be a smooth model with a gradient, create adversarial instances for their model, and then deploy those adversarial examples against our non-smooth model in order to defeat it. The majority of the time, our model will incorrectly categorize these cases as well. At the end of the day, our thought experiment revealed that concealing the gradient didn't do anything.

In most cases, the defense strategies that use gradient masking produce a model that is very smooth in specific directions and neighborhoods of training points, making it more difficult for the adversary to find gradients indicating good candidate directions to perturb the input in a way that is harmful to the model. The opponent, on the other hand, might train a replacement model: a duplicate of the defended model that imitates it by monitoring the labels that the defended model assigns to inputs that have been carefully picked by the adversary.

In the publication on black-box assaults, a technique for carrying out a model extraction attack of this nature was described. The adversary can then utilize the gradients of the replacement model to discover adversarial instances that have been misclassified by the defended model as well as the defended model. We demonstrate this attack technique with a one-dimensional machine learning issue in the image above, which is taken from the discussion of gradient masking found in Towards the Science of Security and Privacy in Machine Learning. The gradient masking phenomena would be increased for issues with more dimensionality, but it would be more difficult to show.

Both adversarial training and defensive distillation, we discover, unintentionally execute a type of gradient masking without realizing it. The use of gradient masking was not expressly intended by either algorithm; nonetheless, it appears that machine learning algorithms may develop a defense that is very simple when they are trained to protect themselves rather than being given precise instructions on how to do so. It is common for attacks to be successful when adversarial instances are transferred from a first model to a second model that has been trained using either adversarial training or defensive distillation. This is true even when a direct assault on the second model would fail. The results show that both training approaches are more effective at flattening out the model and removing the gradient than they are at ensuring that it properly identifies a greater number of points.

10.8 SUMMARY

To recap what we have discussed in this chapter, citations are crucial in a research article not only because they appear in every part, including tables and figures, but also because they offer a basis for the study rationale and methodology and assist readers grasp the implications and value of the study. The major responsibility of authors is to correctly cite relevant and acceptable sources. Due to the importance of references, even reviewers verify the correctness of references, and journal editors employ tools to guarantee that references are cited precisely. Although there are various forms for creating references, writers should become acquainted with the format and style used by the journal to which they plan to submit their paper. Inappropriate, inappropriate, or erroneous reference might jeopardize a manuscript's acceptance for publication.

In addition, we provided an overview of deep learning and adversarial learning techniques. When it comes to artificial intelligence, adversarial learning demonstrates that many contemporary machine learning algorithms may be broken in unexpected ways. These machine learning failures illustrate that even basic algorithms can act in a manner that is very different from what their authors intended. It is our hope that machine learning experts will get engaged and develop strategies for preventing hostile instances in order to bridge the gap between what designers desire and how algorithms actually operate.

CHAPTER 11

Resource, Advisor, and Time Management

CONTENTS

This chapter describes the complementary details for writing research papers like how to acquire the correct resources, how to request help from advisors, and how to manage the time. The common online resources will be introduced and how to efficiently find the proper resources will be illustrated with examples. How to communicate with advisors will also be given with examples. The student will learn how to improve the complementary details for efficiently finish research papers.

11.1 INTRODUCTION

Researchers work in a complicated setting with numerous roles and responsibilities. This setting is prone to distractions, which can derail productivity and reduce efficiency. Effective time management enables researchers to stay focused on their job, which increases research output. As a result, strengthening time management skills is critical to creating and maintaining a successful research program. This article discusses time management techniques that address behaviors related to time evaluation, planning, and monitoring. The editorial board of

DOI: 10.1201/9781003139058-11

the Western Journal of Nursing Research proposes techniques to improve time management, such as setting realistic objectives, prioritizing, and maximizing planning, in this issue. Involving a team, problem-solving hurdles, and early control of possible distractions can all help to keep a research program on track. Researchers can discover areas for improvement and acknowledge progress by continuously reviewing the effectiveness of time management techniques.

11.2 GENERAL TECHNIQUES FOR TIME MANAGEMENTS

"I recommend to you to take care of the minutes; for hours will take care of themselves."

Lord Chesterfield
British statesman

Many researchers encounter competing demands, interruptions, and internal and external distractions when attempting to develop and sustain a successful research program. Time management is a skill required to sustain academic production [37]. It is described as purposeful actions targeted at the effective use of time to complete specified, goal-directed tasks. Furthermore, the advantages of good time management may include increased job satisfaction and less stress [37]. Time management strategies are classified into three main categories: time assessment behaviors, planning behaviors, and monitoring behaviors [37]. To properly manage time, it is necessary to employ a range of individual techniques in each area. Members of the Western Journal of Nursing Research editorial board have submitted essays about time management methods that have helped them succeed in their research. Below summarizes these techniques.

Set achievable and realistic goals.

1. Create long-term scholarship objectives.

2. Create intermediate and urgent actions to attain long-term objectives.

3. Align goals with a well-defined methodology.

4. Establish quantifiable and attainable goals/objectives within a set time frame.

5. Determine what is directly under your control since you will have the most capacity to achieve these objectives.

6. Review objectives on a regular basis for: accomplishment/lack of attainment; and factors that promote or serve as obstacles to achievement.

Enhance realistic planning.

1. Make daily "to-do" lists and tick them off when chores are completed.

2. Divide large assignments, such as manuscripts, into manageable components with clear deadlines.

3. Gather resources before beginning a task.

4. Make a thorough activity timeline.

5. When you finish a work session, write a list of "to-do" things for the following session while it is still fresh in your mind.

6. When you end a session, make a list of what you want to do for the coming session.

7. Automate some procedures (for example, sign up for automatic alerts of funding possibilities or research articles).

8. Early in the process, identify and request essential support.

9. For a more structured approach to work, use an electronic file management system.

Prioritize.

1. Recognize and discriminize the importance of your on-going work.

2. Arrange your objectives/goals in descending order of importance.

3. Work on the most important objective first and persistently until you have attained it or have temporarily exhausted available resources.

4. Priorities should be written down – if a request or opportunity is not in accordance with a priority, say "no."

5. Understand when and how to say "no."

Effective scheduling.

1. Make time for writing.

2. Plan ahead of time to meet deadlines.

3. Choose days that are less difficult than the rest of the week.

4. Make a regular schedule that includes scholarship blocks.

5. Make use of an electronic calendar.

6. Make your electronic calendar accessible to others so that they may see your availability (outside times blocked for scholarly productivity)

7. When meeting with people, make a timed appointment.

8. Consider taking a "research sabbatical" to complete certain research assignments.

Maintain your concentration on the research program.

1. Choose possibilities that will help the research program (e.g., student work, commitments).

2. Engage in teaching and service to help your research.

3. Remove any unnecessary digressions to other "interesting topics."

4. Create a method for working with numerous students on a single assignment that also adds to the research program.

Involve a team

1. Delegate tasks to team members to distribute labor.

2. Seek early peer assessment for any possible changes.

3. Actively seek assistance to improve research output at the school level.

Reward yourself for your efforts.

1. Plan incentives for completing "to-do" lists.

2. Reward completion of portions of huge projects rather than waiting for the full project to be completed.

Control potential distractions.

1. Establish a work environment free of external distractions.

2. Schedule work in a "secure" or cloistered environment.

3. Make a physical space where you can keep your materials set up and ready to go.

4. Turn off visual and auditory distractions (such as email/text alerts and phone calls).

5. Determine potential internal distractions and make a separate list so that when these distractions arise, they can be briefly recorded and dismissed from thought in order to focus on the task at hand.

6. Avoid multitasking because it causes unnecessary distractions and does not improve productivity.

Problem-solving and barrier management

1. Assess barries objectively.

2. Discuss potential solutions with your mentors and peers.

3. Experiment with barrier management strategies and evaluate their efficacy.

Balancing life

1. Get enough rest, sleep, and exercise on a regular basis.

2. Make time for rest and relaxation.

Analyze time management strategies on a regular basis.

1. Reassessment of research productivity after implementing feasible solutions – constant quality improvement

2. Major goals should be reassessed at least quarterly.

3. Consider employing software for "productivity" or "project management."

11.3   PRODUCTIVITY AND RESEARCH WRITING

"There is nothing so useless as doing efficiently that which should not be done at all."

Peter F. Drucker
American educator

Writing activities such as grant submissions, publishing, and evidence-based policy are a good measure of productivity in a research environment. The amount of time needed to write a research grant, a report, or an article also influences productivity in writing research grants, report, and article work.

Thus, research is done through doing the time-consuming process of writing. The scheduling of meetings, committees, and nonrequired teaching commitments cannot be done when calendars are full of meetings, committees, and other nonrequired teaching commitments. To write effectively, you must plan out blocks of two to eight hours. Often, the ideal approach is to first double the time it takes for a piece of writing, and then make a note of that time to be used for writing in your calendar. Be aware of what you plan to do at that time, make sure it is clear on the schedule (i.e., article outline, aim page revision, etc.). Once you have committed to this schedule of restricted time and topics, you should not waver from it.

As it takes time to conduct research, you must make a decision to say "No" to other things that are unnecessary and focus on research. Tasks interrupted take twice as long and have twice as many errors. Let colleagues know you are unavailable during writing times by posting signs that say "Do Not Disturb." Similarly, you should also be mindful and regulate your own self-interruptions, such as turning between different books, articles, or websites (i.e., looking for a reference). Stopping your writing to look for a citation is far more time-consuming than simply jotting a note to search for a source. Interruptions such as phone calls or emails break the conversation flow.

Many faculty remarked they were very happy they had been able to self-coach this valuable piece of advice: "knowing when to stop writing." You will know precisely what you are going to write about as you approach the conclusion of your allotted time. As a result, you can scribble down the many thoughts and ideas instead of penning the last few paragraphs. You won't allow yourself lose time by reviewing or trying to determine the writing flow when you start writing the next time you have a blocked calendar session. So, each time a session is blocked, immediate writing can be started. Making small notes helps you stay on track and create a path for picking up where you left off the following time. Outlines can be useful to certain writers, but most find them too frequently changing to be of any assistance. People typically waste time rewriting outlines. Additionally, you can save yourself valuable time by soliciting peer assessments from your colleagues from time to time as your writing becomes less apparent to you and others.

In addition to the time-saving tips listed above, here are some other suggestions for saving time in your workflow: Using project management software like Basecamp, you can schedule larger projects like data input, preliminary analysis, IRB recertification, and writing time blocks. Schedule your responsibilities on a monthly basis and delegate any that you can. With easy and automated reporting as a result, time can be saved. In addition, software to monitor staff performance grew from $100 million in 2001 to $2 billion in 2005. A productivity software package provided by your research office is a good idea.

A willingness to continue with a project, as well as perseverance, are crucial when it comes to time management. Admitting that writing is difficult and frustrating also alleviates the feelings of discouragement that prevent people from continuing.

Problem solving habits are critical for being able to come up with creative solutions. You need to control the distractions that get in the way of writing, which may include your own multitasking. Lastly, one's ability to tolerate rejection is also related to writing output. More often than not, writing gets rejected before it can be revised. So, revise your writing now!

11.4   THINK TWICE BEFORE ACCEPT A REQUEST – HOW YOU CAN BETTER CONCENTRATE ON YOUR MAIN TIMELINE?

In order to be productive, one must make time to do research, even if that means reducing other commitments. Research productivity is often achieved by prioritizing short-term tasks, which appear urgent, above longer-term goals. It is crucial to know how to decline these time-consuming activities politely. Below, referring to [17], we have listed some methods for warding off time commitments, which are not a high priority. When it comes to implementing new ideas, be selective about how you do it, as it will rely on the circumstances, including the individual making the request.

Delaying your decision provides you time to think about whether or not it's something you want to do. List of sample wording:

1. Let me think about it and get back to you.

2. I will look over my other commitments and let you know.

3. I need to talk with my mentor before making any commitments.

4. That is a terrific opportunity, and I will need to weigh all of my other commitments before deciding if I want to accept it.

5. I need to review my other obligations to ensure that I have enough time to complete quality job; I will notify you on Thursday.

Additional time commitments should be postponed List of sample wording:

1. I am unable to take on any additional tasks until _____ occurs (e.g., my thesis defense happens end of this month).

2. I apologize; I am unable to assist you at the moment; please inquire again after _____ occurs.

Declare that you are not the ideal candidate for the job. List of sample wording:

1. I wish I could assist you, but your situation falls outside of my area of expertise.

2. I'm sorry, but I lack the necessary knowledge to assist you with this issue.

3. I believe _____ would be far more capable of tackling this.

Recognize an outstanding opportunity: this enables you to appreciate the work's significance without becoming directly committed. List of sample wording:

1. That is an excellent opportunity; however, I am unable to participate at the moment.

2. I appreciate the invitation to join in this critical work and regret that I am unable to do so.

3. I appreciate you informing me of this fantastic opportunity; I regret that I am unable to accept it.

Blame your mentor (if they agrees to be blamed). List of sample wording:

1. My mentor advised me not to take on any new volunteer duties at this time

2. Before making a decision, my chair requested that I review all time obligations with her/him.

3. My mentor is adamant that I refrain from joining any further committees until my grant application is filed later this year.

Prior to refusing, compliment the requestor. List of sample wording:

1. I'd want to work with you because I know you're an expert in this field, but I'm unable to participate in this project.

2. I admire your commitment to this subject and regret that I will be unable to collaborate with you at this time.

3. I'd love to work with you, but due to your expertise, I'm forced to deny this amazing chance.

4. I'm delighted you asked, as I like your work, and I'm extremely sorry to have to decline.

5. There is no one else I would prefer work with, and I am disappointed that I will be unable to participate.

Express gratitude for the opportunity, then decline. List of sample wording:

1. While I am glad that you believe I could assist with _____, I am unable to participate.

Avoid detailed excuses unless the justification is self-evident, and especially if the inviter is inclined to disagree about the justification. List of sample wording:

1. I'm grateful for this opportunity, but I'm afraid it's not going to work for me.

2. I am sorry, but I am not able to help you.

3. You are performing critical work; nonetheless, I am unable to assist you.

4. That is not something I do

Recognize that this is a critical issue for the requestor without becoming personally entangled List of sample wording:

1. Knowing how much you care about _____, I'm sorry I'm unable to assist you at this time.

2. While I concur that this is a critical issue, I am unable to assist.

3. I regard this as a significant obstacle. I am confident that you will discover a satisfactory answer. Regrettably, I am unable to assist you in developing a solution.

Assume a role that is less significant than the one offered. List of sample wording:

1. I am unable to serve on the task force, but perhaps I could provide suggestions during a meeting regarding my area of expertise.

2. I am unable to participate as a coinvestigator, but I would gladly attend occasional meetings to discuss _____.

3. While I am unable to serve as a coauthor, I would be willing to provide feedback on a draft of the work.

Negotiate trade-offs in order to meet the requestor's requirements. List of sample wording:

1. If I were released from _____ committee, I could assist you with _____ committee. Can you make that happen?

2. I am unable to join the task force this year; may I join the task force the next year?

Another key thing that people should be kept in mind is that discretion is required to determine which invitations should be accepted and which should be declined. Declining every request is just not appropriate.

11.5 SUMMARY

As we discussed in the last chapter, it is critical that you manage all of your academic resources, especially your precious time, efficiently. We not only provided lists of suggestions, but we also provided advice on how to politely reject proposals that are not really necessary to you at that point in time.

V

Recap and Conclusion

Critical Remarks and Chapters Recap

CONTENTS

With the last chapter of the book, the narrative comes to a satisfying conclusion. We will use this chapter to summarize the main ideas presented in each chapter and bring the book to a successful conclusion.

12.1   OVERVIEW OF THE RECAP

An overview of the recap is shown in Figure 12.1. We begin with a high-level review of the idea of research and then go on to examine the many kinds of study available. We then provided comprehensive examples to illustrate the many types of academic issues you may face when doing research, all while adhering to the highest standards of academic integrity throughout our conversations and presentations.

DOI: 10.1201/9781003139058-12

Figure 12.1: Recap of the three sections of the book

In Part 2, you'll find a step-by-step approach to choosing the subjects and research ideas that are most appropriate for you, as well as a comprehensive handbook on how to perform a solid literature review.

Next that, in the following part, we spoke about how to turn your thoughts into reality. Students learned how to organize their articles and utilize figures and tables to effectively illustrate their points of view in the previous chapter, which they used to their final assignment in the next chapter. During the course of our meeting, we discussed the following topics: This course covers the following topics: 1) algorithm design; 2) computer science experiment kinds; and 3) how to refer to and build your own computer science experimental design.

In order to bring the book to a close, the author included a final chapter in which she addressed the many choices for publishing your research work, how to properly acknowledge others' work, and how to maintain all of your academic resources.

12.2   INTRODUCTION TO COMPUTER SCIENCE RESEARCH

In chapter one, we provided an overview of the writing process for scientific and technical papers. A detailed explanation of all topics covered in this book is provided to help students in obtaining a comprehensive understanding of how to write a research paper for science and engineering from the very beginning of the idea generation process. During our study, we discovered that scientific and engineering research needs a creative and systematic approach, and the findings should be able to add to the body of information already available. According to the general classification, there are two major types of research methods: quantitative and qualitative. We listed four of the most common research methods that you might use (either individually or combined): action research, experiment, case study, and survey. Research can be divided into three categories based on three separate perspectives: the field, the approach, and the character of the research. If you are personally involved in the case study, you should be conscious that you have an impact on it. In the technical section, we brought an overview of Telehealth Systems and their security issues. A buffer overflow attack in Telehealth Systems is discussed. Although a relatively new concept, several compiler add-on tools have recently been made available that work closely with function return address space to prevent such security issues in Telehealth Systems.

An additional important problem that newcomers to the scientific research community and researchers should be aware of before getting started in their careers is academic integrity (also known as academic honesty). Topics that you are unfamiliar with should be presented in an open and inquisitive manner to assist you learn to think first, question second, and act third, as the saying goes. This will help you in learning to think first, question second, and act third, which will improve your overall performance. Throughout this chapter, we worked through a hands-on case study of central processing unit (CPU) task scheduling to get a better understanding of the subject matter (CPUs).

12.3   FIND YOUR IDEAS FOR RESEARCH

The third chapter offers you with a list of study topics, as well as in-depth explanations of each topic. With the goal of providing you with some inspiration, we've put together a list of technical subjects within the field of computer science that we believe you'll find interesting to study on your own time in the future. In the course of debating techniques, the subject of dynamic programming came up, and it was proposed that it might be used in the framework of research and problem-solving.

In Chapter 4, we discussed what a literature review is and how to go about doing one. In order to provide our students with a solid foundation in the topic, we went through all of the different types of literature reviews that might be completed in the first lesson and delved deep. In the aftermath of this conversation, we delved into more detail about the general structure of literature reviews. At the end of the paper, you'll discover a step-by-step example of how to do a successful literature review. From the viewpoint of a system, this portion of the technique section provides a thorough description of adaptive resource allocation in cloud systems. It is organized as follows: Users may learn about a variety of cloud computing services, each of which includes a description of what it can do to help them.

In chapter five, we aim to offer advice on the fundamentals of finding and cultivating fresh ideas for educational purposes, starting with the foundations. This is provided for your convenience. An unusual quantity of information was made accessible via the use of training guides and case studies. In order to bring everything together, we conducted research on buffer overflow attacks.

12.4   BRING YOUR IDEAS TO THE REALITY

While you are doing your duties, it is inevitable that problems may arise. The purpose of chapter six was to demonstrate how to design algorithms that would solve the difficulties stated above, and this was accomplished. We discussed algorithms from a variety of viewpoints, and we summarized the different types. A design algorithm guide, which includes a checklist for algorithm creation, is also available. This guide takes into account a variety of factors that should be considered before formalizing your algorithm. Afterwards, we looked at the methods and issues connected with heterogeneous memory architecture and data distribution, as well as the difficulties that may arise.

In chapter seven, we took a broad look at a variety of different types of computer science experiments in general terms, including: Additionally, this in-depth section on the foundations of machine learning includes a section on experimental pipelines, which is discussed in great detail throughout the book. We addressed the adaptive evolutionary approach for addressing the memory allocation issue in heterogeneous memory systems at the end of the method section, which we detailed in depth.

In Chapter 8, we look at how to successfully incorporate figures and tables into our work, using the basic structure of computer science papers as a reference. In our methodology section, which goes into more depth on machine learning and deep learning experiments, we offer detailed instructions on how to set up a machine learning/deep learning workstation.

12.5   PUT YOUR WORK OUT AND MAKE IMPACTS

How you may choose where to publish your work is covered in depth in chapter nine, which also provides recommendations for finding journals to which you should submit your work for publication. Overall, our aim is to help you in achieving your full academic potential so that you and your family may benefit from a variety of extra services. This section, which includes detailed descriptions of Deep Learning (DL) environments that build on the information covered in the previous chapter, includes step-by-step instructions for setting up a computer-based deep learning environment that builds on the information covered in the previous chapter.

Citations are required in every part of a research work, and they are especially important in tables and figures, as discussed in chapter ten. The most essential responsibility of authors is to correctly reference relevant and approved sources. References are checked for correctness by reviewers, and journal editors employ verification tools to ensure that references are correctly mentioned in their publications. Writers should get acquainted with the structure and style of the magazine to which they will be submitting their work, regardless of the reference style that is being used as a guide. If a manuscript contains references that are inappropriate or even incorrect, the document's publishing acceptance may be jeopardized. We looked through the two advanced learning techniques in depth, which were deep learning and adversarial learning, respectively. Using adversarial learning as an example, researchers found that a number of machine learning systems are in fact susceptible to having their logic broken. In spite of the fact that even basic algorithms may behave in ways that are very different from what their developers had anticipated, these machine learning mistakes serve to demonstrate the point. Machine learning experts may be interested and may come up with ways to fight hostile circumstances, and we hope that they will begin to contribute to bridging the gap between design requirements and algorithm functioning in the future.

In Chapter 11, we discussed the significance of correctly managing your academic resources, especially your precious time. In this chapter, we will discuss how to properly manage your time. Because we provided lists of choices and instructions on how to politely reject nonnecessary offers, we allowed our consumers to make well-informed judgments about their purchases. In the last part, we offer readers with a number of activities that they may use to put their newly acquired abilities and techniques to the test. Learning requires you to put your newfound knowledge into action!

Appendix

Homework assignments are provided in this chapter to help you in finishing the learning process by putting what you've learned into action. You will be given three different kinds of homework assignments to complete in this chapter. It is suggested that you do Homework 1 once you have completed Chapter 3 of your textbook. Following completion of Chapter 6, it is suggested that you complete Homework 2 as well. In order for students to get credit for Chapter 9, they must complete assignment number three. The final project should be presented once the whole session has come to a close, according to the suggested format.

12.6 HOMEWORK AND PRACTICES

In order to assist your learning, you must complete the homework tasks in this book. There are a few of issues in my homework where the solutions are a little out of the ordinary. Quite a few questions have no definitive solution, which is often the purpose. As a result, go all in and make a couple of educated guesses in good faith. However, you should keep your prejudices at bay throughout the report. Enjoy yourself while working on your project! If you're uncertain, don't rely on others to help you (which implies that you are no longer a college freshman). Please feel free to contact me about anything. Let's get to know each other.

After you have finished Chapter 3 in your textbook, it is recommended that you do your assignment one time. You should do Homework 2 once you finish Chapter 6. Students need to complete Assignment 3 in order to get credit for Chapter Nine.

12.6.1 Homework One

Question 1: Please give me one full page to describe yourself and your interests (40 points)

Question 2: For the Figure below, we have 4 nodes A, B, C, and D in

nodes	Time	Cost
A1	2	9
A2	3	5
B1	3	10
B2	4	4
C1	4	9
C2	6	5
D1	2	6
D2	6	2

Figure 12.2: Figure of HW1

a linked list. Each node have two different working modes, for example, node A have modes A1 and A2.

1. Please tell me the minimum total cost while satisfying timing constraints. Please use dynamic program to do it. (40 points)

2. Show and explain **each step** to me. If you just show me results without details steps, you get no point. Please do it step by step by hand. Please give me your detail table with each step. (20 points)

3. 3) What are the mode assignment for all nodes? (20 points)

12.6.2 Homework Two

Question 1: For the Figure below, we have 4 nodes 0, 1, 2, and 3 in a linked list. Each node have two different working modes R1 and R2.

1. Please tell me the minimum total cost while satisfying timing constraints with all guaranteed probabilities. Please use dynamic program to do it. (40 points)

2. Show and explain each step to me. If you just show me results without details steps, you get no point. Please do it step by step by hand. Please give me your detail table with each step. (20 points)

nodes	T	R1 P	C	T	R2 P	C	
0	1	0.8	9	2	0.8	5	
	2	0.2	9	3	0.2	5	
1	1	0.9	10	2	0.7	4	
	3	0.1	10	4	0.3	4	
2	1	0.9	9	2	0.8	5	
	4	0.1	9	6	0.2	5	
3	1	0.2	8	3	0.4	2	
	2	0.8	8	6	0.6	2	

Figure 12.3: Figure of HW2

```
For (i= 1 to N)
 { A[i]=D[i-2]+12;
   B[i]=A[i]*4;
   C[i]=A[i]-10;
   G[i]=A[i]+2
   D[i]=B[i]+C[i]+G[i]; }
```

Figure 12.4: Program of HW3, Q1

3. For the hard real time scenario with timing constraint 19, what are the mode assignment for all nodes to get the minimum cost? (20 points)

12.6.3 Homework three

Question 1: Given the below program W, please draw the corresponding DFG (data flow graph).

Question 2: If we have four processors P1, P2, P3, and P4 available, run program W 100 times, how much is the total execution cycles without retiming? Using retiming, what is the minimum total execution time we can achieve? Please draw the schedule maps step by step to explain.

12.7 FINAL PROJECT

"Wisdom is not about knowing everything but applyting everything you have learned."

Ron Schaefer
American academic

Learning how you may conduct research is only half of the goal of this book. We specially designed a final project section, which provides a specific guideline for applying what you have learned from this book.

Your report should be at least 10-page long with IEEE journal format (double column). You can download the template from IEEE website.

Please don't copy and paste from the original papers. Any full sentence from a paper needs to put a citation. Without doing this, your final points will be heavily reduced. If too many copy and paste, you will fail this project.

Please include any comments and suggestion from yourself. What are the pros and cons of certain approach with comparison of other approaches on this topic? Can you extend this approach with some new ideas? Can you verify the results with new analysis or experiments?

You need prepare slides to present the paper around 20 minutes. We will arrange the presentations at the last four weeks of this semester. I will arrange presentations based on first come first serve policy. Everyone needs to present his project. How to build slides and present your paper is also an important technique to learn.

You should go to the IEEE/ACM web page and start to do literature search. A lot of information is available in the web. This is the beginning of any research. Try to select papers from IEEE/ACM journal and conference papers. For example, the following Transactions (recommend) have many high quality papers on related topics. But you can select papers from other journal or conference. It's better to be recent papers on your selected topic.

IEEE Transactions on Computers

Transactions on Cloud Computing

ACM Transactions on Embedded Computing Systems

You can find them in IEEE Xplore and ACM Digital Library.

12.8   POSSIBLE PROJECTS OR PRESENTATIONS

Here, I just list some possible projects for your considerations. It's better to select one paper within the topics. If your topic is outside of them, it would be a good idea to discuss them with your mentor.

The posssible topics:

1. Cloud Computing: The emerging paradigm of cloud computing provides a new way to address the constraints of limited energy, capabilities, and resources [71, 107, 203, 246].

2. Cyber Security: Security and privacy protection is a critical concern in the development and adoption of cloud computing. Web and Internet security is also an important topic [72, 144, 231, 245].

3. Memory Systems: Study various memory system and cache issues. Check how to improve the performance while satisfying various constraints [13, 218, 219, 285].

4. Telehealth Systems: This industrials has the largest GPD in US economic. Check how to save cost while improve the benefits of the health care systems [28, 100, 198, 224].

5. Mobile Wireless Networks: Many issues in wireless networks, e.g., channel allocations. Design or survey the new approaches such as 6G. Software defined network is a new trend [41, 241, 269, 305].

6. Systems software: A rapid prototyping style which is very popular in industry today. Survey the issues. There are many constraints such as real time, low power, fault tolerance, etc. [131, 147, 195, 274].

7. Low Power Architectures: The synthesis algorithms specifically for low power issues of various computing devices [98, 135, 141, 267].

8. Study of VLIW architectures such as TI DSP, and Intel and HP new IA-64 architectures. It is easy to find related information on the web [194, 207, 266, 306].

9. Loop Scheduling: Optimal scheduling for DFGs and graph transformation techniques such as extended retiming and unfolding [139, 204, 213, 215].

10. Real-time Systems: The issues of designing systems which satisfy all the timing constraints, i.e., hard real-time or soft real-time. Scheduling issues for multiprocessor systems [4, 130, 211, 289].

11. Fault Tolerance: The methodologies of making a system fault tolerant (hardware and software) or Fault diagnosis. I am especially interested in embedded fault tolerant systems [44, 198, 201, 222]

12. Design Space Explorations: Find a good design in a HUGE design space efficiently. Or construct a good computation graph [86, 272, 286, 292]

13. Real-time Networks and Quality of Service: study the implementation issues of QoS. The hardware and software costs [92, 131, 209, 303].

14. Instruction-Level parallelism: Study the code generation techniques for VLIW or super-scaler type of processors [188, 206, 208, 232].

15. Reconfigurable architectures: A good idea to make architectures reconfigurable for various applications and fault tolerance [34, 127, 246].

16. Formal Verification: One of the most important problems in system designs: how to verify the design is correct without doing exhaustive simulations [7, 99, 154, 273]?

17. Case study of some special architecture designs [44, 112, 119, 202].

Bibliography

[1] Computer science conference rankings, http://webdocs.cs.ualberta.ca/zaiane/htmldocs/confranking. html.

[2] Computer science journal rankings, https://www.scimagojr.com/journalrank.php?area=1700.

[3] Moving from assignment to topic, writingcenter.fas.harvard.edu.

[4] Mohammed I Alghamdi, Xunfei Jiang, Xiao Qin, Jifu Zhang, Minghua Jiang, and Meikang Qiu. Tops: Two-phase scheduling for distributed real-time systems. In *2014 IEEE Computers, Communications and IT Applications Conference*, pages 143–148. IEEE, 2014.

[5] Md Liakat Ali, Charles C Tappert, Meikang Qiu, and John V Monaco. Authentication and identification methods used in keystroke biometric systems. In *2015 IEEE 17th International Conference on High Performance Computing and Communications, 2015 IEEE 7th International Symposium on Cyberspace Safety and Security, and 2015 IEEE 12th International Conference on Embedded Software and Systems*, pages 1424–1429. IEEE, 2015.

[6] Md Liakat Ali, Kutub Thakur, John V Monaco, and Meikang Qiu. An approach to minimize crossings in phylogenetic trees. In *2015 IEEE 2nd International Conference on Cyber Security and Cloud Computing*, pages 42–47. IEEE, 2015.

[7] Md Liakat Ali, Kutub Thakur, Charles C Tappert, and Meikang Qiu. Keystroke biometric user verification using hidden markov model. In *2016 IEEE 3rd International Conference on Cyber Security and Cloud Computing (CSCloud)*, pages 204–209. IEEE, 2016.

[8] William Aspray. The institute for advanced study computer: a case study in the application of concepts from the history of technology. In *The first computers: history and architectures*, pages 179–193. 2000.

[9] Victor R Basili. The role of experimentation in software engineering: past, current, and future. In *Proceedings of IEEE 18th International Conference on Software Engineering*, pages 442–449. IEEE, 1996.

[10] Victor R Basili and Marvin V Zelkowitz. Empirical studies to build a science of computer science. *Communications of the ACM*, 50(11):33–37, 2007.

[11] Laszlo A Belady. The disappearance of the "pure" software industry. *ACM Computing Surveys (CSUR)*, 27(1):17–18, 1995.

[12] Loraine Blaxter. *How to research*. McGraw-Hill Education (UK), 2010.

[13] E Cao, Saira Musa, Jianning Zhang, Mingsong Chen, Tongquan Wei, Xin Fu, and Meikang Qiu. Reliability aware cost optimization for memory constrained cloud workflows. In *International Conference on Algorithms and Architectures for Parallel Processing*, pages 135–150. Springer, Cham, 2019.

[14] Yingjie Cao, Yongxin Zhu, Xu Wang, Jiang Jiang, and Meikang Qiu. An fpga based pci-e root complex architecture for standalone sopcs. In *2013 IEEE 21st Annual International Symposium on Field-Programmable Custom Computing Machines*, pages 149–152. IEEE, 2013.

[15] Joao Carreira and Joao Gabriel Silva. Computer science and the pygmalion effect. *Computer*, 31(2):116–117, 1998.

[16] GJ Chaitin. Epistemology as information theory: From leibniz to omega. *arXiv preprint math/0506552*, 2005.

[17] Jo-Ana D Chase, Robert Topp, Carol E Smith, Marlene Z Cohen, Nancy Fahrenwald, Julie J Zerwic, Lazelle E Benefield, Cindy M Anderson, and Vicki S Conn. Time management strategies for research productivity. *Western Journal of Nursing Research*, 35(2):155–176, 2013.

[18] Bryant Chen, Wilka Carvalho, Nathalie Baracaldo, Heiko Ludwig, Benjamin Edwards, Taesung Lee, Ian Molloy, and Biplav Srivastava. Detecting backdoor attacks on deep neural networks by activation clustering. *arXiv preprint arXiv:1811.03728*, 2018.

[19] Hongbo Chen, Hongjun Dai, and Meikang Qiu. A multiple layer sercurity architecture for internet of things into mvc design. In *2018 17th IEEE International Conference On Trust, Security And Privacy In Computing And Communications/12th IEEE International Conference On Big Data Science And Engineering (TrustCom/BigDataSE)*, pages 861–866. IEEE, 2018.

[20] Huili Chen, Cheng Fu, Jishen Zhao, and Farinaz Koushanfar. Deepinspect: A black-box trojan detection and mitigation framework for deep neural networks. In *IJCAI*, pages 4658–4664, 2019.

[21] Longbin Chen, Li-Chiou Chen, Nader Nassar, and Meikang Qiu. An analysis of server-side design for seed-based mobile authentication. In *2016 IEEE 3rd International Conference on Cyber Security and Cloud Computing (CSCloud)*, pages 60–65. IEEE, 2016.

[22] Longbin Chen, Wenyun Dai, and Meikang Qiu. A greedy approach for caching in distributed data stores. In *2017 IEEE International Conference on Smart Cloud (SmartCloud)*, pages 244–249. IEEE, 2017.

[23] Longbin Chen, Yucong Duan, Meikang Qiu, Jian Xiong, and Keke Gai. Adaptive resource allocation optimization in heterogeneous mobile cloud systems. In *2015 IEEE 2nd International Conference on Cyber Security and Cloud Computing*, pages 19–24. IEEE, 2015.

[24] Longbin Chen, Meikang Qiu, Wenyun Dai, and Houcine Hassan. An efficient cloud storage system for telehealth services. *The Journal of Supercomputing*, 73(7):2949–2965, 2017.

[25] Longbin Chen, Meikang Qiu, Wenyun Dai, and Houcine Hassan. Novel online data allocation for hybrid memories on telehealth systems. *Microprocessors and Microsystems*, 52:391–400, 2017.

[26] Longbin Chen, Meikang Qiu, Wenyun Dai, and Ning Jiang. Supporting high-quality video streaming with sdn-based cdns. *The Journal of Supercomputing*, 73(8):3547–3561, 2017.

[27] Longbin Chen, Meikang Qiu, and Jian Xiong. An sdn-based fabric for flexible data-center networks. In *2015 IEEE 2nd International Conference on Cyber Security and Cloud Computing*, pages 121–126. IEEE, 2015.

[28] Min Chen, Meikang Qiu, Linxia Liao, Jongan Park, and Jianhua Ma. Distributed multi-hop cooperative communication in dense wireless sensor networks. *The Journal of Supercomputing*, 56(3):353–369, 2011.

[29] Min Chen, Yin Zhang, Meikang Qiu, Nadra Guizani, and Yixue Hao. Spha: Smart personal health advisor based on deep analytics. *IEEE Communications Magazine*, 56(3):164–169, 2018.

[30] Wencheng Chen, Yi Zeng, and Meikang Qiu. Using adversarial examples to bypass deep learning based url detection system. In *2019 IEEE International Conference on Smart Cloud (SmartCloud)*, pages 128–130. IEEE, 2019.

[31] Xiaoyan Chen, Wei Liang, Jianbo Xu, Chong Wang, Kuan-Ching Li, and Meikang Qiu. An efficient service recommendation algorithm for cyber-physical-social systems. *IEEE Transactions on Network Science and Engineering*, 2021.

[32] Yuanqi Chen, Mohammed I Alghamdi, Xiao Qin, Jifu Zhang, Minghua Jiang, and Meikang Qiu. Tern: A self-adjusting thermal model for dynamic resource provisioning in data centers. In *2015 IEEE 17th International Conference on High Performance Computing and Communications, 2015 IEEE 7th International Symposium on Cyberspace Safety and Security, and 2015 IEEE 12th International Conference on Embedded Software and Systems*, pages 479–490. IEEE, 2015.

[33] Zhi Chen and Meikang Qiu. Spm-aware scheduling for nested loops in cmp systems. *ACM SIGBED Review*, 10(2):13–13, 2013.

[34] Zhi Chen, Meikang Qiu, Zhong Ming, Laurence T Yang, and Yongxin Zhu. Clustering scheduling for hardware tasks in

reconfigurable computing systems. *Journal of Systems Architecture*, 59(10):1424–1432, 2013.

[35] Zhi Chen, Meikang Qiu, Jianwei Niu, Zhonghai Lu, and Yongxin Zhu. Data allocation using genetic algorithm for mpsoc systems with hybrid scratch-pad memory. In *Proceedings of the 18th IEEE real time and embedded technology and applications symposium (RTAS)*, pages 61–64, 2012.

[36] Gang Cheng, Yongxin Zhu, Guoguang Rong, and Meikang Qiu. Prototyping high efficiency cloud computing architecture: Implementation of a content delivery network server on fpga. In *2012 7th International Conference on Computing and Convergence Technology (ICCCT)*, pages 1120–1124. IEEE, 2012.

[37] Brigitte JC Claessens, Wendelien Van Eerde, Christel G Rutte, and Robert A Roe. A review of the time management literature. *Personnel review*, 2007.

[38] Timothy Colburn. *Philosophy and computer science*. Routledge, 2015.

[39] Peijin Cong, Guo Xu, Junlong Zhou, Mingsong Chen, Tongquan Wei, and Meikang Qiu. Personality-and value-aware scheduling of user requests in cloud for profit maximization. *IEEE Transactions on Cloud Computing*, 2020.

[40] Bill Curtis. Measurement and experimentation in software engineering. *Proceedings of the IEEE*, 68(9):1144–1157, 1980.

[41] Hongjun Dai, Qian Li, Meikang Qiu, Zhilou Yu, and Zhiping Jia. A cloud trust authority framework for mobile enterprise information system. In *2014 IEEE 8th International Symposium on Service Oriented System Engineering*, pages 496–501. IEEE, 2014.

[42] Hongjun Dai, Shulin Zhao, Jiutian Zhang, Meikang Qiu, and Lixin Tao. Security enhancement of cloud servers with a redundancy-based fault-tolerant cache structure. *Future Generation Computer Systems*, 52:147–155, 2015.

[43] Wenyun Dai, Longfei Qiu, Ana Wu, and Meikang Qiu. Cloud infrastructure resource allocation for big data applications. *IEEE Transactions on Big Data*, 4(3):313–324, 2016.

[44] Jing Deng, Meikang Qiu, and Gang Wu. Fault tolerant data collection in heterogeneous intelligent monitoring networks. In *2010 IEEE Fifth International Conference on Networking, Architecture, and Storage*, pages 13–18. IEEE, 2010.

[45] Peter J Denning. Acm president's letter: What is experimental computer science? *Communications of the ACM*, 23(10):543–544, 1980.

[46] Peter J Denning. Acm president's letter: performance analysis: experimental computer science as its best. *Communications of the ACM*, 24(11):725–727, 1981.

[47] Peter J Denning. Is computer science science? *Communications of the ACM*, 48(4):27–31, 2005.

[48] Peter J. Denning, Douglas E Comer, David Gries, Michael C. Mulder, Allen Tucker, A. Joe Turner, and Paul R Young. Computing as a discipline. *Computer*, 22(2):63–70, 1989.

[49] Gordana Dodig-Crnkovic. Alan turing's legacy: Info-computational philosophy of nature. In *Computing nature*, pages 115–123. Springer, 2013.

[50] Wei Dong, Xin Li, Yanbin Li, Meikang Qiu, Lei Dou, Lei Ju, and Zhiping Jia. Minimizing update bits of nvm-based main memory using bit flipping and cyclic shifting. In *2015 IEEE 17th International Conference on High Performance Computing and Communications, 2015 IEEE 7th International Symposium on Cyberspace Safety and Security, and 2015 IEEE 12th International Conference on Embedded Software and Systems*, pages 290–295. IEEE, 2015.

[51] Min Du, Ruoxi Jia, and Dawn Song. Robust anomaly detection and backdoor attack detection via differential privacy. *arXiv preprint arXiv:1911.07116*, 2019.

[52] Thomas A Easton. Beyond the algorithmization of the sciences. *Communications of the ACM*, 49(5):31–33, 2006.

[53] Xin Fang, Xiong Jian, Bo Liu, Lin Gui, Meikang Qiu, and Zhiping Shi. Channel estimation over doubly selective channels based on basis expansion model and compressive sensing. In *International*

Forum on Digital TV and Wireless Multimedia Communications, pages 299–311. Springer, Singapore, 2018.

[54] Stephen Feinson. National innovation systems overview and country cases. *Knowledge flows and knowledge collectives: understanding the role of science and technology policies in development*, 1:13–38, 2003.

[55] Dror G Feitelson. Experimental computer science: The need for a cultural change. *Internet version: http://www. cs. huji. ac. il/ feit/papers/exp05.pdf*, pages 1–37, 2006.

[56] Jerome A Feldman and William R Sutherland. Rejuvenating experimental computer science: a report to the national science foundation and others. *Communications of the ACM*, 22(9):497–502, 1979.

[57] Norman Fenton, Shari Lawrence Pfleeger, and Robert L. Glass. Science and substance: A challenge to software engineers. *IEEE software*, 11(4):86–95, 1994.

[58] Peter Fletcher. Readers' corner: The role of experiments in computer science. *Journal of Systems and Software*, 30(1-2):161–163, 1995.

[59] Jeremy on January Fox. Advice: how to decide where to submit your paper, Jan 2013.

[60] Peter A Freeman. Back to experimentation. *Communications of the ACM*, 51(1):21–22, 2008.

[61] Keke Gai, Zhihua Du, Meikang Qiu, and Hui Zhao. Efficiency-aware workload optimizations of heterogeneous cloud computing for capacity planning in financial industry. In *2015 IEEE 2nd International Conference on Cyber Security and Cloud Computing*, pages 1–6. IEEE, 2015.

[62] Keke Gai, Zhihui Lu, Meikang Qiu, and Liehuang Zhu. Toward smart treatment management for personalized healthcare. *IEEE Network*, 33(6):30–36, 2019.

[63] Keke Gai, Longfei Qiu, Hui Zhao, and Meikang Qiu. Cost-aware multimedia data allocation for heterogeneous memory using

genetic algorithm in cloud computing. *IEEE transactions on cloud computing*, 8(4):1212–1222, 2016.

[64] Keke Gai and Meikang Qiu. Optimal resource allocation using reinforcement learning for iot content-centric services. *Applied Soft Computing*, 70:12–21, 2018.

[65] Keke Gai and Meikang Qiu. Reinforcement learning-based content-centric services in mobile sensing. *IEEE Network*, 32(4):34–39, 2018.

[66] Keke Gai, Meikang Qiu, Li-Chiou Chen, and Meiqin Liu. Electronic health record error prevention approach using ontology in big data. In *2015 IEEE 17th International Conference on High Performance Computing and Communications, 2015 IEEE 7th International Symposium on Cyberspace Safety and Security, and 2015 IEEE 12th International Conference on Embedded Software and Systems*, pages 752–757. IEEE, 2015.

[67] Keke Gai, Meikang Qiu, and Houcine Hassan. Secure cyber incident analytics framework using monte carlo simulations for financial cybersecurity insurance in cloud computing. *Concurrency and Computation: Practice and Experience*, 29(7):e3856, 2017.

[68] Keke Gai, Meikang Qiu, Saravanan Jayaraman, and Lixin Tao. Ontology-based knowledge representation for secure self-diagnosis in patient-centered teleheath with cloud systems. In *2015 IEEE 2nd International Conference on Cyber Security and Cloud Computing*, pages 98–103. IEEE, 2015.

[69] Keke Gai, Meikang Qiu, Meiqin Liu, and Zenggang Xiong. In-memory big data analytics under space constraints using dynamic programming. *Future Generation Computer Systems*, 83:219–227, 2018.

[70] Keke Gai, Meikang Qiu, Meiqin Liu, and Hui Zhao. Smart resource allocation using reinforcement learning in content-centric cyber-physical systems. In *International Conference on Smart Computing and Communication*, pages 39–52. Springer, Cham, 2017.

[71] Keke Gai, Meikang Qiu, Lixin Tao, and Yongxin Zhu. Intrusion detection techniques for mobile cloud computing in heterogeneous 5g. *Security and communication networks*, 9(16):3049–3058, 2016.

[72] Keke Gai, Meikang Qiu, Bhavani Thuraisingham, and Lixin Tao. Proactive attribute-based secure data schema for mobile cloud in financial industry. In *2015 IEEE 17th International Conference on High Performance Computing and Communications, 2015 IEEE 7th International Symposium on Cyberspace Safety and Security, and 2015 IEEE 12th International Conference on Embedded Software and Systems*, pages 1332–1337. IEEE, 2015.

[73] Keke Gai, Meikang Qiu, Zenggang Xiong, and Meiqin Liu. Privacy-preserving multi-channel communication in edge-of-things. *Future Generation Computer Systems*, 85:190–200, 2018.

[74] Keke Gai, Meikang Qiu, Hui Zhao, and Wenyun Dai. Anti-counterfeit scheme using monte carlo simulation for e-commerce in cloud systems. In *2015 IEEE 2nd International Conference on Cyber Security and Cloud Computing*, pages 74–79. IEEE, 2015.

[75] Keke Gai, Meikang Qiu, Hui Zhao, and Meiqin Liu. Energy-aware optimal task assignment for mobile heterogeneous embedded systems in cloud computing. In *2016 IEEE 3rd international conference on cyber security and cloud computing (CSCloud)*, pages 198–203. IEEE, 2016.

[76] Keke Gai, Meikang Qiu, Hui Zhao, and Longfei Qiu. Smart energy-aware data allocation for heterogeneous memory. In *2016 IEEE 18th International Conference on High Performance Computing and Communications; IEEE 14th International Conference on Smart City; IEEE 2nd International Conference on Data Science and Systems (HPCC/SmartCity/DSS)*, pages 136–143. IEEE, 2016.

[77] Keke Gai, Meikang Qiu, Hui Zhao, and Xiaotong Sun. Resource management in sustainable cyber-physical systems using heterogeneous cloud computing. *IEEE Transactions on Sustainable Computing*, 3(2):60–72, 2017.

[78] Keke Gai, Meikang Qiu, Hui Zhao, Lixin Tao, and Ziliang Zong. Dynamic energy-aware cloudlet-based mobile cloud computing

model for green computing. *Journal of Network and Computer Applications*, 59:46–54, 2016.

[79] Keke Gai, Yulu Wu, Liehuang Zhu, Meikang Qiu, and Meng Shen. Privacy-preserving energy trading using consortium blockchain in smart grid. *IEEE Transactions on Industrial Informatics*, 15(6):3548–3558, 2019.

[80] Keke Gai, Yulu Wu, Liehuang Zhu, Zijian Zhang, and Meikang Qiu. Differential privacy-based blockchain for industrial internet-of-things. *IEEE Transactions on Industrial Informatics*, 16(6):4156–4165, 2019.

[81] Keke Gai, Kai Xu, Zhihui Lu, Meikang Qiu, and Liehuang Zhu. Fusion of cognitive wireless networks and edge computing. *IEEE Wireless Communications*, 26(3):69–75, 2019.

[82] Keke Gai, Liehuang Zhu, Meikang Qiu, Kai Xu, and Kim-Kwang Raymond Choo. Multi-access filtering for privacy-preserving fog computing. *IEEE Transactions on Cloud Computing*, 2019.

[83] Puneet Gandhi, S Adarsh, and KI Ramachandran. Performance analysis of half car suspension model with 4 dof using pid, lqr, fuzzy and anfis controllers. *Procedia Computer Science*, 115:2–13, 2017.

[84] Jiajun Gao, Yongxin Zhu, Meikang Qiu, Kuen Hung Tsoi, Xinyu Niu, Wayne Luk, Ruizhe Zhao, Zhiqiang Que, Wei Mao, Can Feng, et al. Reconfigurable hardware generation for tensor flow models of cnn algorithms on a heterogeneous acceleration platform. In *International Conference on Smart Computing and Communication*, pages 87–96. Springer, Cham, 2018.

[85] Yihang Gao, Hui Zhao, Qian Zhou, Meikang Qiu, and Meiqin Liu. An improved news recommendation algorithm based on text similarity. In *2020 3rd International Conference on Smart BlockChain (SmartBlock)*, pages 132–136. IEEE, 2020.

[86] Yuxiang Gao, Saeed Iqbal, Peng Zhang, and Meikang Qiu. Performance and power analysis of high-density multi-gpgpu architectures: A preliminary case study. In *2015 IEEE 17th International*

Conference on High Performance Computing and Communications, 2015 IEEE 7th International Symposium on Cyberspace Safety and Security, and 2015 IEEE 12th International Conference on Embedded Software and Systems, pages 66–71. IEEE, 2015.

[87] David Hillel Gelernter. The aesthetics of computing. 1998.

[88] Robert L Glass. A structure-based critique of contemporary computing research. *Journal of Systems and Software*, 28(1):3–7, 1995.

[89] Herman H Goldstine. *The computer from Pascal to von Neumann.* Princeton University Press, 2008.

[90] Fei Gu, Jianwei Niu, Zhenxue He, Meikang Qiu, and Cuijiao Fu. Clmrs: Designing cross-lan media resources sharing based on dlna. In *2015 IEEE 2nd International Conference on Cyber Security and Cloud Computing*, pages 133–140. IEEE, 2015.

[91] Tianyu Gu, Brendan Dolan-Gavitt, and Siddharth Garg. Badnets: Identifying vulnerabilities in the machine learning model supply chain. *arXiv preprint arXiv:1708.06733*, 2017.

[92] Xiaoqi Gu, Yongxin Zhu, Shengyan Zhou, Chaojun Wang, Meikang Qiu, and Guoxing Wang. A real-time fpga-based accelerator for ecg analysis and diagnosis using association-rule mining. *ACM Transactions on Embedded Computing Systems (TECS)*, 15(2):1–23, 2016.

[93] Wenbo Guo, Lun Wang, Xinyu Xing, Min Du, and Dawn Song. Tabor: A highly accurate approach to inspecting and restoring trojan backdoors in ai systems, 2019.

[94] Yibo Guo, Qingfeng Zhuge, Jingtong Hu, Juan Yi, Meikang Qiu, and Edwin H-M Sha. Data placement and duplication for embedded multicore systems with scratch pad memory. *IEEE Transactions on Computer-Aided Design of Integrated Circuits and Systems*, 32(6):809–817, 2013.

[95] Jens Gustedt, Emmanuel Jeannot, and Martin Quinson. Experimental methodologies for large-scale systems: a survey. *Parallel Processing Letters*, 19(03):399–418, 2009.

[96] Ian Hacking. Experimentation and scientific realism. In *Science and the Quest for Reality*, pages 162–181. Springer, 1984.

[97] Zhimin He, Haozhen Situ, Yan Zhou, Jinhai Wang, Fei Zhang, and Meikang Qiu. A fast security evaluation of support vector machine against evasion attack. In *2018 IEEE 4th International Conference on Big Data Security on Cloud (BigDataSecurity), IEEE International Conference on High Performance and Smart Computing,(HPSC) and IEEE International Conference on Intelligent Data and Security (IDS)*, pages 258–263. IEEE, 2018.

[98] Fei Hu, Shruti Lakdawala, Qi Hao, and Meikang Qiu. Low-power, intelligent sensor hardware interface for medical data preprocessing. *IEEE Transactions on Information Technology in Biomedicine*, 13(4):656–663, 2009.

[99] Jingtong Hu, Chun Jason Xue, Meikang Qiu, Wei-Che Tseng, and Edwin Hsing-Mean Sha. Algorithms to minimize data transfer for code update on wireless sensor network. *Journal of Signal Processing Systems*, 71(2):143–157, 2013.

[100] Jingtong Hu, Chun Jason Xue, Meikang Qiu, Wei-Che Tseng, Cathy Qun Xu, Lei Zhang, and Edwin H-M Sha. Minimizing transferred data for code update on wireless sensor network. In *International Conference on Wireless Algorithms, Systems, and Applications*, pages 349–360. Springer, Berlin, Heidelberg, 2008.

[101] Jingtong Hu, Chun Jason Xue, Wei-Che Tseng, Meikang Qiu, Yingchao Zhao, and Edwin H-M Sha. Minimizing memory access schedule for memories. In *2009 15th International Conference on Parallel and Distributed Systems*, pages 104–111. IEEE, 2009.

[102] Jingtong Hu, Chun Jason Xue, Qingfeng Zhuge, Wei-Che Tseng, and Edwin H-M Sha. Towards energy efficient hybrid on-chip scratch pad memory with non-volatile memory. In *2011 Design, Automation & Test in Europe*, pages 1–6. IEEE, 2011.

[103] Jingtong Hu, Chun Jason Xue, Qingfeng Zhuge, Wei-Che Tseng, and Edwin H-M Sha. Data allocation optimization for hybrid scratch pad memory with sram and nonvolatile memory. *IEEE Transactions on Very Large Scale Integration (VLSI) Systems*, 21(6):1094–1102, 2012.

[104] Jingtong Hu, Qingfeng Zhuge, Chun Jason Xue, Wei-Che Tseng, and Edwin H-M Sha. Management and optimization for non-volatile memory-based hybrid scratchpad memory on multicore embedded processors. *ACM Transactions on Embedded Computing Systems (TECS)*, 13(4):1–25, 2014.

[105] Long Hu, Meikang Qiu, Jeungeun Song, M Shamim Hossain, and Ahmed Ghoneim. Software defined healthcare networks. *IEEE Wireless Communications*, 22(6):67–75, 2015.

[106] Wei Hu, Yu Gan, Yuan Wen, Xiangyu Lv, Yonghao Wang, Xiao Zeng, and Meikang Qiu. An improved heterogeneous dynamic list schedule algorithm. In *International Conference on Algorithms and Architectures for Parallel Processing*, pages 159–173. Springer, Cham, 2020.

[107] Tian Huang, Yan Zhu, Qiannan Zhang, Yongxin Zhu, Dongyang Wang, Meikang Qiu, and Lei Liu. An lof-based adaptive anomaly detection scheme for cloud computing. In *2013 IEEE 37th Annual Computer Software and Applications Conference Workshops*, pages 206–211. IEEE, 2013.

[108] Tian Huang, Yongxin Zhu, Yajun Ha, Xu Wang, and Meikang Qiu. A hardware pipeline with high energy and resource efficiency for fmm acceleration. *ACM Transactions on Embedded Computing Systems (TECS)*, 17(2):1–20, 2018.

[109] Yu Huang, Wanxing Sheng, Peipei Jin, Baicuan Nie, Meikang Qiu, and Guangquan Xu. A node-oriented discrete event scheduling algorithm based on finite resource model. *Journal of Organizational and End User Computing (JOEUC)*, 31(3):67–82, 2019.

[110] Hevel Jean-Baptiste, Meikang Qiu, Keke Gai, and Lixin Tao. Model risk management systems-back-end, middleware, front-end and analytics. In *2015 IEEE 2nd International Conference on Cyber Security and Cloud Computing*, pages 312–316. IEEE, 2015.

[111] Hao Jiang, He Nai, Jing Wu, and Meikang Qiu. Ai and machine learning for industrial security with level discovery method. *IEEE Internet of Things Journal*, 8(8):6167–6177, 2020.

[112] Xianyang Jiang, Peng Xiao, Meikang Qiu, and Gaofeng Wang. Performance effects of pipeline architecture on an fpga-based binary32 floating point multiplier. *Microprocessors and Microsystems*, 37(8):1183–1191, 2013.

[113] A Jiayin Li, Meikang Qiu, B Zhong Ming, C Gang Quan, D Xiao Qin, et al. Online optimization for scheduling preemptable tasks on iaas cloud systems. 2012.

[114] Katarzyna Kapusta, Han Qiu, and Gerard Memmi. Secure data sharing by means of fragmentation, encryption, and dispersion. In *IEEE INFOCOM 2019-IEEE Conference on Computer Communications Workshops (INFOCOM WKSHPS)*, pages 1051–1052. IEEE, 2019.

[115] Barbara Ann Kitchenham. Evaluating software engineering methods and tool part 1: The evaluation context and evaluation methods. *ACM SIGSOFT Software Engineering Notes*, 21(1):11–14, 1996.

[116] Chin-Feng Lai, Min Chen, Meikang Qiu, Athanasios V Vasilakos, and Jong Hyuk Park. A rf4ce-based remote controller with interactive graphical user interface applied to home automation system. *ACM Transactions on Embedded Computing Systems (TECS)*, 12(2):1–19, 2013.

[117] Bing Li, Jian Xiong, Bo Liu, Lin Gui, Meikang Qiu, and Zhiping Shi. On services pushing and caching in high-speed train by using converged broadcasting and cellular networks. In *2017 IEEE International Symposium on Broadband Multimedia Systems and Broadcasting (BMSB)*, pages 1–7. IEEE, 2017.

[118] Chong Li and Meikang Qiu. Reinforcement learning for cyber-physical systems: with cybersecurity case studies, 2019.

[119] Jiayin Li, Zhong Ming, Meikang Qiu, Gang Quan, Xiao Qin, and Tianzhou Chen. Resource allocation robustness in multi-core embedded systems with inaccurate information. *Journal of Systems Architecture*, 57(9):840–849, 2011.

[120] Jiayin Li, Meikang Qiu, Jian-Wei Niu, Laurence T Yang, Yongxin Zhu, and Zhong Ming. Thermal-aware task scheduling in 3d chip multiprocessor with real-time constrained workloads. *ACM*

Transactions on Embedded Computing Systems (TECS), 12(2):1–22, 2013.

[121] Jiayin Li, Meikang Qiu, Jian-Wei Niu, Yongxin Zhu, Meiqin Liu, and Tianzhou Chen. Three-phase algorithms for task scheduling in distributed mobile dsp system with lifetime constraints. *Journal of Signal Processing Systems*, 67(3):239–253, 2012.

[122] Jiayin Li, Meikang Qiu, Jianwei Niu, Meiqin Liu, Bin Wang, and Jingtong Hu. Impacts of inaccurate information on resource allocation for multi-core embedded systems. In *2010 10th IEEE International Conference on Computer and Information Technology*, pages 2692–2697. IEEE, 2010.

[123] Jiayin Li, Zhiyang Zhang, Meikang Qiu, Ping Zhang, Gang Quan, and Yongxin Zhu. Optimizing scheduling in embedded cmp systems with phase change memory. In *2012 IEEE 18th International Conference on Parallel and Distributed Systems*, pages 532–539. IEEE, 2012.

[124] Xia Li, Jian Xiong, Bo Liu, Lin Gui, and Meikang Qiu. A capacity improving and energy saving scheduling scheme in push-based converged wireless broadcasting and cellular networks. In *2016 IEEE International Symposium on Broadband Multimedia Systems and Broadcasting (BMSB)*, pages 1–6. IEEE, 2016.

[125] Xiuqiao Li, Limin Xiao, Meikang Qiu, Bin Dong, and Li Ruan. Enabling dynamic file i/o path selection at runtime for parallel file system. *The Journal of Supercomputing*, 68(2):996–1021, 2014.

[126] Yibin Li, Min Chen, Wenyun Dai, and Meikang Qiu. Energy optimization with dynamic task scheduling mobile cloud computing. *IEEE Systems Journal*, 11(1):96–105, 2015.

[127] Yibin Li, Keke Gai, Meikang Qiu, Wenyun Dai, and Meiqin Liu. Adaptive human detection approach using fpga-based parallel architecture in reconfigurable hardware. *Concurrency and Computation: Practice and Experience*, 29(14):e3923, 2017.

[128] Yibin Li, Yan Song, Lei Jia, Shengyao Gao, Qiqiang Li, and Meikang Qiu. Intelligent fault diagnosis by fusing domain adversarial training and maximum mean discrepancy via

ensemble learning. *IEEE Transactions on Industrial Informatics*, 17(4):2833–2841, 2020.

[129] Yiming Li, Tongqing Zhai, Baoyuan Wu, Yong Jiang, Zhifeng Li, and Shutao Xia. Rethinking the trigger of backdoor attack. *arXiv preprint arXiv:2004.04692*, 2020.

[130] Ying Li, Jianwei Niu, Xiang Long, and Meikang Qiu. Energy efficient scheduling with probability and task migration considerations for soft real-time systems. In *2014 IEEE Computers, Communications and IT Applications Conference*, pages 287–293. IEEE, 2014.

[131] Ying Li, Jianwei Niu, Meikang Qiu, and Xiang Long. Optimizing tasks assignment on heterogeneous multi-core real-time systems with minimum energy. In *2015 IEEE 17th International Conference on High Performance Computing and Communications, 2015 IEEE 7th International Symposium on Cyberspace Safety and Security, and 2015 IEEE 12th International Conference on Embedded Software and Systems*, pages 577–582. IEEE, 2015.

[132] Wei Liang, Songyou Xie, Jiahong Cai, Jianbo Xu, Yupeng Hu, Yang Xu, and Meikang Qiu. Deep neural network security collaborative filtering scheme for service recommendation in intelligent cyber-physical systems. *IEEE Internet of Things Journal*, 2021.

[133] Lingxia Liao, Meikang Qiu, and Victor CM Leung. Software defined mobile cloudlet. *Mobile Networks and Applications*, 20(3):337–347, 2015.

[134] Kai Lin, Wenjian Wang, Yuanguo Bi, Meikang Qiu, and Mohammad Mehedi Hassan. Human localization based on inertial sensors and fingerprints in the industrial internet of things. *Computer Networks*, 101:113–126, 2016.

[135] Guanglei Liu, Ming Fan, Gang Quan, and Meikang Qiu. On-line predictive thermal management under peak temperature constraints for practical multi-core platforms. *Journal of Low Power Electronics*, 8(5):565–578, 2012.

[136] Jianqi Liu, Jiafu Wan, Bi Zeng, Qinruo Wang, Houbing Song, and Meikang Qiu. A scalable and quick-response software

defined vehicular network assisted by mobile edge computing. *IEEE Communications Magazine*, 55(7):94–100, 2017.

[137] Kang Liu, Brendan Dolan-Gavitt, and Siddharth Garg. Fine-pruning: Defending against backdooring attacks on deep neural networks. In *International Symposium on Research in Attacks, Intrusions, and Defenses*, pages 273–294. Springer, 2018.

[138] Meilin Liu, Edwin H-M Sha, Chun Xue, and Meikang Qiu. Loop fusion technique with minimal memory cost via retiming. In *24th International Conference on Computers and Their Applications 2009, CATA 2009*, pages 92–98, 2009.

[139] Meilin Liu, Edwin H-M Sha, Qingfeng Zhuge, Yi He, and Meikang Qiu. Loop distribution and fusion with timing and code size optimization. *Journal of Signal Processing Systems*, 62(3):325–340, 2011.

[140] Xiao-Yang Liu, Xiaodong Wang, Linghe Kong, Meikang Qiu, and Min-You Wu. An ls-decomposition approach for robust data recovery in wireless sensor networks. *arXiv preprint arXiv:1509.03723*, 2015.

[141] Xingang Liu, Kwanghoon Sohn, Meikang Qiu, Minho Jo, and Hoh Peter In. Low-cost h. 264/avc inter frame mode decision algorithm for mobile communication systems. *Mobile Networks and Applications*, 17(1):110–118, 2012.

[142] Yan Liu, Xu-Dong Wang, Meikang Qiu, and Hui Zhao. Machine learning for cancer subtype prediction with fsa method. In *International Conference on Smart Computing and Communication*, pages 387–397. Springer, Cham, 2019.

[143] Yingqi Liu, Wen-Chuan Lee, Guanhong Tao, Shiqing Ma, Yousra Aafer, and Xiangyu Zhang. Abs: Scanning neural networks for back-doors by artificial brain stimulation. In *Proceedings of the 2019 ACM SIGSAC Conference on Computer and Communications Security*, pages 1265–1282, 2019.

[144] Yueming Liu, Peng Zhang, and Meikang Qiu. Fast numerical evaluation for symbolic expressions in java. In *2015 IEEE 17th International Conference on High Performance Computing and Communications, 2015 IEEE 7th International Symposium on*

Cyberspace Safety and Security, and 2015 IEEE 12th International Conference on Embedded Software and Systems, pages 599–604. IEEE, 2015.

[145] Hui Lu, Xiaoteng Wang, Zongming Fei, and Meikang Qiu. The effects of using chaotic map on improving the performance of multiobjective evolutionary algorithms. *Mathematical Problems in Engineering*, 2014, 2014.

[146] Michael S Mahoney. The histories of computing(s). *Interdisciplinary science reviews*, 30(2):119–135, 2005.

[147] Kaili Mao, Jianwei Niu, Xuejiao Wang, Lei Wang, and Meikang Qiu. Cross-domain sentiment analysis of product reviews by combining lexicon-based and learn-based techniques. In *2015 IEEE 17th International Conference on High Performance Computing and Communications, 2015 IEEE 7th International Symposium on Cyberspace Safety and Security, and 2015 IEEE 12th International Conference on Embedded Software and Systems*, pages 351–356. IEEE, 2015.

[148] Daniel D McCracken, Peter J Denning, and David H Brandin. An acm executive committee position on the crisis in experimental computer science. *Communications of the ACM*, 22(9):503–504, 1979.

[149] James Montanaro, Richard T Witek, Krishna Anne, Andrew J Black, Elizabeth M Cooper, Daniel W Dobberpuhl, Paul M Donahue, Jim Eno, W Hoeppner, David Kruckemyer, et al. A 160-mhz, 32-b, 0.5-w cmos risc microprocessor. *IEEE Journal of Solid-State Circuits*, 31(11):1703–1714, 1996.

[150] James H Moor. Three myths of computer science. *The British Journal for the Philosophy of Science*, 29(3):213–222, 1978.

[151] Clayton T Morrison and Richard T Snodgrass. Computer science can use more science. *Communications of the ACM*, 54(6):36–38, 2011.

[152] Tausif Muzaffar, Mohammed I Alghamdi, Ajit Chavan, Xunfei Jiang, Xiao Qin, Jifu Zhang, Meikang Qiu, and Minghua Jiang. itad: I/o thermal aware data center model. In *Proceedings of the 2014 IEEE International Conference on Internet of*

Things (iThings), and IEEE Green Computing and Communications (GreenCom) and IEEE Cyber, Physical and Social Computing (CPSCom), pages 502–509, 2014.

[153] Guo Niu, Meikang Qiu, and Yanchun Gu. Kernel learning method on riemannian manifold with geodesic distance preservation. In *2018 IEEE 4th International Conference on Big Data Security on Cloud (BigDataSecurity), IEEE International Conference on High Performance and Smart Computing,(HPSC) and IEEE International Conference on Intelligent Data and Security (IDS)*, pages 89–94. IEEE, 2018.

[154] Jianwei Niu, Yuhang Gao, Meikang Qiu, and Zhong Ming. Selecting proper wireless network interfaces for user experience enhancement with guaranteed probability. *Journal of Parallel and Distributed Computing*, 72(12):1565–1575, 2012.

[155] Prashant Palvia, En Mao, AF Salam, and Khalid S Soliman. Management information systems research: what's there in a methodology? *Communications of the Association for Information Systems*, 11(1):16, 2003.

[156] Chen Pan, Mimi Xie, Jingtong Hu, Meikang Qiu, and Qingfeng Zhuge. Wear-leveling for pcm main memory on embedded system via page management and process scheduling. In *2014 IEEE 20th International Conference on Embedded and Real-Time Computing Systems and Applications*, pages 1–9. IEEE, 2014.

[157] Junjie Peng, Jinbao Chen, Shuai Kong, Danxu Liu, and Meikang Qiu. Resource optimization strategy for cpu intensive applications in cloud computing environment. In *2016 IEEE 3rd International Conference on Cyber Security and Cloud Computing (CSCloud)*, pages 124–128. IEEE, 2016.

[158] Junjie Peng, Yongchuan Dai, Yi Rao, Xiaofei Zhi, and Meikang Qiu. Modeling for cpu-intensive applications in cloud computing. In *2015 IEEE 17th International Conference on High Performance Computing and Communications, 2015 IEEE 7th International Symposium on Cyberspace Safety and Security, and 2015 IEEE 12th International Conference on Embedded Software and Systems*, pages 20–25. IEEE, 2015.

[159] Shari Lawrence Pfleeger. Albert einstein and empirical software engineering. *Computer*, 32(10):32–38, 1999.

[160] John Plaice. Computer science is an experimental science. *ACM Computing Surveys (CSUR)*, 27(1):33, 1995.

[161] George Polya and John Horton Conway. *How to solve it: A new aspect of mathematical method*. Princeton University Press Princeton, NJ, 1957.

[162] Ximing Qiao, Yukun Yang, and Hai Li. Defending neural backdoors via generative distribution modeling. In *Advances in Neural Information Processing Systems*, pages 14004–14013, 2019.

[163] Han Qiu, Tian Dong, Tianwei Zhang, Jialiang Lu, Gerard Memmi, and Meikang Qiu. Adversarial attacks against network intrusion detection in iot systems. *IEEE Internet of Things Journal*, 2020.

[164] Han Qiu and Gerard Memmi. Fast selective encryption method for bitmaps based on gpu acceleration. In *2014 IEEE International Symposium on Multimedia*, pages 155–158. IEEE, 2014.

[165] Han Qiu, Hassan Noura, Meikang Qiu, Zhong Ming, and Gerard Memmi. A user-centric data protection method for cloud storage based on invertible DWT. *IEEE Transactions on Cloud Computing*, 2019.

[166] Han Qiu, Meikang Qiu, Meiqin Liu, and Gerard Memmi. Privacy-preserving health data sharing for medical cyber-physical systems. *arXiv preprint arXiv:1904.08270*, 2019.

[167] Han Qiu, Meikang Qiu, Meiqin Liu, and Gerard Memmi. Secure health data sharing for medical cyber-physical systems for the healthcare 4.0. *IEEE journal of biomedical and health informatics*, 24(9):2499–2505, 2020.

[168] Han Qiu, Meikang Qiu, Meiqin Liu, and Zhong Ming. Lightweight selective encryption for social data protection based on ebcot coding. *IEEE Transactions on Computational Social Systems*, 7(1):205–214, 2019.

[169] Han Qiu, Meikang Qiu, and Ruqian Lu. Secure v2x communication network based on intelligent pki and edge computing. *IEEE Network*, 34(2):172–178, 2019.

[170] Han Qiu, Meikang Qiu, and Zhihui Lu. Selective encryption on ecg data in body sensor network based on supervised machine learning. *Information Fusion*, 55:59–67, 2020.

[171] Han Qiu, Meikang Qiu, Gerard Memmi, Zhong Ming, and Meiqin Liu. A dynamic scalable blockchain based communication architecture for iot. In *International Conference on Smart Blockchain*, pages 159–166. Springer, 2018.

[172] Han Qiu, Yi Zeng, Shangwei Guo, Tianwei Zhang, Meikang Qiu, and Bhavani Thuraisingham. Deepsweep: An evaluation framework for mitigating dnn backdoor attacks using data augmentation. In *Proceedings of the 2021 ACM Asia Conference on Computer and Communications Security*, pages 363–377, 2021.

[173] Han Qiu, Yi Zeng, Tianwei Zhang, Yong Jiang, and Meikang Qiu. Fencebox: A platform for defeating adversarial examples with data augmentation techniques. *arXiv preprint arXiv:2012.01701*, 2020.

[174] Han Qiu, Yi Zeng, Qinkai Zheng, Shangwei Guo, Tianwei Zhang, and Hewu Li. An efficient preprocessing-based approach to mitigate advanced adversarial attacks. *IEEE Transactions on Computers*, 2021.

[175] Han Qiu, Yi Zeng, Qinkai Zheng, Tianwei Zhang, Meikang Qiu, and Gerard Memmi. Mitigating advanced adversarial attacks with more advanced gradient obfuscation techniques. *arXiv preprint arXiv:2005.13712*, 2020.

[176] Han Qiu, Qinkai Zheng, Gerard Memmi, Jialiang Lu, Meikang Qiu, and Bhavani Thuraisingham. Deep residual learning-based enhanced jpeg compression in the internet of things. *IEEE Transactions on Industrial Informatics*, 17(3):2124–2133, 2020.

[177] Han Qiu, Qinkai Zheng, Tianwei Zhang, Meikang Qiu, Gerard Memmi, and Jialiang Lu. Toward secure and efficient deep learning inference in dependable iot systems. *IEEE Internet of Things Journal*, 8(5):3180–3188, 2020.

[178] Mei Kang Qiu, Guang Lei Song, Jun Kong, and Kang Zhang. Spatial graph grammars for web information transformation. In *IEEE Symposium on Human Centric Computing Languages and Environments, 2003. Proceedings. 2003*, pages 84–91. IEEE, 2003.

[179] Meikang Qiu, Diqiu Cao, Hai Su, and Keke Gai. Data transfer minimization for financial derivative pricing using monte carlo simulation with gpu in 5g. *International Journal of Communication Systems*, 29(16):2364–2374, 2016.

[180] Meikang Qiu, Longbin Chen, Yongxin Zhu, Jingtong Hu, and Xiao Qin. Online data allocation for hybrid memories on embedded telehealth systems. In *2014 IEEE Intl Conf on High Performance Computing and Communications, 2014 IEEE 6th Intl Symp on Cyberspace Safety and Security, 2014 IEEE 11th Intl Conf on Embedded Software and Syst (HPCC, CSS, ICESS)*, pages 574–579. IEEE, 2014.

[181] Meikang Qiu, Min Chen, Meiqin Liu, Shaobo Liu, Jiayin Li, Xue Liu, and Yongxin Zhu. Online energy-saving algorithm for sensor networks in dynamic changing environments. *Journal of Embedded Computing*, 3(4):289–298, 2009.

[182] Meikang Qiu, Zhi Chen, and Meiqin Liu. Low-power low-latency data allocation for hybrid scratch-pad memory. *IEEE Embedded Systems Letters*, 6(4):69–72, 2014.

[183] Meikang Qiu, Zhi Chen, Zhong Ming, Xiao Qin, and Jianwei Niu. Energy-aware data allocation with hybrid memory for mobile cloud systems. *IEEE Systems Journal*, 11(2):813–822, 2014.

[184] Meikang Qiu, Zhi Chen, Jianwei Niu, Ziliang Zong, Gang Quan, Xiao Qin, and Laurence T Yang. Data allocation for hybrid memory with genetic algorithm. *IEEE Transactions on Emerging Topics in Computing*, 3(4):544–555, 2015.

[185] Meikang Qiu, Zhi Chen, Laurence T Yang, Xiao Qin, and Bin Wang. Towards power-efficient smartphones by energy-aware dynamic task scheduling. In *2012 IEEE 14th International Conference on High Performance Computing and Communication & 2012 IEEE 9th International Conference on Embedded Software and Systems*, pages 1466–1472. IEEE, 2012.

[186] Meikang Qiu, Wenyun Dai, and Keke Gai. Mobile applications development with android: Technologies and algorithms, 2016.

[187] Meikang Qiu, Wenyun Dai, and Athanasios V Vasilakos. Loop parallelism maximization for multimedia data processing in mobile vehicular clouds. *IEEE Transactions on Cloud Computing*, 7(1):250–258, 2016.

[188] Meikang Qiu and Jing Deng. Key establishment in multi-core parallel systems. In *2008 The 4th International Conference on Mobile Ad-hoc and Sensor Networks*, pages 122–128. IEEE, 2008.

[189] Meikang Qiu, Jing Deng, and Edwin H-M Sha. Failure rate minimization with multiple function unit scheduling for heterogeneous wsns. In *IEEE GLOBECOM 2008-2008 IEEE Global Telecommunications Conference*, pages 1–5. IEEE, 2008.

[190] Meikang Qiu, Keke Gai, Bhavani Thuraisingham, Lixin Tao, and Hui Zhao. Proactive user-centric secure data scheme using attribute-based semantic access controls for mobile clouds in financial industry. *Future Generation Computer Systems*, 80:421–429, 2018.

[191] Meikang Qiu, Keke Gai, Hui Zhao, and Meiqin Liu. Privacy-preserving smart data storage for financial industry in cloud computing. *Concurrency and Computation: Practice and Experience*, 30(5):e4278, 2018.

[192] Meikang Qiu, Wenzhong Gao, Min Chen, Jian-Wei Niu, and Lei Zhang. Energy efficient security algorithm for power grid wide area monitoring system. *IEEE Transactions on Smart Grid*, 2(4):715–723, 2011.

[193] Meikang Qiu, Minyi Guo, Meiqin Liu, Chun Jason Xue, Laurence T Yang, and Edwin H-M Sha. Loop scheduling and bank type assignment for heterogeneous multi-bank memory. *Journal of Parallel and Distributed Computing*, 69(6):546–558, 2009.

[194] Meikang Qiu, Zhiping Jia, Chun Xue, Zili Shao, Ying Liu, and Edwin H-m Sha. Loop scheduling to minimize cost with data mining and prefetching for heterogeneous dsp. 2006.

[195] Meikang Qiu, Yunjiang Jiang, and Wenyun Dai. Cost minimization for heterogeneous systems with gaussian distribution execution time. In *2015 IEEE 17th International Conference on High Performance Computing and Communications, 2015 IEEE 7th International Symposium on Cyberspace Safety and Security, and 2015 IEEE 12th International Conference on Embedded Software and Systems*, pages 547–552. IEEE, 2015.

[196] Meikang Qiu, Sun Yuan Kung, and Jack Dongarra. Message from the general chairs of hpcc/icess/css 2015. In *Proceedings-2015 IEEE 17th International Conference on High Performance Computing and Communications, 2015 IEEE 7th International Symposium on Cyberspace Safety and Security and 2015 IEEE 12th International Conference on Embedded Software and Systems, HPCC-CSS-ICESS 2015*, page xxix, 2015.

[197] Meikang Qiu, Hao Li, and Edwin H-M Sha. Heterogeneous real-time embedded software optimization considering hardware platform. In *Proceedings of the 2009 ACM symposium on Applied Computing*, pages 1637–1641, 2009.

[198] Meikang Qiu, Jianning Liu, Jiayin Li, Zongming Fei, Zhong Ming, and HM Edwin. A novel energy-aware fault tolerance mechanism for wireless sensor networks. In *2011 IEEE/ACM International Conference on Green Computing and Communications*, pages 56–61. IEEE, 2011.

[199] Meikang Qiu, Xinxin Liu, Yiren Qi, Hui Zhao, and Meiqin Liu. Ai enhanced blockchain (ii). In *2020 3rd International Conference on Smart BlockChain (SmartBlock)*, pages 147–152. IEEE, 2020.

[200] Meikang Qiu, Zhong Ming, Jiayin Li, Keke Gai, and Ziliang Zong. Phase-change memory optimization for green cloud with genetic algorithm. *IEEE Transactions on Computers*, 64(12):3528–3540, 2015.

[201] Meikang Qiu, Zhong Ming, Jiayin Li, Jianning Liu, Gang Quan, and Yongxin Zhu. Informer homed routing fault tolerance mechanism for wireless sensor networks. *Journal of Systems Architecture*, 59(4-5):260–270, 2013.

[202] Meikang Qiu, Zhong Ming, Jiayin Li, Shaobo Liu, Bin Wang, and Zhonghai Lu. Three-phase time-aware energy minimization with

dvfs and unrolling for chip multiprocessors. *Journal of Systems Architecture*, 58(10):439–445, 2012.

[203] Meikang Qiu, Zhong Ming, Jihe Wang, Laurence T Yang, and Yang Xiang. Enabling cloud computing in emergency management systems. *IEEE Cloud Computing*, 1(4):60–67, 2014.

[204] Meikang Qiu, Jian-Wei Niu, Laurence T Yang, Xiao Qin, Senlin Zhang, and Bin Wang. Energy-aware loop parallelism maximization for multi-core dsp architectures. In *2010 IEEE/ACM Int'l Conference on Green Computing and Communications & Int'l Conference on Cyber, Physical and Social Computing*, pages 205–212. IEEE, 2010.

[205] Meikang Qiu and Han Qiu. Review on image processing based adversarial example defenses in computer vision. In *2020 IEEE 6th Intl Conference on Big Data Security on Cloud (BigDataSecurity)*, pages 94–99. IEEE, 2020.

[206] Meikang Qiu and Edwin Sha. Heterogeneous parallel embedded systems: Time and power optimization, 2008.

[207] Meikang Qiu, Edwin H-M Sha, Meilin Liu, Man Lin, Shaoxiong Hua, and Laurence T Yang. Energy minimization with loop fusion and multi-functional-unit scheduling for multidimensional dsp. *Journal of Parallel and Distributed Computing*, 68(4):443–455, 2008.

[208] Meikang Qiu, Zili Shao, Qingfeng Zhuge, Chun Xue, Meilin Liu, and Edwin H-M Sha. Efficient assignment with guaranteed probability for heterogeneous parallel dsp. In *Proc. ICPADS*, pages 623–630, 2006.

[209] Meikang Qiu, Jiande Wu, Fei Hu, Shaobo Liu, and Lingfeng Wang. Voltage assignment for soft real-time embedded systems with continuous probability distribution. In *2009 15th IEEE International Conference on Embedded and Real-Time Computing Systems and Applications*, pages 413–418. IEEE, 2009.

[210] Meikang Qiu, Jiande Wu, Jingtong Hu, Yi He, and Edwin H-M Sha. Dynamic and leakage power minimization with loop voltage scheduling and assignment. In *2008 IEEE/IFIP International*

Conference on Embedded and Ubiquitous Computing, volume 1, pages 192–198. IEEE, 2008.

[211] Meikang Qiu, Jiande Wu, Chun Jason Xue, Jingtong Hu, Wei-Che Tseng, and Edwin Hsing-Mean Sha. Qos for networked heterogeneous real-time embedded systems. In *ISCA PDCCS*, pages 135–140, 2008.

[212] Meikang Qiu, Jiande Wu, Chun Jason Xue, Jingtong Aaron Hu, Wei-Che Tseng, and Edwin H-M Sha. Loop scheduling and assignment to minimize energy while hiding latency for heterogeneous multi-bank memory. In *2008 International Conference on Field Programmable Logic and Applications*, pages 459–462. IEEE, 2008.

[213] Meikang Qiu, Chun Xue, Zili Shao, Meilin Liu, and Edwin H-M Sha. Energy minimization for heterogeneous wireless sensor networks. *Journal of Embedded Computing*, 3(2):109–117, 2009.

[214] Meikang Qiu, Chun Xue, Zili Shao, Qingfeng Zhuge, Meilin Liu, and Edwin H-M Sha. Efficent algorithm of energy minimization for heterogeneous wireless sensor network. In *International Conference on Embedded and Ubiquitous Computing*, pages 25–34. Springer, Berlin, Heidelberg, 2006.

[215] Meikang Qiu, Chun Xue, Qingfeng Zhuge, Zili Shao, Meilin Liu, and Edwin H-M Sha. Voltage assignment and loop scheduling for energy minimization while satisfying timing constraint with guaranteed probability. In *IEEE 17th International Conference on Application-specific Systems, Architectures and Processors (ASAP'06)*, pages 178–181. IEEE, 2006.

[216] Meikang Qiu, Laurence T Yang, and Edwin H-M Sha. Rotation scheduling and voltage assignment to minimize energy for soc. In *2009 International Conference on Computational Science and Engineering*, volume 2, pages 48–55. IEEE, 2009.

[217] Meikang Qiu, Laurence T Yang, Zili Shao, and Edwin H-M Sha. Dynamic and leakage energy minimization with soft real-time loop scheduling and voltage assignment. *IEEE Transactions on Very Large Scale Integration (VLSI) Systems*, 18(3):501–504, 2009.

[218] Meikang Qiu, Lei Zhang, Minyi Guo, Fei Hu, Shaobo Liu, and Edwin H-M Sha. Global variable partition with virtually shared scratch pad memory to minimize schedule length. In *2009 International Conference on Parallel Processing Workshops*, pages 478–483. IEEE, 2009.

[219] Meikang Qiu, Lei Zhang, and Edwin H-M Sha. Ilp optimal scheduling for multi-module memory. In *Proceedings of the 7th IEEE/ACM international conference on Hardware/software codesign and system synthesis*, pages 277–286, 2009.

[220] Herbert Schorr. Experimental computer science. In *Proc. of a symposium on Computer culture: the scientific, intellectual, and social impact of the computer*, pages 31–46, 1984.

[221] Panjin Song, Jian Xiong, Lin Gui, Meikang Qiu, and Yue Zhang. Resource scheduling for hybrid broadcasting and cellular networks. In *2015 IEEE International Symposium on Broadband Multimedia Systems and Broadcasting*, pages 1–6. IEEE, 2015.

[222] Yan Song, Yibin Li, Lei Jia, and Meikang Qiu. Retraining strategy-based domain adaption network for intelligent fault diagnosis. *IEEE Transactions on Industrial Informatics*, 16(9):6163–6171, 2019.

[223] George Stibitz. Introduction to the course on electronic digital computers. *The Moore School Lectures*, pages 6–18, 1985.

[224] Hai Su, Meikang Qiu, and Honggang Wang. Secure wireless communication system for smart grid with rechargeable electric vehicles. *IEEE Communications Magazine*, 50(8):62–68, 2012.

[225] Bo Sun, Tao Ban, Chansu Han, Takeshi Takahashi, Katsunari Yoshioka, Jun'ichi Takeuchi, Abdolhossein Sarrafzadeh, Meikang Qiu, and Daisuke Inoue. Leveraging machine learning techniques to identify deceptive decoy documents associated with targeted email attacks. *IEEE Access*, 2021.

[226] Xiaoyong Tang, Kenli Li, Meikang Qiu, and Edwin H-M Sha. A hierarchical reliability-driven scheduling algorithm in grid systems. *Journal of Parallel and Distributed Computing*, 72(4):525–535, 2012.

[227] Yuechen Tao, Hongjun Dai, Bingyong Sun, Shulin Zhao, Meikang Qiu, and Zhilou Yu. A head record cache structure to improve the operations on big files in cloud storage servers. In *2015 IEEE 17th International Conference on High Performance Computing and Communications, 2015 IEEE 7th International Symposium on Cyberspace Safety and Security, and 2015 IEEE 12th International Conference on Embedded Software and Systems*, pages 46–51. IEEE, 2015.

[228] Matthew Telles and Yuan Hsieh. *The science of debugging*. Coriolis Group Books, 2001.

[229] Kutub Thakur, Md Liakat Ali, Keke Gai, and Meikang Qiu. Information security policy for e-commerce in saudi arabia. In *2016 IEEE 2nd International Conference on Big Data Security on Cloud (BigDataSecurity), IEEE International Conference on High Performance and Smart Computing (HPSC), and IEEE International Conference on Intelligent Data and Security (IDS)*, pages 187–190. IEEE, 2016.

[230] Kutub Thakur, Md Liakat Ali, Ning Jiang, and Meikang Qiu. Impact of cyber-attacks on critical infrastructure. In *2016 IEEE 2nd International Conference on Big Data Security on Cloud (BigDataSecurity), IEEE International Conference on High Performance and Smart Computing (HPSC), and IEEE International Conference on Intelligent Data and Security (IDS)*, pages 183–186. IEEE, 2016.

[231] Kutub Thakur, Meikang Qiu, Keke Gai, and Md Liakat Ali. An investigation on cyber security threats and security models. In *2015 IEEE 2nd International Conference on Cyber Security and Cloud Computing*, pages 307–311. IEEE, 2015.

[232] Yun Tian, Shu Yin, Jiong Xie, Ji Zhang, Xiao Qin, Mohammed I Alghamdi, Meikang Qiu, and Yiming Yang. Secure fragment allocation in a distributed storage system with heterogeneous vulnerabilities. In *2011 IEEE Sixth International Conference on Networking, Architecture, and Storage*, pages 170–179. IEEE, 2011.

[233] Zhihong Tian, Mohan Li, Meikang Qiu, Yanbin Sun, and Shen Su. Block-def: A secure digital evidence framework using blockchain. *Information Sciences*, 491:151–165, 2019.

[234] Walter F Tichy, Paul Lukowicz, Lutz Prechelt, and Ernst A Heinz. Experimental evaluation in computer science: A quantitative study. *Journal of Systems and Software*, 28(1):9–18, 1995.

[235] Brandon Tran, Jerry Li, and Aleksander Madry. Spectral signatures in backdoor attacks. In *Advances in Neural Information Processing Systems*, pages 8000–8010, 2018.

[236] Sumesh Udayakumaran and Rajeev Barua. Compiler-decided dynamic memory allocation for scratch-pad based embedded systems. In *Proceedings of the 2003 international conference on Compilers, architecture and synthesis for embedded systems*, pages 276–286, 2003.

[237] Waler G Vincenti. What engineers know and how they know it analytical studies from aeronautical history. 1990.

[238] Ellen M Voorhees. Trec: Continuing information retrieval's tradition of experimentation. *Communications of the ACM*, 50(11):51–54, 2007.

[239] Bolun Wang, Yuanshun Yao, Shawn Shan, Huiying Li, Bimal Viswanath, Haitao Zheng, and Ben Y Zhao. Neural cleanse: Identifying and mitigating backdoor attacks in neural networks. In *2019 IEEE Symposium on Security and Privacy (SP)*, pages 707–723. IEEE, 2019.

[240] Chang Wang, Yongxin Zhu, Jiang Jiang, Meikang Qiu, and Xu Wang. Dynamic application allocation with resource balancing on noc based many-core embedded systems. *Journal of Systems Architecture*, 79:59–72, 2017.

[241] Jihe Wang, Bing Guo, and Meikang Qiu. An probability-based energy model on cache coherence protocol with mobile sensor network. *International Journal of Distributed Sensor Networks*, 9(4):362649, 2013.

[242] Jihe Wang, Bing Guo, Meikang Qiu, and Zhong Ming. Design and optimization of traffic balance broker for cloud-based telehealth platform. In *2013 IEEE/ACM 6th International Conference on Utility and Cloud Computing*, pages 147–154. IEEE, 2013.

[243] Jihe Wang, Meikang Qiu, and Bing Guo. High reliable real-time bandwidth scheduling for virtual machines with hidden markov predicting in telehealth platform. *Future Generation Computer Systems*, 49:68–76, 2015.

[244] Jihe Wang, Meikang Qiu, and Bing Guo. Enabling real-time information service on telehealth system over cloud-based big data platform. *Journal of Systems Architecture*, 72:69–79, 2017.

[245] Jihe Wang, Meikang Qiu, Bing Guo, Yan Shen, and Qiang Li. User-level side channel attack on workflow system in data-center. In *2015 IEEE 17th International Conference on High Performance Computing and Communications, 2015 IEEE 7th International Symposium on Cyberspace Safety and Security, and 2015 IEEE 12th International Conference on Embedded Software and Systems*, pages 1430–1435. IEEE, 2015.

[246] Jihe Wang, Meikang Qiu, Bing Guo, and Ziliang Zong. Phase-reconfigurable shuffle optimization for hadoop mapreduce. *IEEE Transactions on Cloud Computing*, 8(2):418–431, 2015.

[247] Jihe Wang, Meng Zhang, and Meikang Qiu. A diffusional schedule for traffic reducing on network-on-chip. In *2018 5th IEEE International Conference on Cyber Security and Cloud Computing (CSCloud)/2018 4th IEEE International Conference on Edge Computing and Scalable Cloud (EdgeCom)*, pages 206–210. IEEE, 2018.

[248] Jinhai Wang, Yanchuan Gu, Zhimin He, and Meikang Qiu. A resource scheduling algorithm based on maximum discrete vm in heterogeneity cloud. In *2018 IEEE 4th International Conference on Big Data Security on Cloud (BigDataSecurity), IEEE International Conference on High Performance and Smart Computing,(HPSC) and IEEE International Conference on Intelligent Data and Security (IDS)*, pages 171–176. IEEE, 2018.

[249] Luguang Wang, Zhiping Jia, Xin Li, Yang Li, and Meikang Qiu. Dynamic temperature-aware task scheduling based on sliding window model for mpsocs. In *2011 3rd International Conference on Advanced Computer Control*, pages 98–103. IEEE, 2011.

[250] Tianhao Wang, Yi Zeng, Ming Jin, and Ruoxi Jia. A unified framework for task-driven data quality management. *arXiv preprint arXiv:2106.05484*, 2021.

[251] Tianyi Wang, Qiushi Han, Shi Sha, Wujie Wen, Gang Quan, and Meikang Qiu. On harmonic fixed-priority scheduling of periodic real-time tasks with constrained deadlines. In *2016 53nd ACM/EDAC/IEEE Design Automation Conference (DAC)*, pages 1–6. IEEE, 2016.

[252] Tianyi Wang, Soamar Homsi, Linwei Niu, Shaolei Ren, Ou Bai, Gang Quan, and Meikang Qiu. Harmonicity-aware task partitioning for fixed priority scheduling of probabilistic real-time tasks on multi-core platforms. *ACM Transactions on Embedded Computing Systems (TECS)*, 16(4):1–21, 2017.

[253] Xu Wang, Yongxin Zhu, Yajun Ha, Meikang Qiu, and Tian Huang. An fpga-based cloud system for massive ecg data analysis. *IEEE Transactions on Circuits and Systems II: Express Briefs*, 64(3):309–313, 2016.

[254] Zixiang Wang, Senlin Zhang, Meikang Qiu, and Meiqin Liu. Scheduling active nodes of clusters in wsns to minimize energy.

[255] Eric Winsberg. *Science in the age of computer simulation*. University of Chicago Press, 2010.

[256] Claes Wohlin, Per Runeson, Martin Host, Magnus C Ohlsson, Bjorn Regnell, and Anders Wesslen. *Experimentation in software engineering*. Springer Science & Business Media, 2012.

[257] Tom Wolfe. *The right stuff*. Random House, 2018.

[258] Pin Wu, Zhihui Lu, Quan Zhou, Zhidan Lei, Xiaoqiang Li, Meikang Qiu, and Patrick CK Hung. Bigdata logs analysis based on seq2seq networks for cognitive internet of things. *Future Generation Computer Systems*, 90:477–488, 2019.

[259] Runqiu Wu, Jian Xiong, Lin Gui, Bo Liu, Meikang Qiu, Wenfeng Ma, and Zhiping Shi. On services unequal error protecting and pushing by using terrestrial broadcasting network. In *2018 IEEE International Symposium on Broadband Multimedia Systems and Broadcasting (BMSB)*, pages 1–5. IEEE, 2018.

[260] Jianxun Xia, Fei Wu, Zenggang Xiong, Meikang Qiu, and Changsheng Xie. Modeling recommender systems via weighted bipartite network. *Concurrency and Computation: Practice and Experience*, 29(14):e3895, 2017.

[261] Song Xia, Meikang Qiu, and Hao Jiang. An adversarial reinforcement learning based system for cyber security. In *2019 IEEE International Conference on Smart Cloud (SmartCloud)*, pages 227–230. IEEE, 2019.

[262] Jian Xiong, Meikang Qiu, Lin Gui, and Xia Li. On resource scheduling of wireless converged broadcasting and cellular networks with popular services being preferentially delivered. In *2015 IEEE 17th International Conference on High Performance Computing and Communications, 2015 IEEE 7th International Symposium on Cyberspace Safety and Security, and 2015 IEEE 12th International Conference on Embedded Software and Systems*, pages 509–514. IEEE, 2015.

[263] Ronghua Xu, Hongjun Dai, Zhiping Jia, Meikang Qiu, and Bin Wang. A piecewise geometry method for optimizing the motion planning of data mule in telehealth wireless sensor networks. *Wireless networks*, 20(7):1839–1858, 2014.

[264] Wanxin Xu, Meikang Qiu, Zhi Chen, and Hai Su. Intelligent vehicle detection and tracking for highway driving. In *2012 IEEE International Conference on Multimedia and Expo Workshops*, pages 67–72. IEEE, 2012.

[265] Yuming Xu, Kenli Li, Tung Truong Khac, and Meikang Qiu. A multiple priority queueing genetic algorithm for task scheduling on heterogeneous computing systems. In *2012 IEEE 14th International Conference on High Performance Computing and Communication & 2012 IEEE 9th International Conference on Embedded Software and Systems*, pages 639–646. IEEE, 2012.

[266] Chun Xue, Zili Shao, MeiLin Liu, Mei Kang Qiu, and Edwin H-M Sha. Optimizing nested loops with iterational and instructional retiming. In *International Conference on Embedded and Ubiquitous Computing*, pages 164–173. Springer, Berlin, Heidelberg, 2005.

[267] Lina Yang, Shining Li, Zenggang Xiong, and Meikang Qiu. Hht-based security enhancement approach with low overhead for coding-based reprogramming protocols in wireless sensor networks. *Journal of Signal Processing Systems*, 89(1):13–25, 2017.

[268] Peihao Yang, Linghe Kong, Meikang Qiu, Xue Liu, and Guihai Chen. Compressed imaging reconstruction with sparse random projection. *ACM Transactions on Multimedia Computing, Communications, and Applications (TOMM)*, 17(1):1–25, 2021.

[269] Xi Yin, Binxing Fang, Shuyuan Jin, Meikang Qiu, Athanasios V Vasilakos, and Yongjun Xu. Keep all mobile users' whereabouts secure: A radio frequency identification protocol anti-tracking in 5g. *International Journal of Communication Systems*, 29(16):2375–2387, 2016.

[270] Xiaojing Yin, Yongxin Zhu, Liang Xia, Jingwei Ye, Tian Huang, Yuzhuo Fu, and Meikang Qiu. Efficient implementation of thermal-aware scheduler on a quad-core processor. In *2011 IEEE 10th International Conference on Trust, Security and Privacy in Computing and Communications*, pages 1076–1082. IEEE, 2011.

[271] Lujin You, Junjie Peng, Ming Chen, and Meikang Qiu. A strategy to improve the efficiency of i/o intensive application in cloud computing environment. *Journal of Signal Processing Systems*, 86(2-3):149–156, 2017.

[272] Kai Yu, Yuxiang Gao, Peng Zhang, and Meikang Qiu. Design and architecture of dell acceleration appliances for database (daad): A practical approach with high availability guaranteed. In *2015 IEEE 17th international conference on high performance computing and communications, 2015 IEEE 7th international symposium on cyberspace safety and security, and 2015 IEEE 12th international conference on embedded software and systems*, pages 430–435. IEEE, 2015.

[273] Zhilou Yu, Hongjun Dai, Xiaoming Xi, and Meikang Qiu. A trust verification architecture with hardware root for secure clouds. *IEEE Transactions on Sustainable Computing*, 5(3):353–364, 2018.

[274] Zhilou Yu, Qiao Wang, Ying Fan, Hongjun Dai, and Meikang Qiu. An improved classifier chain algorithm for multi-label

classification of big data analysis. In *2015 IEEE 17th International Conference on High Performance Computing and Communications, 2015 IEEE 7th International Symposium on Cyberspace Safety and Security, and 2015 IEEE 12th International Conference on Embedded Software and Systems*, pages 1298–1301. IEEE, 2015.

[275] Ivan Zecena, Ziliang Zong, Rong Ge, Tongdan Jin, Zizhong Chen, and Meikang Qiu. Energy consumption analysis of parallel sorting algorithms running on multicore systems. In *2012 International Green Computing Conference (IGCC)*, pages 1–6. IEEE, 2012.

[276] Marvin V Zelkowitz and Dolores Wallace. Experimental validation in software engineering. *Information and Software Technology*, 39(11):735–743, 1997.

[277] Marvin V Zelkowitz and Dolores R. Wallace. Experimental models for validating technology. *Computer*, 31(5):23–31, 1998.

[278] Yi Zeng, Huaxi Gu, Wenting Wei, and Yantao Guo. $deep-full-range$: A deep learning based network encrypted traffic classification and intrusion detection framework. *IEEE Access*, 7:45182–45190, 2019.

[279] Yi Zeng, Won Park, Z Morley Mao, and Ruoxi Jia. Rethinking the backdoor attacks' triggers: A frequency perspective. *arXiv preprint arXiv:2104.03413*, 2021.

[280] Yi Zeng, Han Qiu, Shangwei Guo, Tianwei Zhang, Meikang Qiu, and Bhavani Thuraisingham. Deepsweep: An evaluation framework for mitigating dnn backdoor attacks using data augmentation. *arXiv preprint arXiv:2012.07006*, 2020.

[281] Yi Zeng, Han Qiu, Gerard Memmi, and Meikang Qiu. A data augmentation-based defense method against adversarial attacks in neural networks. In *International Conference on Algorithms and Architectures for Parallel Processing*, pages 274–289. Springer, 2020.

[282] Yi Zeng, Meikang Qiu, Zhong Ming, and Meiqin Liu. Senior2local: A machine learning based intrusion detection method

for vanets. In *International conference on smart computing and communication*, pages 417–426. Springer, Cham, 2018.

[283] Yi Zeng, Meikang Qiu, Dan Zhu, Zhihao Xue, Jian Xiong, and Meiqin Liu. Deepvcm: a deep learning based intrusion detection method in vanet. In *2019 IEEE 5th Intl Conference on Big Data Security on Cloud (BigDataSecurity), IEEE Intl Conference on High Performance and Smart Computing, (HPSC) and IEEE Intl Conference on Intelligent Data and Security (IDS)*, pages 288–293. IEEE, 2019.

[284] Daigu Zhang, Xiaofeng Liao, Meikang Qiu, Jingtong Hu, and Edwin H-M Sha. Randomized execution algorithms for smart cards to resist power analysis attacks. *Journal of Systems Architecture*, 58(10):426–438, 2012.

[285] Lei Zhang, Meikang Qiu, Edwin H-M Sha, and Qingfeng Zhuge. Variable assignment and instruction scheduling for processor with multi-module memory. *Microprocessors and Microsystems*, 35(3):308–317, 2011.

[286] Peng Zhang, Yuxiang Gao, and Meikang Qiu. A data-oriented method for scheduling dependent tasks on high-density multi-gpu systems. In *2015 IEEE 17th International Conference on High Performance Computing and Communications, 2015 IEEE 7th International Symposium on Cyberspace Safety and Security, and 2015 IEEE 12th International Conference on Embedded Software and Systems*, pages 694–699. IEEE, 2015.

[287] SenLin Zhang, ZiXiang Wang, MeiQin Liu, and MeiKang Qiu. Energy-aware routing for delay-sensitive underwater wireless sensor networks. *Science China Information Sciences*, 57(10):1–14, 2014.

[288] Senlin Zhang, Zixiang Wang, Meikang Qiu, and Meiqin Liu. Ber-based power scheduling in wireless sensor networks. *Journal of Signal Processing Systems*, 72(3):197–208, 2013.

[289] Senlin Zhang, Zixiang Wang, Meikang Qiu, and Meiqin Liu. Energy-efficient soft real-time scheduling for parameter estimation in wsns. *International Journal of Distributed Sensor Networks*, 9(4):814807, 2013.

[290] Wei Zhang, Jian Xiong, Lin Gui, Bo Liu, Meikang Qiu, and Zhiping Shi. On popular services pushing and distributed caching in converged overlay networks. In *2018 IEEE International Symposium on Broadband Multimedia Systems and Broadcasting (BMSB)*, pages 1–6. IEEE, 2018.

[291] Wei Zhang, Jian Xiong, Lin Gui, Bo Liu, Meikang Qiu, and Zhiping Shi. Distributed caching mechanism for popular services distribution in converged overlay networks. *IEEE Transactions on Broadcasting*, 66(1):66–77, 2019.

[292] Wentao Zhang, Hua Huang, and Meikang Qiu. Design and implementation of virtual pottery space based on ceramic cloud service platform. In *2020 7th IEEE International Conference on Cyber Security and Cloud Computing (CSCloud)/2020 6th IEEE International Conference on Edge Computing and Scalable Cloud (EdgeCom)*, pages 145–150. IEEE, 2020.

[293] Yin Zhang, Yujie Li, Ranran Wang, Jianmin Lu, Xiao Ma, and Meikang Qiu. Psac: Proactive sequence-aware content caching via deep learning at the network edge. *IEEE Transactions on Network Science and Engineering*, 7(4):2145–2154, 2020.

[294] Yin Zhang, Meikang Qiu, Chun-Wei Tsai, Mohammad Mehedi Hassan, and Atif Alamri. Health-cps: Healthcare cyber-physical system assisted by cloud and big data. *IEEE Systems Journal*, 11(1):88–95, 2015.

[295] Yiwen Zhang, Chunhui Yin, Zhihui Lu, Dengcheng Yan, Meikang Qiu, and Qifeng Tang. Recurrent tensor factorization for time-aware service recommendation. *Applied Soft Computing*, 85:105762, 2019.

[296] Yue Zhang, Keke Gai, Meikang Qiu, and Kai Ding. Understanding privacy-preserving techniques in digital cryptocurrencies. In *International Conference on Algorithms and Architectures for Parallel Processing*, pages 3–18. Springer, Cham, 2020.

[297] Hui Zhao, Meikang Qiu, Min Chen, and Keke Gai. Cost-aware optimal data allocations for multiple dimensional heterogeneous memories using dynamic programming in big data. *Journal of computational science*, 26:402–408, 2018.

[298] Hui Zhao, Meikang Qiu, and Keke Gai. Empirical study of data allocation in heterogeneous memory. In *International Conference on Smart Computing and Communication*, pages 385–395. Springer, Cham, 2017.

[299] Hui Zhao, Meikang Qiu, Keke Gai, and Xin He. Optimal solution to intelligent multi-channel wireless communications using dynamic programming. *The Journal of Supercomputing*, 75(4):1894–1908, 2019.

[300] Hua Zheng, Zhong Ming, Meikang Qiu, and Xi Zhang. Research on optimizing last level cache performance for hybrid main memory. In *International Conference on Smart Computing and Communication*, pages 144–153. Springer, Cham, 2017.

[301] Weili Zhou, Zhen Zhu, and Peiying Liang. Speech denoising using bayesian nmf with online base update. *Multimedia Tools and Applications*, 78(11):15647–15664, 2019.

[302] Xuyang Zhou and Meikang Qiu. A k-anonymous full domain generalization algorithm based on heap sort. In *International Conference on Smart Computing and Communication*, pages 446–459. Springer, Cham, 2018.

[303] Ming Zhu, Xiao-Yang Liu, Meikang Qiu, Ruimin Shen, Wei Shu, and Min-You Wu. Traffic big data based path planning strategy in public vehicle systems. In *2016 IEEE/ACM 24th International Symposium on Quality of Service (IWQoS)*, pages 1–2. IEEE, 2016.

[304] Ming Zhu, Xiao-Yang Liu, Meikang Qiu, Ruimin Shen, Wei Shu, and Min-You Wu. Transfer problem in a cloud-based public vehicle system with sustainable discomfort. *Mobile Networks and Applications*, 21(5):890–900, 2016.

[305] Xiao Zhu, Duo Liu, Liang Liang, Kan Zhong, Meikang Qiu, and Edwin H-M Sha. Swapbench: The easy way to demystify swapping in mobile systems. In *2015 IEEE 17th International Conference on High Performance Computing and Communications, 2015 IEEE 7th International Symposium on Cyberspace Safety and Security, and 2015 IEEE 12th International Conference on Embedded Software and Systems*, pages 497–502. IEEE, 2015.

[306] Qingfeng Zhuge, Chun Xue, Zili Shao, Meikang Qiu, and Edwin H-M Sha. Pipelining nested loops on timing and code-size optimizations for dsp applications.

Index

Italicized pages refer to figures.

Printed in the United States
by Baker & Taylor Publisher Services